The Visitor's Guide
to
NORWAY

THE VISITOR'S GUIDE TO NORWAY

MPC

HUNTER
PUBLISHING INC.

Kunzmann-Lange, Katharina
    The visitor's guide to Norway. —
    (MPC visitor's guide series)
    1. Norway — Description and
    travel — 1945- — Guide-books
    I. Title II. Norwegen. *English*
    914.81′0448   DL407

Author: Katharina Kunzmann-
    Lange
Translator: A.J. Shackleton

© Goldstadtverlag   Karl A.
    Shäfer, Pforzheim
© Moorland Publishing Co Ltd
    1987 (English edition)

Published by
Moorland Publishing Co Ltd,
Moor Farm Road,
Airfield Estate,
Ashbourne, Derbyshire
DE6 1HD, England

ISBN   0 86190 171 1 (paperback)
ISBN   0 86190 172 X (hardback)

Published in the USA by
Hunter Publishing Inc,
300 Raritan Center Parkway,
CN94, Edison, NJ 08818
ISBN   0 935161 15 5 (paperback)

Printed in the UK by
Butler & Tanner Ltd
Frome, Somerset

Cover illustration:
Waterfall in the Briksdal Valley,
Nordfjord (Jeanetta Baker,
    International Photobank).
Colour illustrations have been supplied
by the Norwegian National Tourist
Office (Bodø, Bardal), the remainder by
Peter Lumley.
All the black and white illustrations
have been supplied by the Norwegian
National Tourist Office.

CONTENTS

Key to symbols used in margin

⚛ Items of cultural or historical interest — usually indicated by signposts with white lettering on a blue background, or sometimes black lettering on a white background.

⊠ This part of the route is forbidden to caravans or at least not recommended, whether because of steep roads, sheer drops, narrow bends or unmade surfaces.

🌲 A beautiful view or interesting natural phenomenon.

❄ Information about winter closure of certain mountain routes.

FOREWORD

Norway is one of the most fascinating countries in the world, as this guidebook attempts to show. A holiday in Norway provides a welcome contrast to lazing beneath the palms on sun-drenched beaches. For Norway is a country of activity and travel. There are so many different ways of getting about - by train, by bus, by car or on foot; and there are so many different kinds of holiday available - backpacking, camping, caravanning, staying in hotels, or hiring a cabin. And the dormobile has become increasingly popular in recent years.

Norway offers an enormous variety of scenic landscapes, making it difficult to choose between them when planning your route. For Norway is much more than just Oslo, the North Cape or the Geirangerfjord. I have tried to make a selection of all the best tourist routes, and these are described here with as much detailed information as possible. I have also put together a suggested round trip, which includes a wide variety of central Norwegian landscapes.

This guide does not include every road, every town or every fjord, simply because there are far too many to include in one book. But the routes I have suggested leave plenty of opportunity for you to explore this delightful country for yourself.

I have used Oslo as the starting point for all the routes. However, if you start from somewhere else in the country — Bergen, for example — you should have no problem in working out your own route from the information given.

It only remains for me to wish you a very enjoyable holiday in Norway.

Katharina Kunzmann-Lange

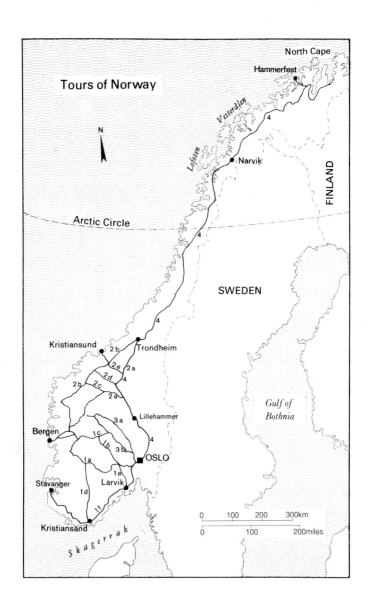

Tours of Norway

N

North Cape
Hammerfest
Vesterålen
4
Lofoten
Narvik
FINLAND

Arctic Circle

4

SWEDEN

4

Kristiansund
2 b
Trondheim
2 e   2 a
2 d
2 b   2 c   4
2 a
3 a
Lillehammer
Bergen
1 c
1 b   3 b
4
OSLO
1 a
1 e
Stavanger
Larvik
1 d
1 f
Kristiansand
Skagerrak

Gulf of
Bothnia

0   100   200   300km
0   100   200miles

INTRODUCTION

1. The country and its people

High waterfalls, deep lakes and fjords, high mountains, narrow valleys, dense forests, bare plateaux and glaciers — often in close proximity — are just some of the features that go together to make up the delightful and sometimes bizarre landscape of southern and central Norway. And a trip to the far north of the country — the land of the midnight sun — will make your holiday an unforgettable experience.

You will be overwhelmed by all the splendours that nature has to offer, tempting you to linger. Norway is a country that gets into your blood. You might pay no more than a flying visit to the south, or you might travel the whole length of the country as far as the North Cape — but you will always feel the need to go back.

Norway is the longest country in Europe. The distance from north to south is about 1,800km as the crow flies, spanning about 13° of latitude. This corresponds roughly to the distance from London to Gibraltar. The Arctic Circle crosses the country roughly in the middle. In contrast to its

Sognefjord, Norway's longest fjord

length, Norway becomes increasingly narrow as you travel north, measuring only 6.3km wide at its narrowest point.

Norway is bounded by the sea to the south, west and north, while in the east it has common borders with Sweden (1,600km), Finland (700km) and the Soviet Union (200km). The coastline, with its many fjords and bays, is 33,800km long.

Norway is indeed a land of superlatives. Jotunheimen, for instance, has 200 summits over 2,000m above sea level, and is thus the highest mountain range in Northern Europe — while the nearby Jostedal Glacier is the largest in the whole of Europe. Norway's highest road is also in this area. Although its altitude is 1,434m, you need only travel 35km to reach sea level at the Sognefjord, which itself is the longest and deepest fjord in the world (180km long and 1,308m deep). The fjords attain incredible depths, far beyond that of the North Sea which borders them; and the same is true of the numerous mountain lakes. Hornindalsvatn, for example, at 514m, is the deepest lake in Europe. The Hardangervidda, with an area of 12,000sq km, is the largest plateau in Europe (*vidda* = expanse).

Some facts about Norway

Form of government:	constitutional monarchy since 1905
Area:	324,000sq km (UK 224,000sq km)
Population:	4.1 million (UK 56.3 million)
Population density:	12.7 inhabitants per sq km (UK 251 per sq km)
Length:	1,800km as the crow flies; coastline including fjords and islands over 33,800km
Breadth:	narrowest point only 6.3km
	widest point 430km
Borders:	with Sweden 1,600km
	with Finland 700km
	with the Soviet Union 200km
Latitude:	southernmost point 57° 57′ 31″
	North Cape 71° 10′ 21″
Longest river:	Glomma approximately 600km
Longest fjord:	Sognefjord approximately 180km
Deepest lake:	Hornindalsvatn 514m (deepest in Europe)
Highest mountains:	Jotunheim (Glittertind 2472m; Galdhøpiggen 2469m) Dovrefjell (Snøhetta 2286m)
Land use:	arable land, pastures and meadows 3.3 per cent
	forest and woodland 21.7 per cent
	barren land, lakes and rocks 74 per cent
Religion:	94 per cent Protestant Lutheran; 11,000 Roman Catholics; 900 Jews
National holiday:	17 May (Constitution Day)

The jagged peaks of Skagastølstindene

The people

Of the 4.1 million Norwegians (about half the population of the London conurbation), fifty-three per cent live in the towns and a third in the Oslo area. Thus the population density, which is about 13 per sq km for the country as a whole, varies enormously, from 80 per sq km around the Oslofjord, to 1 per sq km in Finnmark, Norway's northernmost region. Because of the kind of country they live in, the Norwegians love solitude. Hill farmers are accustomed to it, since their farms are often a long way from the nearest settlement, which may consist of no more than a few brightly painted cottages scattered across the landscape. But the townspeople are also fond of solitude, retreating to their weekend cabins, where they are loth to be disturbed.

Almost every house or cabin is supplied with a flagpole, on which the national flag is hoisted on every possible occasion. The patriotism of the Norwegians finds expression in everything. They even decorate their Christmas trees with little flags. The Norwegian national flag is one of the most beautiful in the world, with its blue cross outlined in white on a red background.

Although individuals vary considerably, the Norwegians are clearly recognisable as a people, with their fair hair and blue eyes. But they share

Young Lapps in a Finnmark encampment

their country with a people of a completely different appearance, language and culture - the Lapps or in their own language the *Sameh*. The Lapps are traditionally nomadic herders of reindeer, and look almost mongoloid with their yellowish skin, black hair and small slit eyes.

The Lapps are short and stocky, with short legs and dark hair, and are fond of bright colours and ornaments. They are not as a rule particularly interested in state education or in politics, and live mostly in extended families or clans, each of which forms a political and economic unit. The Lapps are cunning and vivacious, and businesslike too if they put their mind to it.

Their origins are still debated, but they are most probably a nomadic people who wandered into Scandinavia from central Russia - perhaps from Siberia and certainly from beyond the Urals. This theory is supported by their predominantly nomadic lifestyle, their clan structure and their language, which is in many ways similar to Finnish. Finnish is also known to be related to Estonian, and probably to Hungarian as well. The resemblance between these languages indicates a probable common origin among the nomadic peoples that lived in the regions beyond the Urals.

It is now known that the Lapps had already moved into northern Scandinavia by the early Middle Ages, and trade links with them have been traced back as far as the Bronze Age. They were continually being driven further north by the Germanic immigrants. The mountain Lapps are the best known group, and their lifestyle of herding reindeer is probably the most typical.

In Finland, and also to a smaller extent in Sweden, the Lapps have become permanently settled, and have thus become fully integrated with the rest of the population. The Lapps of Norway are divided into two main groups - the mountain Lapps and the forest Lapps - on the basis of the kinds of reindeer they have. The forest Lapps lead a more settled existence, herding only the reindeer that live in the forest. The mountain Lapps, on the other hand, move to and fro according to the seasons, herding their reindeer from one feeding place to the next, completely ignoring the political boundaries. There is a third, much smaller, group known as the lake Lapps, who do not have reindeer but fish from the lake shores and coasts.

There is a special group of Lapps called the Skolt Lapps, who originally came from Karelia, now part of Russia. They are of Russian Orthodox faith, and live in the north-eastern corner of Finnish Lapland.

Attempts by the churches to convert the Lapps have left them with a veneer of Christianity which they maintain alongside traditional shamanistic beliefs. The Norwegians have also tried to settle and integrate them into Norwegian society. However, although the ancient traditions of the Lapps have been strongly influenced and modified by modern economic and cultural ideas, attempts to assimilate them have long since been abandoned. This was firstly because the cultural barriers were so enormous, and secondly because it was eventually realised that such integration was not in fact desirable.

Attitudes to the Lapps have changed completely. Governments, for example, have granted them a number of important privileges, similar to those granted to American Indians in their reservations. There are boarding schools for Lapps at certain central points, and their special way of life is taken into account by the customs, currency and tax authorities. This is unfortunately only true of the Scandinavian countries. The vast area of the Kola Peninsula in Russia has now been closed off to the Lapps and their reindeer.

Tourists have little opportunity to see the Lapps in their true element, since in summer the reindeer herds are on the move. They wander continually throughout the region, even swimming across fjords; but they never come near to any of the main tourist routes.

If you do come across Lapps, they are likely to be there especially for the tourists, living picturesquely in tents erected close to the main tourist centres. Well-scrubbed men, women and children appear in brightly embroidered costumes, and allow themselves to be photographed in exchange for the appropriate fee. They offer a whole range of skilfully made artifacts, which they barter in a manner reminiscent of more southern climes.

The brightly coloured traditional dress which the Lapps display is in fact their winter costume, and is only brought out for the tourists' benefit. There are all sorts of goods on offer to tourists: various articles of reindeer leather, such as purses, handbags and shoes; articles of clothing, usually brightly embroidered, and some even mass-produced; a few whole reindeer skins - and of course the inevitable reindeer antlers, without which a trip across the Arctic Circle is hardly complete!

The further you go northwards, the further from the main road the Lapp settlements are, the more traditional the lifestyle, the less colourful the clothes (jeans have taken over here too), and the less you have to pay for souvenirs. The villages are usually less picturesque, and tents have long since been replaced by wooden cabins.

Today there are probably about 30,000 to 35,000 Lapps in Scandinavia altogether, and most of them (about 22,000) live on Norwegian territory. An exact count is impossible because of their lifestyle and their indifference towards national boundaries.

Also worthy of mention are the 12,000 *Kvæner*, who are of Finnish origin.

Customs

Woodcarving is the most typical of the Norwegian handicrafts. There are some particularly valuable examples of this in the Norwegian Folk Museum in Oslo. Jewellery work also has a long tradition, while costumes have only been introduced fairly recently.

Thanks to their isolation, the bizarre scenery, the long, dark winters, and their glorious Viking history, the Norwegians have a rich collection of sagas and fairy tales, in which the troll plays a significant part.

You will come across these terrifying little figures in every souvenir shop. But trolls — or mountain spirits — are not dwarves, but giants who live in the mountain forests and waterfalls. You never see them face to face, but they make their presence felt in all the nasty tricks that they play on humans.

The long, dark winter awakens a yearning for the light, vividly expressed during the Norwegian Christmas — or Yuletide — when there is a rich display of candles. At this time of year, when even Oslo in the south has no

The opening of the Storting, Norway's national assembly

---

more than an hour or two of daylight, all the rooms in the houses are bright with the warm glow of candlelight.

The summer solstice is similarly celebrated during the time of the midnight sun. And nowhere is the Christian faith so closely allied to nature as it is in Norway.

The constitution

Norway is a constitutional monarchy. The Norwegian constitution was passed in **Eidsvoll** in 1814, and as such is the oldest formal constitution in Europe. The monarch has the so-called executive power, while the legislative power lies with the Norwegian parliament or Storting, and independent judicial power is exercised by the courts. The Storting is elected once every 4 years, and cannot be dissolved in the interim.

All Norwegians over 20 years of age are allowed to vote. The Storting consists of 150 members, all of which are elected from individual consituencies by proportional representation, with a specific number of seats allocated to each constituency.

All routine matters are dealt with by the whole house in plenary session. But constitutional matters and basic budget decisions are dealt with by the Odelsting, which is made up of 112 Members of Parliament. Parliamentary bills must first be considered by the Odelsting, and must then be submitted for agreement to the Lagting, which consists of the remaining thirty-eight Members of Parliament. Thus Norway possesses a modified form of the single-chamber system.

The government is formally appointed by the monarch, who acts on the advice of the leader of the winning party or coalition.

The Norwegian political parties are as follows: the Labour Party (DNA), the conservative Høyre Party, the Christian People's Party (CVP), the Centre Party (Senterparti), the socialist Left Party, the liberal socialist Venstre Party, the Progressive Party, the Red Democratic Alliance, the Liberal People's Party and the Communist Party. King Olav V has been head of state since 1957. It is the job of the monarch to exercise executive power in conjunction with the Privy Council and the government, whose majority decision he must follow. He cannot make an appointment to the Privy Council without the approval of parliament. He has the right to veto legislation, but his veto can serve only to delay it. He is commander-in-chief of the armed forces and head of the state church. His person is inviolable, which means that according to the constitution he cannot be impeached. He is succeeded by his nearest male heir.

Economy and trade

Up to World War II, the Norwegian economy was based on fisheries, marine transport, agriculture and forestry. But since then industrial technology has become increasingly important. In the last ten years or so, the harnessing of rich oil and natural gas resources off the Norwegian coast has brought about a complete change in the country's economic structure. The well-known Ekofisk oilfield alone produces more oil than Norway can use, with the result that about forty per cent of Norway's exports are of oil and natural gas. The vast income from this mineral wealth has not only helped to improve Norway's balance of trade, but has also enabled industry to flourish. Norway is now one of the world's four biggest exporters of natural gas, and one of the results of this sudden boom is a population explosion in many of Norway's small fishing towns as they have been transformed into large industrial complexes.

Ignoring those countries with flags of convenience (Liberia and Panama), Norway has the fourth-largest merchant fleet in the world, with a gross tonnage of over 20 million. Most of these ships are commissioned overseas and are thus an important source of income.

It is significant that the average ship size of the Norwegian merchant

Fishing fleet in harbour

fleet, at about 16,000 gross tonnage, is almost twice that of any other fleet. About half of the ships are tankers, with the result that Norwegian shipping has been affected by the oil crisis. You can travel deep into the central mountains, only to find a supertanker which has been laid up in some isolated fjord. The golden age of shipbuilding is over too; in recent years, although ships have still accounted for one-sixth of total exports, the trend is very much downwards. But a switch to building oil platforms has come sufficiently early to prevent the slump being worse.

Industry has now become the largest factor in the Norwegian economy, and also employs the most workers. The enormous growth of industry is due partly to the use of the country's vast water resources for hydroelectric power, and partly to the income from oil and natural gas. Apart from the wood-processing industries, the electrometallurgical and electrochemical industries are also very important. The metals worked include aluminium, zinc, nickel and copper.

Other important industrial products are nitrogen, nitrates and plastics. The textile and food industries work to satisfy home requirements.

Norwegian factories manufacture an increasing variety of products, but there are no obvious concentrations of industry. Smaller and medium-sized firms are still very much the norm. There is relatively little damage to the environment, since electricity is the chief power source.

Electricity production is not only important for industry, but also for domestic consumers. Norway boasts the highest electricity consumption *per capita* of any country in the world. Almost every individual farmstead, and even the remotest fishing village, has been connected to the electricity grid. And yet barely a third of the country's available water is being harnessed for electricity.

Fisheries are an important source of income, with a catch of 2.65 million tonnes in the early 1980s. The fish most commonly caught are herring, cod and mackerel. Only a quarter of the catch is used for food, the majority being rendered down to fish meal and fish oil. Ten to fifteen per cent of edible fish products are consumed at home, the rest being for export.

In the past, fish used to be salted, dried and preserved, either on the rocks (as klipfish), or in large wooden structures (as stockfish). But nowadays it is deep frozen in modern processing plants or while still at sea. Stockfish and klipfish are now produced only in small quantities at home, and are exported to a few countries in Africa, Latin America and the Mediterranean.

The Norwegian whaling fleet, with its home ports of Sandefjord and Tønsberg, was at one time of world importance, but is of little significance today because of international restrictions.

Barely a quarter of Norway is covered with the forests which form the basis of the forestry industry. Most of these forests are privately owned. The felled tree trunks are transported by water to processing plants, where wood pulp, paper and cardboard are produced. The tree population is unfortunately becoming much too old. But reforms are afoot to rejuvenate the forests, which will make them more viable, especially where rare woods are concerned.

Agriculture, which occupies only three per cent of the land area of the country, is predominantly involved in livestock production — though there are a few small arable farms, and some fruit is grown in the Hardanger region. Larger farms are only to be found in Gudbrandsdal in the east of the country, while countless small farms have been abandoned in recent years.

The arts

The arts in Norway are seldom practised for their own sake, and more often take the form of applied art. Thus in Norway arts are inseparable from handicrafts. Sculpture and engraving are the oldest of the Norwegian arts; they began with wood carving. Some of the oldest carvings known have been found on old Viking longboats off the Norwegian coast (see the Bygdøy Museum on page 155). The important finds which have been discovered both in and around these ships reveal amazing artistry and a love of ornamentation. The sledges and chariots found near the ships are

'Young Couple', sculpture by Vigeland

engraved with scenes depicting human figures and well-known sagas.

Similar carvings are to be found in stave churches (see page 27), where the artistic abilities of the wood carvers are perhaps best displayed in the marvellous animal heads which grace the doorposts.

'Snow Shovelers' (1910-11) by Edvard Munch

Traditional sculpture unfortunately declined at the same time as many other rural traditions. More recently, however, thanks to the work of a sculptor called Gustav Vigeland (1869-1943), sculpture has become important again.

Vigeland's work is of such tremendous breadth and variety that it is impossible to sum up in a few words. Much of his enormous output can only be understood if its typically Norwegian features are fully appreciated. Much of it clearly reveals the tragedy of his loneliness as an artist. The son of a smallholder, he first devoted himself to wood carving, and only later went on to work in stone. His most significant works are *The Kiss, Man and Woman*, and his monument to the mathematician Niels Henrik Abel. With such works he made a name for himself, and the City of Oslo commissioned him to design a fountain for the city. The result was greeted with such enthusiasm that they went on to commission a much larger work, for which a large section of the Royal Park was put at his disposal. In a veritable frenzy of creative activity, he produced so many sculptures that they soon outgrew the Royal Park, and an area was set aside for him in what is now called the Frogner Park. Here his sculptures are displayed in what might best be described as a vast outdoor exhibition, of which his original commission - the fountain - is only a tiny feature.

Vigeland's most famous work is the tall monolith symbolising the course of a human life, which he took barely ten months to produce. But if this monolith is ample proof of his incredible creative drive, it also bears witness to the fact that at this stage in his career Vigeland had ceased to be aware of his artistic limitations. If you compare the fine detail of his earlier works, which stand comparison with those of the great sculptor Rodin, you are forced to admit that his art had at this point declined into a form of mass production.

The nearby Vigeland Museum gives yet further insights into the artist's life and works. His brilliance and dynamism are possibly what made him Norway's only well-known sculptor for decades on end, while others were forced to remain in the sidelines. Contemporary sculptors studied mostly in Paris, where they were chiefly influenced by Rodin and his followers.

Well-known modern sculptors include Rolf Lunde; Wilhelm Rasmussen, who for many years worked on the restoration of the cathedral in Trondheim; Emil Lie, who created the large bronze and granite female statues in the square in front of Oslo's City Hall; Stinius Fredriksen; Gunnar Janson; and many others.

The figures which decorate the City Hall in Oslo include some of the finest examples of modern Norwegian art, which brought many new artists to the fore. One of these was the sculptor Anne Grimdalen. Born into a poor country family, she worked hard to gain recognition as one of the topmost sculptors of her day. Her most famous work is the statue of King Harald Hårdråde on horseback, which is to be found on the west wall of the City Hall. Apart from that, she is well known for her animal figures, and especially for her representations of bears. She died in 1961. The number of modern artists is far too great to be listed here.

Just as Vigeland is considered the most significant of the Norwegian sculptors, so Johann Christian Dal (1788–1857) was the greatest of the Norwegian romantic painters. He is indeed looked on as the father of Norwegian painting. We cannot include the many nineteenth-century painters, who for their inspiration drew partly on the Paris academy and partly on the powerful style of depiction which has characterised Norwegian art since the Middle Ages.

The most famous modern Norwegian artist is Edvard Munch (1863–1944), who was a pioneer of Impressionism, both in his painting and in his graphic designs. Almost all his works are to be found in the Munch Museum in Oslo, which contains almost 24,000 paintings, drawings and water colours, together with a number of his personal effects. There are so many modern artists that it is impossible to name them all, and a whole book would be needed to do justice to their work.

Only a few names need to be mentioned as representative of Norwegian literature, not because little has been produced, but because their work has played such a significant role in world literature. The most important names are Henrik Ibsen, Sigrid Undset, Knut Hamsun, Bjørnstjerne

Genuine Norwegian handicrafts make ideal souvenirs

Bjørnson, Kristofer Uppdal, Jonas Lie and Alexander Kielland. Clearly, Norway cannot hope to provide a large readership for its writers and poets. So it is all the more remarkable that Norwegian authors have produced so many literary masterpieces that have gained a permanent place in world literature.

Norway's musical output can be summed up in just one name — Edvard

Grieg (1843–1907). This outstanding composer gained great inspiration from the folk music of his country. He is considered a master of the art of the miniature - songs and *lieder*, for example. He wrote only one piano concerto, but it is one of those most frequently played. And his incidental music to Ibsen's play *Peer Gynt* has brought him immortality. *Peer Gynt* has also been set to music by the modern composer Harald Sæverud, while other well-known modern composers include Klaus Egge and Fartein Valen.

Norway's two most famous musical interpreters have been the now legendary violin virtuoso Ole Bull (1810–1880) and the opera soprano Kirsten Flagstad. Norway has a long musical tradition, which it continues to cultivate. The famous concert seasons in Oslo and Bergen draw international audiences.

As regards the dramatic arts, most of the important dramatists have already been mentioned. Only one more name needs to be added - that of Ludvig Holberg (1684–1754), the creator of many fine plays. Bilingualism creates problems in the dramatic arts — problems which are particularly acute in traditional theatre.

Norwegian handicrafts are deeply rooted in the Old Norse figures and engravings. Their simple style and clear, traditional lines, expressed in modern terms, have made them into one of the most important of the Norwegian art forms, and they are treasured throughout the world. The most popular examples of Norwegian handicraft are silverware and glassware, and also furniture and other goods.

One interesting institution is the Norwegian Design Centre, which is located on Drammensveien in the centre of Oslo. It provides a comprehensive exhibition of the creative output of Norwegian industry. A large number of handicraft businesses are involved in an organisation called PLUS, which promotes co-operation between artists, craftsmen, designers and industry. You will see lots of children enjoying the toys and models, and working out how they are made up. This institution is indicative of the vitality and creativity of the Norwegian handicrafts industry, and ensures that it retains its position among the arts.

2.   A short history

The history of Norway has almost always been bound up with that of Denmark and Sweden. The Scandinavian countries went through a whole series of unions, federations and bloody feuds before they eventually achieved their present state of mutual friendship and trust.

The history of Norway really began with the immigration of Germanic tribes, who first settled in the south and later began to displace the native Finns and Lapps. By the Bronze Age, Norway was already fully occupied by Germanic peoples. But the land remained divided up between the various tribes until Harald Hårfagre (Fairhair) (AD870-930) founded the first unified kingdom by subduing many of the tribal princes. He appointed his own nobles to administer the *fylker* (districts), demanded oaths of fealty and imposed laws. However, he divided the succession equally between his three sons and the consequence of this was war between them and dissolution of the Kingdom. The theme of central authority, contested by nobles and other dissatisfied elements, runs through Norwegian history for a considerable time after this.

At about the same time the Vikings began to plunder the coasts of the North Sea and Baltic, later moving down the French coast and into the Mediterranean. The Norwegian Vikings went via Iceland to Greenland, and eventually to North America under Leif Erikson. By the year AD 1000, King Olav was ruling from his capital at Trondheim; while fighting to unite the country, he fell to the Danes and Swedes off the island of Rügen (on the Baltic coast of what is now Germany). This was also the time when Christianity was first introduced to Norway from Denmark; the country was Christianised by King Olav the Holy (1015–1028). Oslo was probably founded in 1050 by Harald Hårdråde, who fell in 1066 in a bid for the throne of England. Bergen was founded around 1070.

Further periods of disorder were partly due to the increased political influence of the church, which, after the institution of an archbishopric at Trondheim, became more and more concerned with the selection of sovereigns, and partly due to an increase of influence amongst the larger and more powerful families. Further problems were caused by bands of adventurers.

The struggles continued well into the fourteenth century, both to unify the country and to defend it against the Danes. This was also the time when large farms and stave churches were built in Norway. Between 1349 and 1350, nearly half the population died of the plague. At the end of the fourteenth century, Queen Margaret of Denmark inherited the Norwegian throne in the Union of Kalmar. Sweden was also part of this union until 1523.

From then onwards, Norway remained in personal union with Denmark, which exerted a strong cultural and economic influence. But the Norwegians held on stubbornly to their individual identity, and never allowed themselves to be 'swallowed up' by Denmark. The isolated situation of much of the country helped in this. The costs of the struggles between Denmark and Sweden were often borne by the Norwegians, which kindled their hatred against both peoples, and fuelled their desire for national autonomy. These feelings came to a head during the continental blockade in the Napoleonic Wars, when Norway's shipping and trade collapsed. The Norwegians blamed the Danes for this because of their alliance with Napoleon. Denmark lost Norway after Napoleon's defeat, and in 1814 Norway was ceded to Sweden.

There was widespread resentment against the Swedes, indeed, the Norwegians refused to recognise the treaty, declared their independence, and at the Storting in Eidsvoll they drew up a liberal constitution which

Eidsvoll, site of Norway's Constitution

suited their own tastes. However, Carl Johan Bernadotte of Sweden compelled the Norwegians to recognise their personal union with Sweden, while at the same time allowing them considerable autonomy. It made no difference to the Norwegians whether they were ruled by the Danes or the Swedes, provided that their rights were respected — so they eventually complied. But the Norwegian Storting was to remain in continual conflict with the government in Stockholm.

The nineteenth century saw a great flowering in art, literature and music and also the development of a written national language. The king was

Fredriksten Fortress in Halden has sealed many historic decisions

forced to grant Norway a parliament during this time, although this still did not satisfy Norwegian aspirations. In a national referendum in 1905, the vast majority of Norwegians expressed their desire for independence. This was ratified in the Treaty of Karlstad in the October of that year. Prince Carl, who was a member of the Danish royal family, was elected king of Norway, taking the name of Håkon VII.

King Håkon VII was married to the British Princess Maud, who died in 1938. King Håkon himself died in 1957 at the age of 85. He was succeeded by his only son, born in 1903, who became King Olav V. King Olav, the 'smiling monarch', had been married to Princess Märthe of Sweden, who had died in 1954 before his accession to the throne. There were three children of this marriage: Crown Prince Harald, born in 1937; Princess Ragnhild, born in 1930; and Princess Astrid, born in 1932. Both Norwegian princesses are married to commoners from prominent families.

The Norwegian royal family is distinguished by its plain and unpretentious lifestyle. Crown Prince Harald is said to be a sporting character of liberal persuasions. The Norwegian parliament has granted him express permission to marry a commoner without prejudicing his right of accession to the throne. Like his father, he is a skilful and enthusiastic yachtsman; he studied at Oxford and at the Norwegian Military Academy. The Norwegian monarchy, like that of the other Scandinavian countries, is predominantly unaffected by party-political conflicts, and enjoys considerable popularity at all levels of society.

Norway remained neutral during World War I, but suffered severe economic hardship due to the British blockade of her fish exports to Germany. Norway also lost the greater part of her trade with the Allies. During World War I, Norway remained very much in sympathy with Britain and somewhat hostile to Germany. But relations with Germany improved between the wars. Swedish ores were loaded onto ships at the ice-free harbour at Narvik, and transported directly to Germany in Norwegian vessels.

In World War II, this relationship was soon in jeopardy. In 1940 the country was occupied by the German army, while Britain planned a counter-action and to a certain extent carried it out. The result of this was heavy fighting, especially in the area of Narvik, and the eventual outcome was a total German occupation of Norway. After 125 years of peace, the Norwegian population suffered considerably during the 5 years of Nazi occupation.

The king went into exile and did not return until the country was liberated in 1945 and took part in the founding of the United Nations. Norway joined NATO in 1949, was a founding member of EFTA in 1969 and of the Nordic Passport and Customs Union in 1958. They have a free trade agreement with the EEC, but a referendum in 1972 decided against full membership of the community. In recent years, Norway's history and prosperity has been closely connected with the discovery and development of North Sea oil and natural gas.

3. Stave churches and storehouses: a legacy of the Middle Ages

When you visit the Norwegian Folk Museum, which is an open-air museum on Oslo's Bygdøy peninsula, this will possibly be your first chance to see an example of a strange kind of church that is virtually exclusive to Norway. The building in question was originally built in 1200 at Gol in Hallingdal, 120km north-west of Oslo, and was brought to the Folk Museum on the initiative of King Oskar II. At first sight this church might be considered more in keeping with the South Seas than with Norway. It is an example of a stave church — a type of building that is almost peculiar to southern and central Norway. (In the interests of accuracy, it should be noted that there is a stave church in Sweden not far from Gothenburg, and another in the Giant Mountains of Silesia in Poland. The latter was brought there over 100 years ago from Vang in the Grindane Mountains of southern Norway.)

In the Middle Ages, around 1300, there were probably about a thousand

Borgund stave church, Lærdal

of these strange churches in Norway. But only about twenty-five of them have survived to the present day, and some of these are in poor condition or have been considerably altered. Research suggests that these Norwegian stave churches were modelled on the early Germanic village halls, where the tribal chiefs and elders assembled. Each is an enormous wooden building made up of a single rectangular structure supported by a large number of columns.

The interior of the building opens right up into the roof area; the walls are made up of vertical planks or staves, which fit together ingeniously to form an extremely strong structure. You can tell from the construction how familiar the Norwegians were with building in timber, and especially with building ships. Timber structures have severe limitations on the height of the walls, but this problem was overcome by supporting them with crossbeams and building a series of roofs in step formation, one on top of another. This increased the potential height of the building in the same way that a dome does in a stone structure. The shingle roofs usually end in a single central stave, the top of which is richly carved, usually in the form of a horse or dragon, reminiscent of the prow of a Viking ship. Indeed, the whole structure gives the impression of having been constructed by the people who built the Viking longboats.

There were no windows to the interior of the building, since window glass was unknown in Norway at the time. The only natural light was that which entered through one or two dormers in the roof. The congregation would stand in semi-darkness in a church which normally lacked benches, while the carved wooden altar and the preacher stood out in the only available light.

These stave churches, whose structure and form make them feel like part of the forest, lend an incomparable beauty to the mountainous landscape of southern Norway. They have mostly been enlarged or extended at a later date, so that they now possess side-aisles and entrance halls. Most of the really old churches had a circular aisle all the way round, and separate entrances for men and women. The interior timbers are often richly painted and engraved. The designs used hark back to ancient runes, and many pre-Christian motifs such as the Midgard Serpent can be picked out among the rich ornamentation.

On the outside of these churches, the wood has been covered with pitch, which over the centuries has become dark blue in colour. The roof is made up of a complex of gables and smaller roofs, and is steeply pitched to prevent the snow lying, giving the impression from a distance of a high wooden pyramid.

If you visit the stave church at the Folk Museum in Oslo, you will find the drawings on the wall near the altar to be of particular interest. These were not discovered until the church was moved to its present site. They include drawings of human and animal figures, and also runic inscriptions. The staves are also frequently inscribed with runes giving the names of long-forgotten generations.

The biggest stave church is at **Heddal** in the county of Telemark. Its own records show that it was consecrated in 1147. Another remarkable stave church is the one at **Borgund** in Lærdal (not to be confused with Borgund near Ålesund). This is probably the most beautiful of the stave churches that remain in Norway, and it is also in the most beautiful of settings. You will come across several stave churches in the course of the tours that are described later in the book. They are all worth visiting, because every stave church is different.

The thinly populated mountain regions of southern Norway were quite different from elsewhere in Europe, where the beautiful churches were created by a special class of master builders. The people who built these stave churches were used to wielding an axe and to making a ship seaworthy; so they naturally had their own ideas about building churches. The fact that stave churches are confined to the south of the country is probably because the northern regions came to Christianity very much later, at a time when stone churches had already become the norm.

There are yet more buildings in Norway that hark back to the Middle Ages. They were built for purely secular purposes, but many have remained in much the same form as that in which they were originally built. Known in Norwegian as *stabburer* or storehouses, they are built on stilts and were designed for storing winter fodder. They can be found all over southern Norway. Some of them have been preserved intact since the Middle Ages, while others are modern constructions built according to the traditional design. Sometimes they have been converted into houses or stables. Presumably they were built on stilts so that they were easier to enter through deep snow, and to protect them from hungry wild animals. Access was provided via a ladder or staircase. In the far north, farmers needed to lay up vast stores of winter fodder for their cattle, which might otherwise perish during the long, hard winters. There are incidents recorded of farmers whose animals were too weak to walk when the snow had melted, so that they had to be carried out bodily to the pastures.

You will still notice today how the rich meadows are fenced off, with no livestock grazing on them. The fences are in fact to keep cattle out rather than in, while the animals themselves are forced to feed along the grass verges and forest fringes. The hay meadows are set aside specifically for winter fodder. In the meantime, tourists have to cope with meandering herds of cattle, which sometimes block the road completely. To stop the cattle wandering into towns and villages, there are cattle grids on all the roads. The motorist is given ample warning of these by means of signs which say *Fe-Rist*.

4. Geology

Geologically speaking, the whole of the west coast of Norway looks rather like a giant rampart which acts as a bulwark against the ocean. This idea is by no means absurd if you consider the way in which the land was actually formed.

During the Silurian period, a fold mountain range was formed, which

Cattle and goats roam Norway's roadsides

approximately followed the coastlines of Scotland and Norway. It is known as the Caledonian fold, and is made up of porphyry and granite dating from between 1,000 and 2,000 million years ago, covered by sediments from the Cambrian and Silurian periods (about 300 to 400 million years ago). A part of this mountain range later sank below the sea, with the result that Scotland and Norway became separated. The coastline of Norway can thus be compared to a vast sloping barrier of rock sticking up from the sea.

This rock barrier was full of faults and fissures, which were further opened up by the action of the sea; also, the whole land area began to sink, thus creating the belt of rocks and islands that lines the Norwegian coast today, amounting to as many as 150,000 in all. Even the Lofoten Islands owe their origin to this geological process.

The sinking of the land was also responsible for that other characteristic feature of the Norwegian coast, the *fjords*. These were originally valleys, which were flooded as the land sank. During the ice ages, the fjords were gouged out by glaciers, making them even deeper and more complex in structure. As a result, they often became much deeper than the sea bordering the coast.

The ice also eroded the mountains which form the land mass of Norway, levelling them out into the vast plateaux which the Norwegians call *fjells*. These are on average about 1,000m above sea level, and their higher parts

Lille Finnjerka, rock formation on the Nordkinn Peninsula

---

are still covered with glaciers. A typical example in central Norway is the Jostelbre (*bre* = glacier).

The present shape of the land surface is largely the result of glaciation during the ice ages. The mountain peaks were eroded down to form plateaux, and all the loose rocks were carried away by the glaciers, which gouged out the river valleys into vast U-shaped trenches. As you travel through Norway, the effects of the glaciers are still clearly to be seen in the rounded summits of the mountains.

After the last ice age was over, the whole of Scandinavia became subject to isostatic forces, which caused the land mass generally to rise in a process that is still going on today. This can be explained by the fact that, during the last ice age, Scandinavia was weighed down by a vast ice sheet between 1 and 2km thick, which exerted a pressure of more than 200 atmospheres. With time, the continuous pressure forced the earth's crust downwards at the centre of the ice sheet, while the rocks deep down in the crust were pushed outwards towards the ice-free areas that surrounded the ice, so that these in turn were pushed upwards.

When the ice melted, the release of pressure on the centre of the land mass caused it to rise again, while the rocks in the earth's crust returned to the centre. Thus the centre of the land mass rose while the edges began to

The harbourside, Bergen

Aurland village. The road leads over the mountains to Sognefjord

A farmhouse near Voss

The 'Reka', known as the strangest mountain in Norway

sink again.

The many glaciers that remain form an inexhaustible water source to supply the many waterfalls that plunge hundreds of metres over the cliffs and valley faces. Mardalsfoss, which plunges 655m, is the highest waterfall

Olden, Western Norway

---

in Europe. It falls into Eikesdalsvatn between Åndalsnes and Sunndalsøra.

The many rivers are usually very short and fast-flowing. They are not usually navigable, but are useful for transporting timber and for energy production. They break up the Norwegian landscape, and often contribute to the strangeness of the scenery. Norway's vast water resources are also contained in its numerous lakes, which are mostly narrow, deep and fjord-like. They are very cold, crystal clear and oxygenated, and thus form the ideal habitat for the large fish populations. Taken together, they cover an area almost as large as the old county of Yorkshire, and larger than Norway's total area of agricultural land.

5.   Fauna and flora

Barely a quarter of Norway's land area is occupied by forest, most of which is made up of firs and pines. Birch trees form the last bastions in the far north, where the treeline is usually made up of dwarf birches of stunted growth. The treeline is at about 1,000m in the south of the country, dropping gradually to 300m at the Arctic Circle, while the extreme north is totally bare of trees.

The west coast of Norway is characterised by rich vegetation, and grain and fruit crops are also to be found. Grain crops can be cultivated on the west coast as far north as 71° whereas in inland Scandinavia 65° is the northernmost limit. Apart from grain crops, a variety of vegetables are grown too, including carrots, while potatoes are cultivated right up to the North Cape. The growing period is very short for all these crops, but thanks to the long summer days, the actual ripening time is almost comparable with that in the southern Mediterranean and growth is still possible during the night.

The same applies to tree growth, and this is the reason why Scandinavian timber is so much prized for its quality, especially that from foliage trees. These trees grow relatively slowly in Scandinavia, so the growth rings are very close together, creating a very fine grain and making the wood very hard.

When you travel through Norway, you will notice that the vegetation of temperate Central Europe extends a long way north, while at the same time typically Arctic flora can also be found a long way south.

The fjells, which make up nearly a third of Norway's land surface, have their own special flora, which is characterised by bushes and shrubs such as the dwarf pine, the dwarf birch, the arctic willow, the juniper, and the cranberry bush, the fruit of which has such a special place on Norwegian menus.

In the far north, the plant life develops much later with the summer being so short, but when it eventually starts growing it does so more quickly. Nature seems suddenly to explode into life, and you will be amazed at the rich greenery that can spring from the finest of cracks in a vertical cliff.

The treeless expanses of the fjells and the far north are often boggy and covered in cotton grass. Mosses and lichens are also typical of these areas. These ground-cover plants tend to flower in the autumn, covering the fjells with a rich orange carpet. The **Hardangervidda** forms an enormous nature reserve, with numerous rare species of plants and animals. At a height of 1,200 to 1,400m, it covers an area of nearly 12,000sq km to form the largest

Lake Strynsvannet, Hjelle

plateau in Europe; its flora is typical of moorlands and subarctic regions: dwarf birch, woolly willow, northern monk's hood and alpine crowfoot.

The fauna of southern Norway is similar to that of Central Europe. Game animals include hares, foxes, badgers and martens, not to mention roe-deer and red deer. The extensive forests are the habitat of Scandinavia's

The mountains and fjords of Sogndalsdalen

largest indigenous wild animal — the elk. There are numerous signs to warn tourists of a possible sudden encounter, for although the elk is a shy animal and rarely seen, the dangers should not be underestimated. A fully-grown male can weigh as much as 500kg, and may reach a shoulder height of up to two metres. During the summer the elk move well away from civilisation, but in winter they may come right into the towns.

The reindeer are not fully wild, having been partially domesticated by the Lapps; they move in herds across northern regions. They are also seen occasionally on the plateaux of central Norway, though only in groups of three or four. The northern parts of the mountains are the habitat of lynxes, wolves and gluttons (or wolverines), and at one time of brown bears, though these are now confined to a small area in Hallingdal (120km from Oslo). Another animal which has almost disappeared is the musk-ox, which has been reintroduced to **Dovrefjell**. These shaggy, bull-like creatures are becoming increasingly numerous, but to see them you must hike across the inhospitable fjell and wait patiently for hours.

Norway has much the same bird species as we do, but the coast is particularly interesting with its many bird islands. The inaccessible rocks and cliffs are the nesting grounds for gannets, razorbills, guillemots, puffins and numerous species of gull.

Another creature which is typical of Norway is the salmon. This fish is in its element in the many fast-flowing rivers, which it climbs to get to its spawning grounds. At points where its progress is hindered by unusually

Reindeer at Danebu, Valdres

steep rapids or waterfalls, salmon ladders have been installed which enable the fish to jump up to higher levels. Another important freshwater fish is the trout. The rivers are so rich in fish that they provide an angler's paradise, but this sometimes means that they do not grow to full size because there are simply too many of them. The fjords are the home of saltwater fishes such as herring, cod and mackerel — and also of seals. Seals have been seen in the Nærøyfjord — a branch of the Sognefjord.

Most domestic animals are much the same as those found in this country. Sheep and goats are particularly important as sources of wool, milk, cheese and meat. The upland ponies are of special interest. They are small, pale-coloured and compact in build.

Some other creatures are pests — particularly the midges, which are especially common in Norway. On quiet summer evenings they swarm around lake shores and across marshes and bogs. They do not become a nuisance every year, but it is difficult to predict when there are going to be a lot of them. A suitable insect repellent is a wise precaution.

6. The midnight sun

Because the earth's axis of rotation is tilted, the length of day and night varies considerably from one place to another, and according to the season of the year.

At the equator, there is hardly any noticeable difference between summer and winter, and day and night each last for 12 hours at all times of the year. But the seasonal variations become greater as you travel towards the poles. Thus, while the North Pole enjoys continuous daylight from March to September, the South Pole remains in constant darkness. On 22 September the two switch over, and the North Pole is plunged into darkness while the South Pole enjoys continuous daylight until 21 March.

In all places north of the Arctic Circle (latitude 66° 33'), the sun never sets on Midsummer Day (23 June). The further you go north of this line, the longer the period of continuous daylight. The midnight sun lasts:

in Tromsø	from 20 May to 23 July;
in Hammerfest	from 16 May to 27 July;
at the North Cape	from 14 May to 29 July;
on Spitzbergen	from 21 April to 22 August.

This phenomenon is mathematically and astronomically very interesting, but it also affects everyday life. Even in the south of Norway, the nights in summer are perceptibly shorter and brighter than in England; and in Trondheim July nights are barely more than a fleeting period of dusk.

People, animals and plants are naturally affected by this. During the midsummer period, the whole of Scandinavia is full of the joys of life. People sleep less, and seem to be in a constant state of high spirits. It is a time of unrestrained celebration throughout Scandinavia, and this most serious-minded of races becomes quite uncharacteristically festive.

The plant life, which has been asleep during the long, dark winter, suddenly explodes into life with the first warm sunshine, so that budding, flowering and ripening are compressed into a much shorter period. In northern latitudes there is a period of luxuriant plant growth, in which as

Puffins inhabit the Lofoten bird-rocks

Midsummer's night at Hjertøy near Bodø

much is achieved in three to four weeks as would take several months in countries further south.

On the other hand, during the long, dark winter, day can often be little more than a fleeting period of dawn, while areas north of the Arctic Circle must endure whole periods of continuous darkness. There are rarely any tourists around at this time of year. Life becomes hard for the inhabitants, who must put up with extreme cold as well as continuous darkness. No wonder, therefore, that the return of the sun is celebrated as a resurrection.

Technology has made things somewhat easier these days. Electricity for lighting is cheap, thanks to the country's vast resources of hydroelectric power, so that even the smallest village in Norway is supplied with more than adequate street lighting. Every Norwegian house is filled with lights, some of which remain constantly lit for months on end. Hammerfest, the northernmost town in the world, was the first town in Europe to be completely lit by electricity. With a consumption of 16,000 kilowatt-hours per person per year, Norwegians are by far the greatest consumers of electricity in the world.

Another common occurrence in the north is the northern lights. This phenomenon has baffled scientists down the centuries. The sky first becomes filled with yellow and red light, which is then transformed into an intense medley of bands of light. All colours and intensities are represented, so that the night sky is filled with an amazingly bright display of lights like a vast theatre stage. You need only to experience it to

Spring in Telemark

understand why it was once thought to be supernatural in origin. This ghostlike curtain of coloured lights, spreading like a shimmering veil across the sky, and often seeming like a reflection of distant fires, was enough to fill all onlookers with dread, and was thought to be an omen of great evil.

Even today, the origin of the northern lights (more correctly named polar lights, since they occur in the Southern Hemisphere too) is yet to be fully understood. They appear to have something to do with sunspots — gigantic disturbances in the sun's atmosphere. Huge quantities of protons are hurled into space and travel towards the earth at speeds appoaching that of light. As these particles come into the earth's magnetic field, they are deflected towards the earth's two magnetic poles. This is the reason why the phenomenon occurs most frequently in those latitudes bordering the magnetic poles. At heights of between 100 and 1,000km, the particles come into contact with the outermost layer of the earth's atmosphere, where they cause ionisation, giving off light. The colour pattern which emerges depends on the wavelengths of the light rays produced, but the composite result is the incredible display of variegated light bands that make up the northern lights. Neon lamps work according to a similar principle.

Nordfjord, Western Norway

7. Climate and travel

It would be wrong to look on a holiday in Norway as a form of arctic expedition. On the contrary, high summer in Norway can often rise to near-Mediterranean temperatures, especially in the far north. This is one of the reasons for the explosion of luxuriant growth during the few weeks of summer. In May 1984, maxima of 25°C were recorded in Lapland, though these were exceptional. But the old idea that Norway is always cold is an unfounded prejudice based solely on its northerly location. The climate of most of Norway is strongly influenced by the Atlantic Ocean and the Gulf Stream. It is because of the Gulf Stream that the fjords and harbours remain ice-free for most of the winter, even in the most northerly regions, while harbours bordering on the Gulf of Bothnia remain iced up for many months, even those lying much further south. This is why Swedish ores from Kiruna are exported via the Norwegian port of Narvik. The effects of the Gulf Stream are coastal only; thus the deep valleys in central Norway such as Gudbrandsdal have a continental climate, with cold winters and hot summers, and quick alternations between sunshine and rain.

Chalet in the Jotunheimen mountains

The climatic differences can be so extreme that almost every fjord or valley might be said to have its own climate. You might leave a valley in bright sunshine, only to run suddenly into fog and cloud over the pass, and to find heavy rain on the other side. But the valley after that might be bathed in sunshine again. It is interesting to note, for example, that in the area around Lom in Ottadal, the climate is so dry that irrigation is required, while the mountains only 60km to the west are one of the wettest regions in the whole country.

Although Norway spans as many as 13° of latitude, there is surprisingly little difference in temperature between the north and the south, especially in the summer. This fact is even more amazing if you consider the enormous distances between north and south. The North Cape is as far north of Norway's southernmost point near Kristiansand as Rome is to the south.

Mount Gausta, tallest in Telemark

In May, while the high mountain passes are still cut off by snow, with average temperatures of around 10°C, the valleys are already warm enough to be comfortable in the open air. The driest month is June, when temperatures suddenly leap up. July is the warmest month, with average temperatures of 17.3°C in Oslo and 15°C in Bergen (London 17.8°C). But averages are only useful for statistical purposes, and July temperatures of 35°C have been recorded. After all, it is impossible to predict what the weather is going to do.

The best time for travelling to Norway is during the long days of summer. The best weather is between the middle of June and the second half of August. Even when it is wet, the rain never lasts long. Outside the summer season, however, there is always a risk of cold nights inland and prolonged rainfall on the coast. Many of the mountain passes remain closed until the beginning of June.

The water temperatures also vary considerably. The mountain lakes are usually very deep and are supplied by water from glaciers and melting snow, while the fjords that go deep inland are similarly only suitable for the hardiest of swimmers. On the other hand, the North Sea coast is usually perfectly all right for swimming, and thanks to the Gulf Stream, it warms up quickly in the summer.

Norway is also very attractive in the winter. From the beginning of December until well into the spring, it provides ideal conditions for skiers.

1 OSLO TO BERGEN

1 (a) The Haukeli route

Oslo ● Kongsberg (Larvik) ● Haukeligrend (Kristiansand) ● Røldal
(Haugesund) ● Kinsarvik ● Bergen (about 550km)

What the route has to offer:
The road via **Telemark** forms the southern route from Oslo to Bergen.
Though at 550km it is not the shortest route, it is full of interesting scenery.
It can also be approached from Denmark via the ports of Larvik and
Kristiansand. There is a great variety of things to see, from the Spirals of
Drammen to Norway's largest stave church in Heddal; the road passes
through vast pine forests and lovely valleys, across rugged plateaux such as
the Haukelifjell (now open throughout the winter whereas the old
mountain passes were closed for three or four months of the year), past
gorgeous lakes and along the fjord, and finally through Norway's richest
fruit-growing region to the enchanting old city of Bergen.

The road is a new one, and the Norwegians are justifiably proud of it.
Before it was built, the east-west route was closed by snow for much of the
year, but the new road is built to the highest European standards. Although
twisty, it is not difficult for drivers, with one or two long climbs of 10 per
cent or 12 per cent at the most. The E76 from Oslo to Bergen is the ideal
route for the start of a Norwegian tour, offering a foretaste of what is to
follow. Frequent stops are needed to take in the full beauty of the
landscape, so it is worth taking at least 2 days to complete the journey to
Bergen.

The route:

Take the E18 motorway from Oslo to Drammen. Leave the E18 at this
point as it heads off towards Larvik, and follow signs for the E76 for
Kongsberg. The road passes through **Drammen** (population 50,000),
administrative capital of the county of Buskerud. Ancient wall carvings
indicate that there was a settlement here as long as 4,000 or 5,000 years ago.
It is in fact made up of two towns, Stromsø and Bragernes, which
were united in 1811 to form the town of Drammen. The harbour
is important for car imports.

Immediately on leaving the town along the E76, turn sharp right along
the Kongsgata, which leads to the Spirals of Drammen, the town's chief
attraction. The Spirals are in fact a 1,650m long tunnel, which winds in six
enormous spirals to the top of the Bragernesåsen, where there is a
restaurant and a marvellous view. The tunnel is open all the year round.
The Spirals owe their existence to the foresight of the townspeople, who in
1953 stopped quarrying for building stone and began to tunnel for it

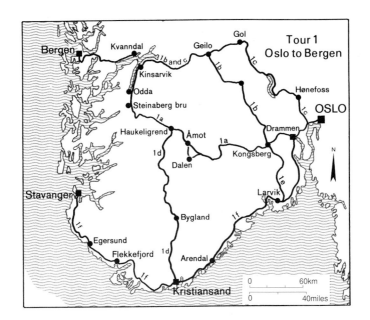

Tour 1
Oslo to Bergen

instead, thus preserving the beauty of the landscape. They continued this highly original method of conservation until 1961.

The E76 continues via Hokksund to **Kongsberg** (population 21,000). Kongsberg is situated on the Lågen river, which forms rapids at several points nearby. The town was founded by King Christian IV in 1624, following the discovery of silver deposits, and has flourished on silver mining ever since. The silver ores were eventually exhausted, and the last mine was closed in 1957. But by this time the metal-working industry had become firmly established.

The eighteenth-century rococo church bears witness to the town's early prosperity. It seats 2,400 people, and is thus one of the largest churches in Norway. The old silver mines are about 6km outside the town. The best-known of these is the Kongsgruve (or King's Pit), part of which is open to the public. It is served by the old mine railway, which plunges 2.3km into the hillside to a depth of 340m. The mine itself is 1,000m deep, and there is still one of the ancient lifts which took the miners down into the pit. In its heyday, the mine employed as many as 4,000 miners. The Pit Museum contains a marvellous silver collection.

From Kongsberg the E8 goes northwards to **Geilo** (see route 1b).

Those wishing to avoid the town centre should turn off just after Krekling Station onto Road 286, which bypasses the town; then at Skollenborg turn right onto the E8, which comes back into the E76 at Saggrenda near the old silver workings.

The road rises gently as far as Meheia, and soon afterwards crosses the county boundary from Buskerud into Telemark. From Meheia the road drops gently to Notodden (population 13,000). This lively little industrial town is supplied by the Tinnelva hydroelectric plant, where three sets of nearby rapids have been harnessed for this purpose. The town's chief industry is the Norsk Hydro saltpetre works.

The E76 continues, eventually skirting Heddalsvatn and arriving at Heddal, which is best known for the incredible **Heddal stave church**. Built probably in the thirteenth century, it is Norway's largest stave church. Like all stave churches (see page 27) it was originally built without windows, but windows were installed when it was restored in the middle of the last century. In 1954 it was restored again, but this time many of its features were restored to their original form.

Visitors are provided with a leaflet in English, but it is rather lacking in information. Especially interesting are the rich ornamentation, the wall paintings and the runic inscriptions. The doorways are decorated with plant and animal motifs. On the bishop's throne in the choir is a carving of a scene from the Nibelung saga showing Gunter and Siegfried riding towards Brunhild's castle. The covered aisle which goes all the way round is typical of stave churches, and has been preserved in its original form. The bell tower is separate and stands on the opposite side of the road. This church is a must for all visitors to this area.

Also worth visiting in Heddal is the open-air museum, with its small collection of old country dwellings. Of special interest is the old farmers' inn, whose walls and ceilings are painted all over with large rose motifs. This is typical of Telemark, where walls, doors and furniture were painted with rose designs, particularly during the eighteenth and nineteenth centuries.

Now drive on to Ørvella and Sauland, where the road into Tuddalsdal goes off to the right. Tuddal has a number of old houses, the oldest of which is a fourteenth-century storehouse (*stabbur* — see page 30).

The E76 now rises continuously to a maximum height of 425m — the highest point along this section of the route. A few bends further along is the village of **Nutheim**, where there is an outstanding view of the Flatdal and the mighty Lifjell. The road now descends to the village of **Seljord** with its medieval church. Seljord is situated by a lake of the same name - one of the finest in Telemark - and is surrounded by the lovely Telemark countryside. There are numerous old houses with grass growing on their roofs, some even with flowers and trees growing out of them.

At **Brunkeberg**, Road 39 to Kristiansand goes off to the left. 8km further on is **Morgedal**, which is where the sport of skiing first began. There is a memorial to Sondre Nordheim, the founder of modern skiing. He demonstrated his new technique in Oslo over a hundred years ago, and it has since become known all over the world as slalom. The Norwegians have an interesting explanation for the word. Apparently, when worried mothers saw their children schussing down steep slopes, they would shout

Morgedal, birthplace of Sondre Nordheim, pioneer of skiing

sla lom, which in Telemark dialect means 'make turns'. The skiing museum also contains a number of memorabilia of Bjåland, the South Polar explorer.

At **Høydalsmo** (Ofte) there is a left turn along Road 45 to **Dalen**. Tourists are recommended to make a short detour from Høydalsmo via Dalen to Åmot. The narrow, winding road is about 26km longer than the direct route along the E76, but it passes through some gorgeous scenery, and there are a number of interesting things to see on the way.

Road 45 goes through a wooded region to **Eidsborg** on the shores of a beautiful lake. There is an open-air museum up the hill to the right of the road. This includes a stave church, some storehouses, several old farmhouses scattered among the hills, and a small indoor museum of costumes and folklore.

The road winds on down towards Dalen. Drivers who can cope with yet more bends may like to go on from Dalen up to Holtebru (500m). All of the bends command a wonderful view over Dalen and the long, winding Bandaksvatn, which forms the top end of the Telemark Canal.

From Dalen the route continues along Road 38 to Liosvingen, where some drivers may wish to turn left and go through Rukkejuvet. This road is narrow and rather rough, but winds through wild and very beautiful scenery; it returns to the E76 near Vinjesvingen.

The most direct route from Liosvingen is to continue along Road 38, returning to the E76 at Åmot (Ytre Vinje). Running parallel to Road 38 is the Ravnejuveien — the road through the Raven's Chasm. This goes off to the right just outside Skålen, and follows a steep, winding track to the top of a vertical cliff. If a paper aeroplane is floated over the edge, the updraught brings it back over the cliff top again.

The Ravnejuveien eventually goes into the E76 at Gøytil, about 4km before Åmot. However, it is probably quicker and easier to go back to Road 38 and continue along it to **Åmot (Ytre Vinje)**. Here, at the confluence of the Tokke and the Vineå, there was once a 90m high waterfall called the Hyllandfoss, which has since been swallowed up by a power station.

The E76 continues along the side of Lake Vinje, and at Vinjesvingen is joined by the little road from Dalen via Rukkejuvet. The road goes on to a tourist centre at Mjonøy and continues through the Smørkleppdal. It then begins to climb gently through the Grungedal. At Edland there is a right turn for Road 362 to Rauland. This road goes along the side of Lake Totak, and passes a large number of houses and storehouses from the fifteenth and seventeenth centuries. Soon after Rauland the road joins Road 37, which leads back south to the E76 at Åmot.

The junction at Edland is soon followed by a crossroads at **Haukeligrend**, where the E76 is joined by Road 12 from Kristiansand (see route 1d). This is the beginning of the famous stretch of road known as the **Haukeli Road**, which first goes over the Haukelifjell, and then passes the edge of the Hardangervidda. This important east-west connection was first made at the end of the last century. The road went over a number of passes that were passable only in high summer. Now the E76 has been made into a really good road, which avoids the highest stretches by means of a long series of tunnels. More adventurous travellers may still prefer to use some of the old roads over the passes, and to get an idea of how wild they used to be. These roads usually come off the E76 just before one of the tunnels. They are still kept in good repair, and act as relief roads during the summer months.

From Haukeligrend (540m) the road climbs gently at first, but soon becomes very much higher. Botn (815m) is in a beautiful setting by a lake, and there are some old storehouses by the road. At **Vågslid** there is a tourist centre, with many holiday huts and a hotel by the lake. This is a good centre for walking across the fjell with its snow-covered mountains.

Soon after that the road passes through a skiing area and comes to another tourist centre at Prestegård. It now aproaches the first tunnel, which is 1.6km long. It crosses the 1,000m line, and comes out of the tunnel to a beautiful view over Haukeliseter. Even in August, it is possible to touch the few bits of snow that cling to the shadows at the side of the road.

At Haukeliseter (980m) there is yet another tourist centre where travellers can stop for a rest. It is situated by the Ståvatn, a lake which is full of fish. A few kilometres further on, at Midtfjellsvollen, is the turning for the old road over the Dyrskar. Provided this road is open (no attempt is made to clear the snow), travellers are recommended to take it rather than go through the 6km long Haukeli Tunnel. The old road goes right over the pass, which at 1,148m offers an outstanding view.

Seljestad Tourist Centre

A short distance beyond the Haukeli Tunnel is the tollbooth where drivers have to pay for using the tunnels. By now the road has reached 1,085m, which is the highest point on the new Haukeli Road. It carries on for 3km through delightful mountain scenery. There may be one or two sheep or goats, either grazing or sunning themselves on the edge of the road. There will sometimes be people on the roadside selling the local brown goat's-milk cheese. Try a little of it before buying any, as it is an acquired taste.

Next comes the Svanndalsflona Tunnel, which leads gently downhill for just over 1km, and comes out at Austmannli. It is worth parking the car in the car park to the left of the road, and taking a look at the old road as it winds down the mountainside below. This road was built over 100 years ago, and now plays hide and seek with the new road. The seven great hairpins reach a maximum gradient of 12 per cent, and every corner offers a breathtaking view.

The road descends steeply to **Røldal**, which lies at 370m beside a lake of the same name. It has a large power station and a thirteenth-century stave church. The church has been heavily restored and is no longer in its original form, but it has become famous as a place of pilgrimage on account of a crucifix that is supposed to bring about miracles.

The E76 runs out along the lake shore, and leaves it near Horda at the point where Road 46 goes straight on for Sand on Sandsfjord. A short way up the hill is the turning for Road 520, which goes past numerous lakes filled with enormous quantities of fish, and eventually comes out at Sauda on the fjord of the same name. Sauda boasts the largest steelworks in Europe.

At Hordadalen the old road again leaves the new one just before the tunnel. It was again built over 100 years ago; it is 3m wide and has a maximum gradient of 10 per cent; the pass is 1,100m high, and there are sixteen hairpins on the way up. The Røldal Tunnel passes 200m below, but the new road eventually meets the old one on Røldalsfjell, reaching a maximum height of 1,067m.

This is followed by a gentle descent to the Seljestad Tunnel. Just before the tunnel the old road turns off, providing yet another opportunity to brave the wild terrain and enjoy the exciting scenery.

Seljestad is another tourist centre, with plentiful overnight accommodation, and numerous paths and ski-lifts in the vicinity. At the side of the main road there is a memorial to a postilion who in January 1903 was buried for $2\frac{1}{2}$ days under an avalanche and managed to dig himself out.

A few kilometres further on, just before **Steinaberg bru** near Jøsendal, the E76 crosses Road 47. At this point the main route goes right along Road 47 and turns northwards in the direction of Odda. Meanwhile, the E76 continues in the direction of Haugesund.

Excursion to Haugesund

Continue along the E76, which goes uphill as far as Vassvik. Here it begins to descend and eventually reaches sea level at Fjæra on Åkrafjord. The road then goes for 24km along the side of the fjord; it is extremely impressive, passing through twelve tunnels and over twenty-four bridges as the mountain drops sheer into the fjord. It also passes Langfoss, an impressive waterfall with a total height of about 400m.

After Kyrping the road leaves the fjord and goes on to Grindheim. Then there is Gjerde (Etne), a small village of 250 people with a lovely old church. This is closely followed by Ølensjøen, from which a ferry serves the islands to the north and Knapphus beyond. From Ølensjøen the road continues past Grindefjord to **Haugesund** (population 27,000).

This town has an important harbour, and is the home of one of Norway's largest herring fleets. Nearby across the Karmsund is the island of Karmøy, which is reached via a bridge 700m long and 45m high. Just before the bridge are five standing stones known as the 'Five Foolish Maidens', which are part of an ancient burial site. At Avaldsnes, just south of Haugesund, there is an old thirteenth-century church which has associations with King Harald Hårfagre (Fairhair).

The island of Karmøy is steeped in history, and has a number of monuments to the same Harald Fairhair, who was the founder of the kingdom of Norway. In the summer there are bus tours round the island, providing an opportunity to visit the historical monuments and appreciate the beauty of the island. At the southern end of the island is the port of Skudeneshavn, from which boats go to Stavanger. There are also hydrofoil trips to Stavanger (1 hour) and Bergen ($2\frac{1}{2}$ hours).

The return route from Haugesund is the same as the outward route. But it is also possible to turn off at Håland on Road 13 for Skånevik and take the ferry to Utåker. From here Road 13 continues along the coast of the peninsula, crossing over inlets and passing lovely little towns such as Uskedal and Rosendal, until it eventually reaches Løfallstrand. Further north along the road are yet further attractions, such as the medieval church at Ænes, the Fureberg Waterfall and the Bondhus Glacier.

From Løfallstrand there is a ferry across the **Hardangerfjord** to Gjermundshamn (25 minutes). Hardangerfjord is probably the best known and certainly one of the most beautiful of the Norwegian fjords. It extends 170km inland, has many branches and is over 800m deep in places. Along its shores there are unusual cliff formations with gushing waterfalls, and also fertile green slopes which form the largest fruit-growing area in Norway. In May, when the orchards are in blossom, one can well understand why those living on the Hardangerfjord have a reputation for being especially musical.

From Gjermundshamn the route continues along Road 13 through Mundheim to Eikelandsosen. Here there is a choice between staying on Road 13, which goes via Tysse to meet the E68 road to Bergen, or else taking Road 552 to Fusa, where there is a ferry to Hatvik (15 minutes). From Hatvik the route goes via Osøyro, where it joins Road 14 for Bergen.

The main route continues along Road 47. A short distance further on there is a marvellous view of the incredible **Låtefoss**. This is one of Norway's most beautiful waterfalls, and forms two branches plunging 165m down the mountainside. It sometimes falls partly on the road, so that drivers with open sun-roofs will suddenly find themselves drenched. Unfortunately, the most photogenic view is marred by a kiosk selling souvenirs. A few kilometres further on is yet another waterfall, called the Vidfoss.

Soon after that the road arrives in **Odda** (population 7,000), which lies at the top end of the Sørfjord, a branch of the Hardangerfjord that comes a long distance inland. Odda is important for its chemical plant. At this point Road 550 branches off along the west shore of the fjord to form the so-called Folgefonn Road. It is narrower than Road 47, but goes through the village of Aga, where several beautiful old houses are kept as a national monument. The road leads eventually to Utne, where a ferry crosses to Kvanndal, which is back on the main route.

The main route from Odda goes along the east shore of the Sørfjord to **Tyssedal**. The main road by-passes the town through a 3km long tunnel. It is an important industrial centre, with an aluminium plant among others. Across the fjord in **Eitrheim** is a zinc plant. The energy for these and other industries is provided by the Tyssedal Power Station, which harnesses the water from the Tysså Falls through three enormous pipes. A second power station is under construction. A little side road goes off from Tyssedal, which rises 556m to the Ringedalsvatn with its enormous dam.

*Vøringfoss Falls in
Hardanger*

Road 47 goes on from Tyssedal to Lofthus, which surprisingly is the centre of Norway's best-known fruit-growing area, with orchards amounting to 100,000 trees in all. They are naturally at their most attractive at the end of May when the trees are in blossom. These orchards owe their existence to the presence of the Gulf Stream, which increases the average yearly temperature by as much as 8°C compared with places of the same latitude on the east coast of Scandinavia. Also in Lofthus is the log house where Edvard Grieg, the composer, lived for a number of years.

Road 47 eventually ends at **Kinsarvik**, where the ferry goes across to **Kvanndal**. For those with a little extra time, it is worth visiting the nearby medieval church, and the Skiparstod, the remains of an ancient Viking boathouse, which is directly on the quay itself. Before the Brimnes-Bruravik ferry was enlarged, this was Norway's busiest ferry port. Just south of the town, the impressive Tveitafoss plunges 103m into the valley.

Excursion to Fossli and the Måbødal

From Kinsarvik it is worth making a short excursion to **Fossli** (about 100km there and back). This combines a lovely journey along the side of the Eidfjord with a trip on one of Norway's most exciting mountain roads.

There are numerous breathtaking views and impressive waterfalls.

The route follows Road 7 from Kinsarvik to **Eidfjord** along the fjord of the same name. There are many wonderful views across the fjord to the sheer mountains opposite, which are between 1,200 and 1,600m high.

People with caravans are recommended to leave them on a camp site at

Eidfjord, or better still at Kinsarvik.

Road 7 goes from Eidfjord across the fertile valley bottom past Eidfjordvatn; then at **Sæbø** it turns up into the glorious **Måbødal** where the mighty **Vøringfoss** plunges more than 180m. The road winds breathtakingly out of the valley, climbing 400m in only 6.7km by means of five hairpins and three tunnels. The best view of the road and the valley is from just before the first bend, but the best view of the waterfall itself is from the Fossli Hotel, which is situated above the rock face and can be reached via a side road that goes off just after Fossli. The waterfall sends out vast clouds of spray, producing rainbow effects in the sunlight. The road up to the hotel is fully metalled throughout, and offers wonderful views of the **Hardangerjøkul** (1862m), a massive snowfield to the north east.

Instead of returning to Kinsarvik, some travellers may prefer to take the ferry across the Eidfjord from **Brimnes** to **Bruravik**, with its attractive views of the Hardangerjøkul, and of the narrow, steep-sided Osafjord, which is a branch of the Eidfjord. The road from Bruravik is a new and very scenic one, which eventually meets the E68 near **Granvin**. The E68 goes left for Bergen, and right for Voss and the Sognefjord.

The ferry from Kinsarvik to Kvanndal takes 35 minutes, stopping briefly at Utne. The crossing provides views of the **Hardangerfjord** with its many branches. It is the best-known and one of the most beautiful fjords. It extends 170km inland, and its branches include Sørfjord, Eidfjord, Osafjord, Samlafjord and Granvinfjord; it reaches depths of up to 830m, making it deeper than the adjoining parts of the North Sea. Its shores offer a variety of scenery, from steep cliffs and waterfalls with glimpses of snow-covered peaks, to pleasant slopes covered in orchards. The people who live by the Hardangerfjord are particularly musical, and have a special sort of violin called a *Hardingfela*.

At **Kvanndal** the route joins the E68, which goes right for **Voss** and Sognefjord, and left for Bergen. The route to Bergen first goes along the shore of the fjord, passing Ålvik and the Bjølvefoss Power Station with its 800m long vertical pipes. It then crosses a suspension bridge over the Fykesund to arrive at Øystese, which is a popular resort. The next place is **Norheimsund**, which is another tourist resort. Here Road 551 branches off and continues along the side of the fjord.

The E68 now climbs, goes through a tunnel, and eventually comes into a gorge called the Tokagjelet. The road passes a waterfall called the Vosselv, and winds on through several tunnels to Kvamskogen — a mountain resort full of weekend cottages, huts and guesthouses.

The road eventually returns to sea level at **Tysse** on the Samnangerfjord, where Road 13 comes in from Stavanger in the south. (This road is also mentioned in the section on **Haugesund** — see page 54.) The E68 skirts the fjord and then passes through a number of tunnels to reach **Indre Arna**, the last station on the railway line to Bergen. The railway goes on to Bergen through an 8km long tunnel beneath Ulriken, Bergen's local mountain resort. The road goes on to Bergen via Espeland and Nesttun.

The city of Bergen is described later in the book in the section on towns and cities.

1 (b)   The Numedal route

Oslo ● Kongsberg ● Geilo ● Kinsarvik ●Bergen

What the route has to offer:

The route from Oslo to Bergen via Kongsberg and Geilo is one of the most varied routes between Norway's two largest cities. It runs up the wild valley of **Numedal**, past the gushing Lågen river, and later crosses the high plateaux of the **Hardangervidda** with its snow-covered peaks and glaciers. The high-point of the journey is the section through Måbødal with its famous waterfall, the Vøringsfoss. After a ferry across the **Hardangerfjord**, the route finally reaches the lovely city of Bergen. The part of the route through the Hardangervidda is closed from mid-October to mid-May.

The route:

Take the E18 motorway from Oslo to Drammen. Leave the E18 at this point as it heads off towards Larvik, and follow signs for the E76 for Kongsberg. The road passes through **Drammen** (population 50,000), administrative capital of the county of Buskerud. Ancient wall carvings indicate that there was a settlement here as long as 4,000 or 5,000 years ago. It is in fact made up of two towns, Stromsø and Bragernes, which were united in 1811 to form the town of Drammen. The harbour is important for car imports.

Immediately on leaving the town along the E76, turn sharp right along the Kongsgata, which leads to the Spirals of Drammen, the town's chief attraction. The Spirals are in fact a 1,650m long tunnel, which winds in six enormous spirals to the top of the Bragernesåsen, where there is a restaurant and a marvellous view. The tunnel is open all the year round. The Spirals owe their existence to the foresight of the townspeople, who in 1953 stopped quarrying for building stone and began to tunnel for it instead, thus preserving the beauty of the landscape. They continued this highly original method of conservation until 1961.

The E76 continues via Hokksund to **Kongsberg** (population 21,000), which is situated on the Lågen. The town was founded by King Christian IV in 1624, following the discovery of silver deposits, and has flourished on silver mining ever since. The silver ores were eventually exhausted, and the last mine was closed in 1957. But by this time the metal-working industry had become firmly established. The eighteenth-century rococo church bears witness to the town's early prosperity. It seats 2,400 people, and is thus one of the largest churches in Norway.

About 6km outside the town are the old silver workings. The best-

Kongsberg Church

known of these is the Kongsgruve (or King's Pit), part of which is open to
the public. It is served by the old mine railway, which plunges 2.3km into
the hillside to a depth of 340m. The mine itself is 1,000m deep, and there is
still one of the ancient lifts which took the miners down into the pit. In its
heyday, the mine employed as many as 4,000 miners. The Pit Museum
contains a marvellous silver collection.

The route leaves the E76 at this point. The E76 goes on via Notodden and
Haukeligrend to Haugesund, with road 47 leading off to **Kinsarvik** (see
route 1a).

This route now turns north along Road 8, which has come up from
Larvik (see route 1f), and carries on through **Numedal**. The valley is heavily
wooded and is drained by the Lågen, which runs parallel to Road 8 and to
the railway as well. At Stengelsrud, Road 37 goes off to the left, forming an
alternative route through Telemark. It eventually comes out into the E76 at
Åmot, and thus makes a delightful alternative to the more southerly route
along the E76 (see route 1a).

Road 8 continues northwards past numerous small waterfalls, crossing
to the east side of the river over the Grettefoss Bridge. A small road
continues along the west bank of the Lågen, leading to several small
tollroads up the nearby Blefjell (800m to 900m high). At Svene there is a
medieval church, which was partly rebuilt in the eighteenth century.

A few kilometres beyond Lampeland, a road turns right for Sigdal. The
next place is **Flesberg**, which has a twelfth-century stave church. Much of

the original building was lost when the interior was replaced in the eighteenth century. Road 8 crosses the river again over the Djupdal Bridge. A short way further on is the Numedal Hotel - a tourist centre, where licences may be obtained for fishing in the Lågen.

At Stærnes a small road turns off across the river and runs parallel to Road 8. It passes numerous old houses, farms and storehouses, and arrives at Rollag, where there is another stave church. This church has again been so heavily remodelled that very little of the original church remains. The road goes on past the church, and continues along the east bank of the river past the Mykstu Power Station. Near **Veggli** it rejoins Road 8, which comes back across the river.

A little further on there are one or two more old wooden houses typical of Numedal. The medieval Kravik Farm has been made a national monument. At Hvåle a small bridge goes across the river to Nore, which has a twelfth-century stave church. This church is particularly worth seeing, being in an unusual style. The interior is richly painted and decorated.

The river is now broader, and from Åsly as far as Sevle it forms the Norefjord. On some of the old farms in the area, there are original medieval storehouses (*stabburer*). Road 8 turns sharply westward and goes past one of Norway's largest power stations, Nore I. There is a road off to the right which goes northwards to the Tunnhovd Reservoir.

The next place is **Rødberg**, which is a small industrial town at the far end of the Numedal Railway. The road now goes west towards **Uvdal**, with its wonderful scenery and its typical stave church standing high on the slope. Although built in the Middle Ages, it was later remodelled, but it is colourfully decorated with flower and garland motifs.

Road 8 goes further into Uvdal, climbing all the time, and flanked by the foothills of the **Hardangervidda**. There are numerous holiday centres on the side of the road, where travellers may rest, and where hikers strike out across the Hardangervidda. This region is Norway's newest and most extensive national park. The high plateau offers breathtaking scenery, while the unusual subarctic flora and fauna are protected over an area of nearly 3,000sq km.

After Åsberg the road winds up over a 1,063m high pass, then drops down into Fetjan. A beautiful view opens up across the Hardangervidda. The road passes by the lakes of Holme and Skuvdal (with its modern chapel on the shore), once again crossing the 1,000m line. Shortly afterwards it arrives at Geilo where it meets the junction with Road 7.

Geilo (population 2,200) is a popular tourist centre and winter resort, with numerous ski-lifts to ski slopes of varying difficulty. In January there is an important winter sports festival in Geilo. The town is the home of Norway's largest ski training centre. Even in the summer there are sports on offer. There is a riding school, and all the larger hotels have swimming pools. Licences can also be obtained for fishing in local waterways. Geilo is an important junction on the railway line to Bergen. Road 7 from Hønefoss

Ski trails at Geilo

via Gol to Kinsarvik also passes through Geilo (see route 1c).

The route goes left at Geilo in the direction of Eidfjord and Kinsarvik. Near Fekjo, soon after Geilo, there are grave mounds from the Viking period.

The road rises as it enters the Hardangervidda. Near the holiday centre of Ustaoset, the Bergen railway reaches its highest point of 991m above sea level. Road and rail run parallel along the shore of Ustavatn. Then at Haugastøl the road and railway divide. The railway skirts the north of the Hardangerjøkul.

Road 7 continues to climb. To the right is the mighty **Hardangerjøkul** (1,862m), with its impressive snowy peaks. Near to the mountain hut at Fagerheim, some Lapps have set up a souvenir stall. At Halne — a mountain hut by a lake of the same name — the road crosses the county boundary from Buskerud into Hordaland. An ancient track called Normannslepet passes directly by the hut.

The road rises even further into the mountains, reaching its highest point near the holiday station of Dyranut (1,250m). In the hard winters, when snowstorms rage across the mountains, the road is blocked by snow from mid-October to mid-May. The road drops only slowly to below 1,000m.

The road then comes to **Fossli** and the **Måbødal**, which together provide the most remarkable scenery of the whole journey between Oslo and Bergen. The Vøringfoss near Fossli is one of Norway's most famous waterfalls, with a height of 182m. The best view of the fall is from a restaurant at the top. There are plans afoot to use this wonderful waterfall for a power station, which would be a dreadful thing to do.

The next part of the route is quite incredible - five hairpins and three tunnels within 6.7km as the road descends rapidly into Måbødal. The road is narrow and difficult for caravans. It has had to be blasted out of the mountainside, and has a gradient of between 10 per cent and 12 per cent.

Only a short distance further on is Sæbø, only 15m above sea level. From here a side road goes off into Hjølmodal, with its steep mountains and numerous waterfalls. This road is very narrow with few passing places, and is not very suitable for caravans or dormobiles.

The road continues along Eidfjordvatn, and through two tunnels to **Eidfjord** on the fjord of the same name, which forms a branch of the **Hardangerfjord**. The town of Eidfjord is surrounded by a typical moraine landscape; it has a medieval church built of sandstone, which is dedicated to James the Apostle. A side road from Eidfjord goes via Kjeåsen, with its beautiful vista across the fjord, to Sima with its power station, and finally to Rembesdalfoss and Skykkedalfoss — two beautiful high waterfalls, which can only be reached on foot.

The route continues along the fjord. Near **Brimnes**, the ferry crosses the fjord to **Bruravik** (10 minutes). A new road goes from Bruravik to Granvin, where it joins the E68 for Bergen. The ferry has been greatly enlarged to take some of the traffic from the Kinsarvik-Kvanndal ferry.

Road 7 continues along the fjord, passing a small open-air museum with old farmhouses at Bu, and eventually arrives at **Kinsarvik**, the chief ferry port on the Hardangerfjord. From here onwards the route follows the same course as that of route 1a until it finally arrives in Bergen.

1 (c)   The Hallingdal route

Oslo ● Hønefoss ● Gol ● Geilo ● Kinsarvik ● Bergen (480km)

What the route has to offer:
Road 7 is the shortest and most frequently-used route between Norway's two largest cities, Oslo and Bergen. It goes past fjord-like lakes, through the varied scenery of **Hallingdal**, and into the mountainous terrain of the **Hardangervidda**. It joins up with route 1b at **Geilo** and with route 1a at Kinsarvik. The section through Hallingdal also forms the first part of route 3b from Oslo to the Sognefjord.

Norway offers skiing opportunities for the whole family

The route:

The route leaves Oslo on the E68 road, which is a dual carriageway as it passes through the outlying suburb of Sandvika. The first towns along the route are all popular resorts, especially at weekends, when the traffic can be very heavy. Immediately outside the city boundary, the ski-lifts and ski-jumping platforms appear. The side branches of the Tyrifjord Lake are popular weekend resorts in the summer for the people of Oslo. The road is a very good one to Sundvollen, where a tollroad goes off to **Kleivstua** (4km). From here it is a 20-minute walk to the Kongensutsikt (King's View), which at 483m commands a view of the lake and the Hole Peninsula. At the top of the hill is the eleventh-century church of **Bønsnes** — an ancient settlement, where the ancestors of Olav the Holy and Harald Hårdråda are supposed to have lived.

The E68 now enters the Ringerike-Hønefoss conurbation (population 27,000), of which **Hønefoss** (population 12,000) forms the centre. The chief industries are wood processing and electrical power. The town lies on the confluence of the Begna and the Randselva. The large waterfall which gives the town its name also supplies the power station. The Riddergården Court Museum is worth visiting, with its ancient medieval buildings. Hønefoss is a station on the Oslo-Bergen railway.

From Hønefoss the E68 goes northwards into Begndal and Lærdal (see route 3a).

The present route goes left along Road 7, which begins at this point. This road goes via Sokna, past one or two small lakes, and at Hamremoen turns right along the eastern shore of the long, winding **Krøderen Lake**. There are some marvellous views of the Norefjell, which is a popular ski and tourist resort for the people of Oslo. It can be reached via a tollroad that goes off at Noresund and bridges the lake at its narrowest point.

Road 7 carries on along the eastern shore of the lake. At Haversting it meets the railway, which has just emerged from a 2.3km long tunnel. Near Gutsvik the road leaves the top end of the lake and joins the River Bromma. Soon after that it arrives at **Flå**. The heavily wooded landscape is the home of brown bears, especially in the area of Vassfaret. The road continues through the forests and comes out at the old town of **Nesbyen** (population 2,000), with its open-air museum. The Hallingdal Museum displays old buildings from the surrounding areas, which are filled with interesting costumes, clothing, weapons and household tools.

The road now really begins to climb, and soon arrives at **Gol** (population 4,000), which is an important road junction. Road 49 goes north to **Leira** and **Fagernes**, forming a connection to route 3a. This road climbs steeply, and winds past a number of mountain huts. Several side roads go up into the nearby mountains and down into Valdresdal. Several viewpoints on the way provide glimpses of the snow-covered peaks of the Jotunheimen Massif to the north.

Road 52 climbs through the breathtaking landscape of the **Hemsedalfjell** (route 3b) and then descends into Lærdal, while the present route goes west along Road 7 in the direction of **Geilo**.

Gol is a busy modern tourist centre. There are organised local excursions to places such as the Hemsil II Power Station; the tourist office also plans walking expeditions and sporting activities. Gol once had an old stave church from the twelfth century, but this was moved to Oslo in 1885 by King Oscar II. It was rebuilt at Bygdøy, where it is now one of the main attractions of the Norwegian Folk Museum.

The route does, however, pass another stave church only a short way further on. For Road 7 carries on west from Gol to **Torpo**, where a twelfth-century stave church stands next to the modern one. Its ceilings are decorated with medieval paintings depicting the legend of St Margaret, to whom the church is dedicated. The doorway and entrance hall are engraved with typical wood carvings, including scrollwork, dragons and semi-heathen symbols.

At the next town of **Ål**, there used to be another stave church of the same period, which was unfortunately destroyed at the end of the last century. However, the present church in Ål is also worth seeing; it is built in the ancient style, and the choir is decorated with copies of paintings from the stave church. The nearby village of Leksvoll has an open-air museum with fifteen old buildings, of which the school, the mill and the seventeenth-century inn are of particular interest.

The valley becomes steeper and the river becomes faster, with rapids in several places. The road arrives at **Hol**, which has a district museum and an

Smallcraft harbour, Bodø

Reine, a Lofoten fishing village

Tind, near to Å

View of the Aurlandsfjord

interesting church built on the remains of the old stave church. Some ancient Viking graveyards have also been found here.

From Hol, Road 288 goes north into Sudndal, leading eventually to **Aurland** on the Sognefjord. It is still partly under construction, and is narrow and unmade in places. But it is an exciting stretch of road through high mountain scenery, rising to 1,600m and then dropping to sea level at the fjord.

Road 7 carries on west along the top of a deep gorge, where the Ustaelva tumbles far below over waterfalls and foaming rapids. The road soon arrives at **Geilo**, from where the route follows the same course as route 1b.

1 (d) From Kristiansand to Haukeligrend

Leading to route 1a (250km)

What the route has to offer:
This route connects with ferries to Kristiansand from Hirtshals and Hanstholm in Denmark and from Newcastle and Harwich in England.

The route from Kristiansand goes along the lake known as the Byglandsfjord, and climbs through **Setesdal**, flanked by steep rocks and beautiful landscapes; at **Haukeligrend** it meets the Haukeli Road, and thus joins route 1a from Oslo to Bergen.

*The training ship
'Sørlandet' at Kristiansand*

The route:

The route leaves Kristiansand (described in detail in the section on towns
and cities) to the north along Road 12. The way from the harbour is along
the Vestre Strandgate, past the railway station, and out of the town along
Setesdalsveien.

Road 12 goes through the small industrial town of Mosby, from which
Road 405 goes off towards Vegusdal. A short way along this road, near
Vennesla, are the impressive Otra Rapids and the Hunsfoss. From here,
Road 454 goes back into Road 12, making it only a short detour.

At Hægeland the road passes a pretty nineteenth-century church on the
right. The Otra becomes wider at this point, and the road follows the west
bank. At Hestvåg there is a left turn for Road 9 to **Egersund**, which leads to
the E18 for **Stavanger** (see route 1f). Just after this junction is **Hornnes**,
which also has an interesting church. Built in 1828, it is octagonal in shape.
Hornnes lies in an idyllic site on the shores of Breiflå, where the Otra has
broadened out to become a lake.

In the small industrial town of Evje, Road 9 goes off to the right towards
Arendal. At this point Road 12 crosses the river and continues along the
east bank of the Otra to Birkeland. This is where the **Setesdal** proper
begins. It is one of the strangest and most beautiful valleys in Norway. The
scenery is truly dramatic. The Otra races downwards along a green valley
hemmed in by steep mountain slopes.

The folklore of the area is interesting too for the people stick closely to their own customs, practices and costumes. Many of the typical houses in the area are centuries old. Among the local craftsmen, the *sylvsmeder* (silversmiths) are particularly flourishing.

At Birkeland the river is very fast-flowing, and just to the north of it is the impressive Syrtveitfoss. There follows a beautiful view of the **Byglandsfjord** - one of the many lakes through which the Otra flows. The next place is Ådal, which has a church built in 1827 and a famous 900 year old oak (Landeeiki). Nearby is Landeskogen, a home for the mentally handicapped. The road continues through a 600m long tunnel and carries on to Bygland. There are a number of grave mounds on the edge of this town, and its museum has a particularly good local collection.

The road then crosses the river, and runs along the western side of the Sandnesfjord to **Ose**, where the Otra plunges over the Reiårsfoss into the fjord. The area is full of old storehouses (*stabburer* — see page 30), many of them 800 years old and more.

Road 12 goes through Granheim-Langeid, and continues through several narrow gorges until it arrives at **Helle** — centre of Setesdal's silversmithing tradition. Both Helle and Rysstad, the next place along, have a number of old houses and silversmiths' workshops.

At Brokke the road passes a power station on the right. Near Flårenden bru it crosses the river again. The surroundings are becoming increasingly wooded, and the mountains on either side are over 1,000m high. The road passes the Hallandsfoss, where the Otra forms a 15m high waterfall, and continues to **Valle**.

Valle is undoubtedly the most beautiful town in the whole valley, with its romantic setting among high mountains rounded by the action of glaciers. 500m beyond the church, and across a suspension bridge over the Prestefoss, is a famous old pine tree known as the 'holy pine'.

Just after the next town of **Flateland** is the turning for the Setesdal Museum, which is housed in a farm of a type found only in this valley. The farm includes a building known as the Rygnestadloft, which was built in the sixteenth century and is the most remarkable wooden construction in the whole valley.

The road passes several more waterfalls and rapids. The scenery becomes wider and the valley very narrow. The next point of interest is the old bridge at Moen, which until 100 years ago was the only way through to the old village of Bykle. Bykle Church was built on the remains of an old stave church, and its interior was painted with traditional rose motifs at the beginning of the last century. The village is full of beautiful old houses and storehouses.

The valley bottom becomes flatter, but the mountains become higher, rising to about 1,400m in height. The countryside becomes wilder and more sparsely populated. In the neighbourhood of **Hovden** are a skiing centre and a reindeer park. Hovden is also a popular starting point for mountain-walking expeditions.

At Sessvatn the road reaches the top of the pass at a height of 917m above sea level. It winds steeply down the other side, reaching a maximum gradient of 10 per cent, until it arrives at **Haukeligrend**. At this point the road meets the E76, the course of which is described in route 1a from Oslo to Bergen.

1 (e) From Larvik to Kongsberg

Leading to routes 1a and 1b (about 100km)

Travellers entering Norway from Denmark via Frederikshavn and Larvik will be able to use this route to join either of two routes from Oslo to Bergen: those via Haukeli (route 1a) and Numedal (route 1b).

Larvik (population 9,000) lies on the fjord of the same name. It was at one time a whaling port, but wood processing is the main industry nowadays. Particularly worth seeing is the Herregården — a large manor house built in 1673 as the Danish governor's residence, which now houses the City Museum. There is also the Maritime Museum, which is housed in the old customs shed. Apart from mementoes of Larvik's maritime past, it also contains models of Thor Heyerdahl's two famous boats *Kon Tiki* and *Ra*. Thor Heyerdahl was actually born in Larvik. There is a painting by Lucas Cranach in the choir of the old church of Larvik, which was built in 1677. Opposite the old church, and in front of the new one, stands a war memorial created by Vigeland.

Not far from Larvik, the small fishing port of **Stavern** is also worth visiting. A charming little town, it still possesses the old sea defences built in the middle of the eighteenth century to protect the wharves and the fleet. Stavern is a popular beach resort, and still houses a military garrison.

The route leaves Larvik along the E18 in the direction of Oslo. Then, just before the E18 crosses the River Lågen, Road 8 for Kongsberg goes off to the left. This is the main route and runs along the west bank of the river, but there is an alternative route running parallel along the east bank. This can be reached by crossing the river on the E18 and turning left along Road 304 immediately after the bridge. This road goes past a twelfth-century Romanesque church in Hedrun, and a waterfall called the Holmfoss, which is a good place for salmon. There are two ways to get back to the main route: either by turning left at Holm and crossing the river to Kvelde, or by continuing to Hvarnes and Hvara bru, where Road 304 enters Road 8 near another old church.

The road passes through Steinsholt, where Road 316 goes off to Skien and to Styrvoll with its medieval church, eventually arriving at Svarstad. 6km further on, at the Fossekroa tourist station, is a turning for the Brufoss, which is another good place for salmon. And near Bekkevar there is another medieval church not far from the road.

The next town is **Hvittingfoss**, with its wood and paper-making

The beech wood – typical of Larvik

industries. There is a waterfall here with some interesting rock paintings. At Hvittingfoss, Road 315 goes off for Holmestrand and Sande, where it joins the E18 for Drammen and Oslo, thus forming the quickest route from Skien to Oslo.

26km further on at **Skollenborg**, Road 286 goes off to the right, bypassing Kongsberg in the direction of Drammen and Oslo. Nearby is the Labru Waterfall, with its associated power station. A short distance further on at Saggrenda, Road 8 comes into the E76. Those wishing to visit **Kongsberg** (see route 1a or 1b) should turn right at this point. The same applies to those who want to travel to Bergen via Numedal (see route 1b). Those wishing to miss Kongsberg and take the Haukeli route to Bergen should turn left here along the E76 for **Notodden** (see route 1a).

1 (f) The coastal route

Oslo ● Larvik ● Kristiansand ● Stavanger (about 600km) ● (Bergen)

What the route has to offer:
The route follows the south coast of Norway along the main E18 road to Flekkefjord, then Road 44 to Stavanger. The many beaches and fishing

ports make it a very popular route in the summer. It sometimes leaves the coast for a little, but the beaches are never far away. This route is described in less detail than the others, since most visitors from outside Norway prefer to drive inland rather than remain on the south coast.

There is a direct ferry from Stavanger to Bergen, and another route via Haugesund (route 1a) is explained at the end here. The route also connects to route 1a via route 1d from Kristiansand or route 1e from Larvik.

The route:

The E18 motorway goes from Oslo to **Drammen** (see route 1a). The E18 then carries on over a range of hills to Sande on Sandebukta, an important branch of the Oslofjord; then it continues along the shore to **Holmestrand**, a pretty little town with a popular beach. Its industry has expanded in a typically Norwegian fashion, in that the harnessing of water power has led to the founding of a vast aluminium industry. The town centre is rather pretty, and still preserves its old wooden buildings intact, which in most towns have been lost through fire.

Road 310 continues along the coast to **Horten** — a naval base with a large harbour and airport, and a very interesting Naval Museum containing a few old curiosities. A national park at **Borre** contains Scandinavia's largest collection of Viking royal graves. Edvard Munch lived a long time in the next town of **Åsgårdstrand**, where his house contains a small museum to his memory.

Tønsberg is Norway's oldest town, and was first mentioned in records from the ninth century. The ruins of the Tønsberghus, the thirteenth-century royal fortress, are on a hill with a fine view. When Oslo had been made the capital, Tønsberg's importance quickly declined until the eighteenth century, when it became the home of Norway's whaling fleet. The Vestfold County Museum contains some interesting exhibits about whaling and seafaring at that time. Møllebakken is the site of an old lawcourt, and some graves found nearby are thought to be those of Harald Hårfagre's sons. Oseberg near Tønsberg is where the famous Viking ship was discovered that is now exhibited at the Maritime Museum at Bygdøy.

15 km further along the E18 is the town of **Sandefjord**. Once an important whaling station, its harbour is now modernised and is used mostly for exporting wood. The Whaling Museum describes the history of whaling. Two other museums are devoted to seafaring and local history respectively. In the suburb of Gokstad yet another Viking ship has been found; it too is on show at Bygdøy.

A short way beyond Sandefjord, the E18 crosses the Lågen, and Road 8 goes off for Kongsberg (see route 1e). The E18 then passes through **Larvik** (see route 1e), the port for ferries from Frederikshavn in Denmark. Here Road 301 goes off to **Stavern**, with its ancient sea defences (see route 1e), and the two lovely seaside resorts of Nevlunghavn and Helgeroa. Between them is the Møten Peninsula, which is worth a detour for the sake of the beach at Oddane Sand and its Bronze Age grave mounds. The road goes

Tønsberg and surrounding islands

back into the E18 near Langangen, which itself is bypassed by the E18.

At Eidanger, Road 36 goes off to **Porsgrunn** (a centre for porcelain manufacture) and **Skien** (Ibsen's birthplace, with the Ibsen Museum at Venstørp), continuing through Telemark to Seljord, where it joins the E76 to Haukeligrend (see route 1a).

The E18 turns southwards along the Eidangerfjord through Heistad to **Brevik**, with its lovely old town hall and its fishermen's houses. A long bridge carries the road 45m above the Brevikstrømmen and into the Høgakei Tunnel near Strathelle.

The E18 now leaves the coast for a little, and it is worth making a short detour via **Kragerø**. Kragerø is a picturesque little coastal town, with narrow streets and lovely wooden cottages, and a number of interesting islands offshore. The ferry to Stabbestad connects with Road 351, which continues along the scenic coastline until it rejoins the E18 at **Søndeled**. There are several more side roads to the coast, going through pretty little fishing ports full of tradition. **Risør**, for example, is one of the oldest, and is famous for having regattas at all seasons of the year. **Tvedestrand** has a home industry producing artificial flowers and Christmas decorations. It also boasts the narrowest house in Norway, commonly known as the 'flat-iron'.

Arendal is reached either via the coast road (410) or along the E18. The oldest town on the south coast, it lives chiefly from wood exports. There is also a ferry to Hanstholm in Denmark. At one time, the different parts of the town were connected by canals. But these were replaced by streets when the town was rebuilt after a fire. The Tyholmen quarter is full of lovely old streets and cottages. On the adjoining island is the Merdøy Museum, which is contained in an old boathouse built in 1700.

The route continues through the pretty coastal resorts of Fevik and Vik, and past Bronze Age graveyards to **Grimstad**, where the Ibsen Museum is housed in an old pharmacy. At Nørholm there is a lovely manor house which was bought by Nobel Prizewinner Knut Hamsun in 1918, and which now contains mementoes of him. **Lillesand** is yet another pretty and rather traditional little fishing port. It has a medieval church and some lovely old burghers' houses. There are also boat trips to Kristiansand.

Further on towards Kristiansand, Road 401 turns off to make a short detour along one of the finest parts of the whole coast, eventually arriving at **Kristiansand** (see the section on towns and cities). At this point route 1d goes off to Haukeligrend.

The E18 continues via Søgne to Mandal, which is Norway's most southerly town. Mandal is a popular holiday resort, with a nature park and a marvellous beach at Sjøsanden. Mandal salmon is a particular speciality. The old town has a number of pretty little houses, and the town hall is housed in the old manor, built in 1766. The City Museum contains among other things a large art gallery, and a monument by Gustav Vigeland, who was born in the town.

The E18 goes inland through Vigeland, where Road 460 goes off to **Lindesnes**, Norway's most southerly point. There is a restaurant on the headland, with an old charcoal beacon from 1822 standing next to the modern lighthouse.

After Lyngdal the E18 rises slightly to give a nice view of the Fedafjord and Kvinesdal. It then goes along the side of the fjord to Feda, and continues towards **Flekkefjord**. The route leaves the E18 to go into the town itself. This ancient town depends for its livelihood on fishing, leather tanning and furniture manufacture. The so-called Hollenderbyen or 'Dutch quarter' on the Grisefjord is especially picturesque.

From Flekkefjord, the E18 takes the inland route via Moi to Stavanger, but the present route uses the coast road (44) via Egersund and Nærbø. This road crosses the Stolsfjord in the centre of Flekkefjord, and leaves the town in a southerly direction. It turns right just outside the town, and passes through several villages to arrive at **Åna-Sira** — a lovely little fishing port next to a large power station.

The next part of the route is especially interesting. Road 18 climbs over a high coastal ridge, rising to a maximum height of 275 m by means of tunnels and several hairpins, at a gradient of up to 10 per cent. The summit provides a marvellous view of the Jøssingfjord, and there is a memorial to a battle in 1940 between an English and a German warship. The road returns to sea

The sunshine coast of Sørlandet – narrow waterways, sheltered creeks and a warm sea

level at **Hauge i Dalane**. There are titanium mines here. The old Sokndal Church was rebuilt in 1803 in the Louis XVI style. Several side roads lead to beaches such as Rekefjord, Sokndalstrand, Nesvåg and Vatland.

The road reaches the coast again at Stapnes, and shortly after that arrives at **Egersund** (population 11,000). This busy little port depends on fisheries (herring, mackerel, salmon and lobsters) and on a large ceramics factory. Egersund Church was originally built in 1605, and in 1700 was ⌘ restored and extended to its present cruciform shape. It also contains an old altar-piece from 1607. The Dalane Folk Museum is in the Egersund suburb of Slettebo on Road 9 (connecting with the E18). It includes buildings filled with local furnishings from the seventeenth and eighteenth centuries.

Road 44 carries on via Hellvik and Sirevåg to **Ogna**, with its glorious beach of fine sand and its small thirteenth-century church. Brusand is also in a fine coastal setting, with a good bathing beach, albeit marred by old wartime defences. At Kvassheim the road passes some Iron Age graveyards. Further up the coast near Grødeland, there is an open-air ⌘

museum showing buildings and customs from earlier times.

At Søyland the roads divide. Road 44 goes straight on to the industrial town of **Bryne**, where the excavations at the nearby prehistoric site at Kasen include Bronze Age grave mounds and first-century farms. The road continues to **Sandnes**, the town for bicycles and mopeds, and then past factories and oil refineries directly to **Stavanger** (see the section on towns and cities).

The coast road goes left at Søyland along Road 507, passing the thirteenth-century church at Orre, and the Jæren Bank with its numerous bird species. At Bore it enters Road 510, which goes on to Stavanger via the airport at Sola and the historic Hafrsfjord, where Harald Hårfagre won his decisive battle against the 'petty kings', uniting the kingdom of Norway under his rule.

Apart from the direct ferry to Bergen, there is a ferry to Skudeneshavn on the island of Karmøy, from which it is possible to join the E76 at **Haugesund**. The E76 eventually joins route 1a to Bergen at **Steinaberg bru**.

2 BERGEN TO TRONDHEIM

2 (a) The mountain route

Bergen ● Dale ● Voss ● Gudvangen ● Sognefjord ● Kaupanger ●
Jotunheimen ● Otta ● Dovrefjell ● Trondheim (about 630km)

What the route has to offer:

Leaving the charming city of **Bergen**, the route follows the Sørfjord,
passing through several tunnels, and offering wonderful views of the island
of Osterøya surrounded by fjords. After **Dale** the route turns inland
towards the mountains. The road becomes steep and narrow, and is in
some places cut out of the rock, as it climbs through the impressive
Bergesdalen, with its waterfalls and gorges. This is followed by a plateau
with lakes, then a breathtaking drop from the Stalheim Pass down into the
wild Nærøydal, a valley peppered with silvery waterfalls, until the road
ends at the ferry port of **Gudvangen**. There follows a marvellous trip along
the branches of the **Sognefjord**, with the opportunity of an excursion to the

Bøverdalen valley runs from Lom to the Jotunheimen

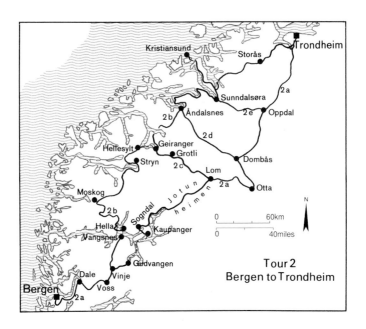

Tour 2
Bergen to Trondheim

very edge of a glacier. At the far end of the Sognefjord, the road suddenly climbs steeply from sea level to 1,430m as it crosses the highest road pass in Norway. Ahead is the bare, wild landscape of **Jotunheimen**. The road is unmade in places as it passes along one of Norway's most exciting mountain routes. The beautiful Bøverdal offers a bold constrast to the wildness of the mountains. The stave church at **Lom** provides some cultural interest. The road runs along the Ottavatn past villages of lovely old cottages, until it comes into the E6 road at **Otta**.

From Otta onwards, the route joins route 4a (Oslo to the North Cape) as far as **Trondheim**. The biggest attraction of this part of the route is the unique and fascinating landscape of the **Dovrefjell**. For a detailed description of the Otta-Trondheim section, turn to route 4a (pages 112-16).

Two parts of the section between Bergen and Voss will pose problems for caravans and dormobiles. Road 13 runs along the Sørfjord through a number of tunnels, some of which have a clearance of only 2.9m. And the mountain road from Dalen to Voss is barely 4m wide in places, making it difficult for caravans to pass. Such problems can, however, be avoided by going to Voss via the E68 (see route 2b), which is safer and more comfortable.

The Jotunheimen section remains closed from about 15 October to 10 June.

76

The route:
From Bergen, the route follows the E68 as far as Trengereid, then turns off on Road 13 for **Dale**. The section which follows is still partly under construction, and the many tunnels are rough though still passable. However, some of the tunnels have a clearance of less than 3m. To the left of the road is a wonderful view of the Sørfjord, which turns into the Veafjord further along. Opposite is the large island of Osterøya, which is completely surrounded by a complex of branching fjords. At **Vaksdal** there is Norway's largest publicly owned mill. The road then passes through a few more tunnels before Stanghelle, where it meets the Dalevågen.

The road now turns inland towards **Dale** (population 25,000), an industrial town producing cotton and knitwear. From Dalen, Road 569 goes off via Stamnes into a wild and isolated valley called Eksingedal. But the route continues along Road 13 as it begins a breathtaking climb. In places the road has had to be blasted out of the mountainside, and is sometimes only 4m wide. On the left there are sharp rock projections, on the right a drop so precipitous that the bottom is out of sight. A deafening noise comes up from the river as it thunders down over rapids. There are one or two passing places, where a driver can take a short break, wipe the sweat from his palms and take a look at the dizzy slopes and the breathtaking views.

The worst part of the route is over when the road tops 588m on a section of finished road as it approaches the Hamlagrø Reservoir. But the highest point of the Dale-Voss route is 10km further on at the far end of the reservoir, where it reaches 625m. The road then drops quickly, passing the Dalane Fjellstue (mountain hut) on the right. Only 10km further on, it has dropped to just 50m above sea level in the valley of the Vosso. The river, and the lake into which it flows, are famous for salmon. The route soon arrives at **Voss**, where Road 13 re-enters the E68, which has come from Bergen along the Hardangerfjord (see route 2b).

Voss is popular both as a winter and a summer resort, and has a station on the railway to Bergen. There is a cable car up to a restaurant on the mountainside, from which a chair lift carries on up to the summit of the Hangur (817m). Given the journey so far, a wonderful view can naturally be expected. The mountains around Voss are a popular skiing area. The town itself boasts a thirteenth-century church, a folk museum which includes an old farm, and other interesting buildings. Not far from the station is Norway's oldest secular wooden building, the Finnloftet. Built in the middle of the thirteenth century, it served as an assembly hall for the neighbouring overlords.

The E68 leaves Voss along a beautiful valley beside the Lønavatn. Just beyond the end of the lake is the beautiful **Tvinnefoss**, which cascades down into the valley over a number of separate falls. At **Vinje** the road divides: Road 13 turns off again in the direction of **Vangsnes** (see route 2b), while the present route continues along the E68 towards **Gudvangen**. There are a number of ski-lifts and cable cars in the neighbourhood of Oppheim.

The next high point of the route is at **Stalheim**, where the legendary hotel commands a breathtaking view from the top of the pass, while the nearby Stalheimsfoss plunges 126m into the valley. The new road no longer goes directly past the hotel and the waterfall, and has taken much of the excitement away from this once notorious pass. But more adventurous drivers may care to negotiate the old road (signposted to the hotel). The 100 year old Stalheimskleiva drops steeply for 1.5km through 13 hairpins, reaching a gradient of over 18 per cent in places. The road is unsurfaced and between 4m and 5m in width, but it is protected by a concrete kerb.

More cautious drivers should avoid the long 'scramble' by using the new road with its many tunnels, and climbing back up from the valley bottom where the road is wider. Caravans should be left in the car park at the bottom. The road turns off across a bridge, and is signposted to the Stalheimsfoss. One need only climb the first few hairpins before the waterfall comes into view. The road is wide enough at this stage for even a dormobile to turn round at one of the hairpins. The nearby Sivlefoss is equally beautiful, and is named after the poet Per Sivle.

The **Nærøydal** is relatively broad and flat, but it is surrounded by steep, almost vertical walls traversed by a vast number of waterfalls. They plunge down the mountainside like a long row of hanging threads — some silver, others in all colours of the rainbow.

At the far end of Nærøydal, the ferry port of **Gudvangen** offers a wide variety of types of accommodation from camping to hotels. Ferries run from here to **Revsnes**, **Kaupanger** and **Aurland**. There are four or five ferries a day to Revsnes and Kaupanger, and three a day to Aurland. Up-to-date information about times and reservations can be obtained from the Norwegian Tourist Office. It is not absolutely essential to book in advance; a ferry can occasionally be full at the height of the season, but the beauty of the surroundings means that it is no hardship to wait for the next crossing.

The trip along the Nærøyfjord is an unforgettable experience. The Nærøyfjord is a branch of the **Sognefjord**, which is the longest (180km) and deepest (1,250m) in Norway. The Nærøyfjord is on average only 500m wide, and the sides drop almost vertically into the sea. As the mountains either side are over 1,000m high, the valley and the fjord remain permanently in the shade for many months of the year. On the $2\frac{1}{2}$ hour journey to Kaupanger, it is worth trying to count all the waterfalls that fall directly into the fjord. Seals can also be seen along this branch of the Sognefjord.

About a third of the way to Kaupanger, the ferry comes out into the Aurlandsfjord. The mountains retreat somewhat, and the boat traffic increases. Then about two thirds of the way, the ferry turns right into the mighty Sognefjord itself. On the right is **Revsnes**, where the E68 road goes off through **Lærdal** to Borgund and Fagernes (see route 3a). The ferry docks at **Kaupanger** on the opposite side of the fjord.

Kaupanger is a village of some 600 inhabitants. Its stave church, built in 1170, is the largest in the region. Its open-air museum includes a collection

Chair-lifts at Voss

of old houses with furniture and tools. Kaupanger offers further ferry connections to Årdalstangen.

Road 5 from Kaupanger goes over a ridge to **Sogndal**, which is the main centre of the area. Sogndal has a number of lovely old houses. Near the church is a runic stone nearly 1,000 years old. Road 5 goes on from Sogndal to Moskog and the North Sea coast, and also connects to route 2b for the **Geirangerfjord**.

The present route turns right at Sogndal along Road 55 for the Sognefjell, passing through a little hamlet called England. The waterfall near Årøy has been tamed by a power station, but the associated river is still full of salmon. It is crossed by several bridges in zigzag formation, which provide an ideal position for a large number of anglers. The next place is Hafslo by a lake, from which a side road goes off to **Solvorn**.

This pretty little town is becoming increasingly popular, thanks to its glorious setting on the banks of the Lustrafjord - another branch of the Sognefjord. A ferry links Solvorn with Årdalstangen. Another ferry goes to **Urnes** on the opposite bank of the fjord (seven trips a day in the summer).

⚜ Urnes has the oldest stave church in Norway, which was built at the beginning of the twelfth century on the site of an even older stave church. Its good state of repair, its beautiful carvings and its gorgeous setting make it a very worthwhile trip.

Road 55 goes over another ridge, and joins the side of the fjord at Marifjøra. At the end of a side branch (the Gaupnefjord), and just before Gaupne, Road 604 turns off into **Jostedal**.

Excursion into Jostedal (about 80km return trip)

The trip through Jostedal takes at least half a day, but it is very much worth it. The valley is narrow and the scenery is wild, with numerous waterfalls on either side.

About 30km along, and just after Gjerden, a small tollroad goes off to the left at the Kroken Hotel, leading up to the Nigardsbre. The glacier has already been visible for some time, peeping between the snowy mountains. The road ends at a car park, from which a boat crosses a lake to the moraine at the end of the glacier. It seems very near at first, but still seems no nearer when the boat arrives at its destination and the parked cars have been left far behind. There follows a climb over rubble and rocks made smooth by ice. Little narrow bridges go over deep crevices and foaming torrents of blue-green water. In damp weather the climb can become slippery and rather dangerous. Strong wellingtons or boots with a good grip are in any case essential. Children should not be allowed too near the glacier. The ice cliff towers higher and higher, and the nearer it becomes, the more difficult and exciting the climb. It is vital to heed all warnings, especially in the summer, when ice can break away from the glacier and crush people beneath it. But even from a respectful distance, the Nigardsbre is an unforgettable sight.

For more adventurous mountaineers, a walk across the glacier is arranged twice a day, and the necessary equipment is provided.

The Nigardsbre forms a tongue of the **Jostedalsbre**, which is the largest ice sheet in Europe. It has an area of 1,000sq km, and the ice is as much as 500m thick in places. The mountain ridge is about 2,000m high, the highest point being Lodalskåpa at 2,080m.

Road 55 continues along the shore of the Lustrafjord, passing through a number of small hamlets. On the other side of the fjord, opposite Nes, is the Feigumfoss — one of Norway's highest waterfalls, plunging 200m into the fjord. The fjord ends at **Skjolden**, which is the furthest point inland that any of the fjords ever come, being 180km from the coast.

Within the next 33km, the road winds and climbs from sea level to a height of 1,430m. The hairpins begin at **Fortun**, which is only 25m above sea level. At Turtagrø, only 11km further on, and after a gradient of between 10 per cent and 12 per cent, the road has already reached 900m. **Turtagrø** is a mountaineering hotel, from which numerous expeditions are undertaken

Norway offers plenty of opportunities for open-air activities

to the surrounding peaks over 2,000m. The hotel has a beautifully carved façade.

The hairpins continue, and the height above sea level is indicated at regular intervals along the side of the road. It is a single-track road with passing places, and from 1,300m it is no longer surfaced. The snow cover increases on the roadside; sometimes, even in summer, the old snow can still be piled up sufficiently to produce a 3m high wall on either side of the road. At 1,400m the road passes the Herva Reservoir, which provides energy for the power station at Fortun. The top of the pass is at the Sognefjell Hut, where the height is given as 1,430m above sea level. It is the highest road pass in Norway, and remains closed from 15 October to 10 June. The snowy peaks to the south and south west are all over 2,000m.

As the road crosses the mountains, there are little stone towers all along the way. These were originally built to indicate the track over the pass. But more little towers have been put up since just for fun, or to add to the ones already there. Many of them have been 'crowned' with an everyday object such as a shoe, an empty tin or a bathing cap. Travellers are encouraged to add towers of their own.

As the road descends, it soon becomes surfaced again. From the mountain huts of Krossbu, Bøvertun and Høydalsdelet, there are numerous tracks into the mountains. Elveseter provides an unusual luxury hotel: an old farm with a mill has been tastefully converted into a building with all modern facilities.

At Galdeshand a little further on, there is a right turn along a tollroad to Juvasshytta, which at 1,841m provides the best access to **Galdhøpiggen** (2,469), Norway's highest peak. It may be only the second-highest, though not even the Norwegians can agree on this. If the permanent ice on **Glittertind** is taken into account, it is 3m higher at 2,472m. The road to Juvasshytte should not, however, be attempted in an ordinary car, but with a Land Rover, Range Rover or equivalent; and the ascent of Galdhøpiggen should only be attempted with the help of an experienced guide.

A short way further on is the old ski hut and tourist station of Røyheim, which is a protected building. From here, yet another tollroad leads off to a mountain hut, from which it is possible to climb to the Svellnos Glacier. This track is similarly closed to caravans and dormobiles. Road 55 has been fully completed from here onwards. It descends through the romantic valley scenery to **Lom** (population 700), where it enters Road 15 from **Otta** to **Grotli** (see route 2c).

Lom is famous for its stave church, which is one of the finest in the country. It was built 800 years ago as a basilica in the Romanesque style. But in the middle of the sixteenth century, the original building was extended into its present cruciform plan. The church has a richly decorated Baroque pulpit and a number of marvellous paintings. The columns and doorposts are decorated with runic inscriptions and medieval ornamentation. One interesting feature is the row of St Andrew's crosses which runs above the central aisle, strengthening the columns either side. Across the street from the church is St Olav's House, which forms part of the Lom Museum. St Olav is said to have stayed here overnight in the eleventh century. Also very unusual is the vast three-storey storehouse, which was once used to store grain. The Fossheim Hotel includes parts of the old Gaukstadstuggu House from 1650.

The route goes right at Lom, and continues in an easterly direction towards Otta. At this point in the valley, the Otta River has widened into a long, winding lake, whose waters are of a bright blue-green colour. The road runs alongside it through hamlets with old farms such as Graffer, after which the local traditional costume is named. **Garmo** is a small village with lovely old cottages, and was the birthplace of Knut Hamsun. At **Randen**, Road 51 goes off through Jotunheimen to **Fagernes**, where it connects with route 3a.

7km further on is **Vågåmo** a picturesque little place with beautiful old houses. Its stave church has been so totally refurbished as to be virtually unrecognisable as such; but the original eleventh-century building was the second-oldest stave church in Norway. There are several large medieval farms nearby, of which the Håkenstad Farm is on show to visitors. There are a few tracks from Vågåmo into the surrounding mountains.

Road 15 crosses to the other side of the river at Vågåmo, and continues for 30km via Lalm, with its quarrying and talcum powder industry, eventually arriving at **Otta.**

Galdhøpiggen, Norway's highest mountain

This is the point where the present route joins route 4a (Oslo to the North Cape), which it follows as far as Trondheim. Road 15 comes into the E6, and the route goes left. It carries on through Dombås and the Dovrefjell to Oppdal, Berkåk Støren and Melhus, eventually arriving at **Trondheim**. A detailed description of this section of the route is given as part of route 4a.

2 (b) The fjord route

Bergen ● Kvanndal ● Voss ● Sognefjord ● Moskog ● Nordfjord ● Hellesylt ● Geirangerfjord ● Trollstigveien ● Åndalsnes ● Sunndalsfjord ● Trondheim (about 880km)

What the route has to offer:

The fjord route is a long and difficult one, and subject to delays on the ferries — but it is also extremely beautiful.

The route goes from Bergen on the E68 to Voss, then crosses a difficult pass over the Vikafjell (closed from 1 December to 15 May) and down to the Sognefjord. The pattern continues as high passes alternate with fjords and wild valleys. The first high point of the route is the **Geirangerfjord**, which is Norway's most beautiful fjord. It can first be enjoyed from the boat, and then from the road as it climbs away up the Eagle's Road.

The **Eagle's Road** leads via fjord and fjell to the next high point of the journey, the **Trollstigveien**. This road used to be notorious for its bends, but has now been considerably improved and is no longer impassable to caravans. The fjord is waiting at the bottom, and the route continues along several fjords, with scenery varying from soft, green woodland to wild, boggy fjells, until it eventually arrives at Trondheim.

The route:

The E68 leaves **Bergen** in the direction of the Hardangerfjord. At **Indre Arna** the railway from Bergen emerges from an 8km long tunnel under Ulriken. After **Tysse**, the E68 climbs over a pass with hairpins and tunnels, passing the attractive Vosselv and the gorge at Tokagjelet. At **Norheimsund** the road meets the **Hardangerfjord**, and follows the shore as far as **Kvanndal**, where a ferry goes across to **Kinsarvik** (see route 1a). The E68 continues along a side branch of the fjord called the Granvinfjord to **Granvin**.

Beyond Granvin, and halfway along the Granvinvatn at Granvin Kirke, there is a turning for Road 572. This road winds through beautiful scenery to the tourist resort of **Ulvik**, continuing to Bruravik, where a 10-minute ferry journey crosses to Road 7 for **Eidfjord**, **Geilo** and **Gol** (see route 1b). Meanwhile, the E68 winds slowly past the waterfall at Skjervet, and over a 260m high pass into the tourist resort of **Voss**. At this point Road 13 comes in from Bergen via Dale (see route 2a).

Voss is popular both as a winter and a summer resort, and has a station on the railway to Bergen. There is a cable car up to a restaurant on the mountainside, from which a chair lift carries on up to the summit of the Hangur (817m). Given the journey so far, a wonderful view can naturally be expected. The mountains round Voss are a popular skiing area. The town itself boasts a thirteenth-century church, a folk museum which includes an old farm, and other interesting buildings. Not far from the station is Norway's oldest secular wooden building, the Finnloftet. Built in the middle of the thirteenth century, it served as an assembly hall for the neighbouring overlords.

The E68 leaves Voss along a beautiful valley beside the Lønavatn. Just beyond the end of the lake is the wonderful **Tvinnefoss**, which cascades down into the valley over a number of separate falls. At **Vinje** the road divides. The E68 continues over the famous **Stalheim Pass** to **Gudvangen**, a ferry port on a branch of the Sognefjord (see route 2a). The present route goes left along Road 13, which immediately begins to climb.

After **Holo** the road becomes especially difficult. About thirty years ago, hairpins were added to make the road less steep (maximum gradient 12 per cent). Just beyond the county boundary, the road reaches the top of the pass (986m). A waterfall at Målsevatn has been harnessed by a power station. The road drops quickly, with several wonderful views across the fjell and the surrounding mountains, and down to the Sognefjord. Shortly before **Viksøyri**, the road comes to the stave church at Hopperstad. Built in the twelfth century, it was heavily restored in 1895. Across the road and

Old traditions survive in the Voss area, east of Bergen

along a path is the site of an ancient pre-Christian cult.

At Viksøyri, the road comes right down to the **Sognefjord**, Norway's longest (180km) and deepest (1,250m) fjord. It runs along the shore to the ferry port of **Vangsnes**, where a 12m high statue of Fridtjof stands above the shore. The ferries are so frequent that little waiting is required. They go to **Hella** (15 minutes), **Dragsvik** (20 minutes) and **Balestrand** (20 minutes). There are also round trips from Vangsnes with the local ferry line Fylkesbåtane Sogn og Fjordane. Information about the routes, times and prices of these services can be obtained from tourist and travel bureaux, and from the Norwegian Tourist Office.

Balestrand on the Sognefjord

Road 5 goes east from **Hella** along the fjord via Leikangen and Hermansverk to **Sogndal**, where it meets route 2a. (A 5km long cable crossing the fjord near Hermansverk is reputed to be the world's longest unsupported electrical cable.) Road 13 goes west along the fjord from **Dragsvik** via Balestrand, leading (via Roads 14 and 607) all the way to the North Sea coast.

The present route goes north along Road 5 from **Dragsvik** to the top end of the Vetlefjord. It then climbs steeply in hairpins (13 per cent gradient) over a 745m high pass, with rest points on the way providing views across the mountains. It passes several lakes including Lanevatn and Haukedalvatn. Three more hairpins follow as it climbs up again to the mountain hut at Rørvik (543m); then it winds down another valley to **Moskog**.

Road 5 carries on from here via Førde to Florø on the coast. But the present route goes right at Moskog along Road 14, skirting the long Jølstravatn and arriving at **Skei** — a popular holiday resort by a lake full of fish. A side road goes off here to Lunde at the foot of the Jostedal Glacier, while Road 14 continues through the wild, impressive scenery of the steepsided Vætedal.

At **Byrkjelo**, the home of brown goat's-milk cheese, Road 14 goes off down to the Nordfjord. The route carries on along Road 60, crossing the Fillefjell, which at 643m has a number of ski-lifts and viewing points. It then winds down to **Utvik** on the Innvikfjord — one of the many branches of the Nordfjord. The road winds along the shore, passing through fishing villages and holiday resorts such as **Olden** and Loen. From Loen there is yet another side road to the foot of the Jostedal Glacier. At **Stryn**, Road 15 goes off to **Grotli**, then on via Ottadal to **Lom** and **Otta** in Gudbrandsdal. This connecting route is described as route 2c.

Road 60 carries on along the fjord. It then begins to climb, and near Bleksvingen it turns away from the fjord. At the same point a side road turns off and climbs along the side of the fjord towards **Nos** which, being situated at 600m almost vertically above the fjord, provides some wonderful views on the way.

But Road 60 has some more sights in store. At Kjøs it meets the shore of Hornindalvatn, which with a depth of 604m is Europe's deepest lake. Here Road 15 goes off along the southern shore of the lake, and on via Nordfjordeid to Måløy on the North Sea. But the route continues along Road 60 through Hornindal and Langedal towards Hellesylt.

At **Tryggestad**, Road 655 goes off into Norangsdal — a strange valley where a landslide has caused a small lake to form. It also destroyed a farm, the remains of which can be seen when the waters are clear. Road 60 soon arrives at **Hellesylt**. Beautifully situated, it is the ferry port for the **Geirangerfjord**. Road 60 goes on towards Ålesund, while the present route follows the busy car ferry route to **Geiranger**.

The 70-minute journey along the Geirangerfjord is one of Norway's greatest attractions. For the Geirangerfjord is the most beautiful of all the fjords. The waters are deep, calm and salty, and hemmed in by almost vertical cliffs. The countless waterfalls that plunge down these cliffs have names such as the Brudeslør (Bridal Veil) and the Syv Søstre (Seven Sisters). They are fed by the meltwater from the surrounding mountains, which remain snow-covered until early summer. Lone farms cling to the mountainside, defying the rocky slopes with a little grazing land. Most of these have long since been abandoned.

The vertical walls of the Prekestol (Pulpit) are decorated with the names of big cruisers that come into the fjord. They come in so close that it is possible to paint their names on the rock face. Keen photographers may be lucky enough to find one of these cruisers lying at anchor at the end of the fjord.

The village of **Geiranger** (population 300) is totally geared towards tourism. The *Turistkontor* opposite where the ferry docks provides information about excursions and other attractions (open in the season from 9am to 8pm).

Road 58 goes south from the village and via the **Dalsnibba** to **Lom** (see route 2c), while the present route goes north via the **Eagle's Road** (Ørneveien) to **Eidsdal**. But both routes offer such marvellous views that it is worth first making a short excursion to a viewing point on the opposite road from the intended route out. So one should at least go as far back along route 2c as the Utsikten Bellevue Hotel, or even to **Flydalsjuvet**.

Geirangerfjord

The view from the **Eagle's Road** becomes more breathtaking with every hairpin, but the best view is that from Ørnesvingen across to the Pulpit and the Seven Sisters. At Korsmyra the Eagle's Road reaches the top of the pass at 624m. Then, as it drops down into Eidsdal, there are more beautiful views of the surrounding mountains and the Norddalsfjord. From **Eidsdal**, there is a 15-minute ferry crossing to **Linge/Valldal**.

Excursion to Ålesund

From Linge, Road 58 goes left for **Ålesund** (population 35,000), which is one of the prettiest fishing towns in Norway. Everything in this town revolves around fishing and seafaring. Ålesund is beautifully situated out among the coastal islands. It is the base, not only of a vast overseas fishing fleet, but also for Arctic expeditions. There are numerous excursions on offer, from a fishing expedition on a trawler to a visit to the famous bird island of **Runde**. The nearby hill of Alska affords a marvellous view of the town and of the islands along the coast. Also worth visiting are the Aquarium, the Municipal Museum and the one-time Bird Rock in the centre of the town.

The route leaves **Valldal/Linge** on Road 63, climbing through Meierdal, where St Olav is supposed to have been active at the beginning of the eleventh century.

There follows the next high point of the journey — the **Trollstigveien**. Here the road plunges over the edge of a strange plateau, and drops 850m down the almost vertical mountainside. There are eleven hairpins, and the maximum gradient is 12 per cent. But this once notorious road has now been made much safer. On the way down, the road crosses the Stigfoss, an impressive 180m high waterfall.

Road 63 comes down near **Soggebru**, where it goes left into the E69 road

The busy fishing port of Ålesund

The Troll Path, Romsdal

from **Dombås** (see route 2d). The next junction is at the side of the Romsdalsfjord: the E69 continues left towards **Ålesund** (see above), while the present route takes Road 64 into **Åndalsnes**. This prettily situated holiday resort has a furniture industry and a wharf where oil platforms are built.

Road 64 continues along the shore of the Isfjord. At Hen, a side road goes off into the beautiful Vengedal at the foot of the snow-covered **Romsdalshorn**. Road 64 leaves the fjord at Torvik, but a side road continues along the shore to Klungsnes, where there is a memorial stone to the Scottish landing in 1612.

Road 64 crosses a small tongue of land, and at Lerheim it meets the Rødvenfjord. Here a side road goes off via Eid to the Rødven Stave Church, with its original interior. The Rødvenfjord opens out into the Langfjord near Åfarnes, where a ferry crosses the Langfjord to Sølsnes. Road 64 goes from Sølsnes to **Molde**, the town famous for its roses.

But the present route stays on the south shore of the Langfjord, continuing along Road 660. The road leaves the fjord, and twists and climbs through Vistdal, where it is still being improved. From Eresfjord, there is the possibility of a short excursion into **Eikesdal** — one of the most beautiful valleys in Norway. Particularly impressive is the Mardalsfoss near Reitan, which can be reached via a ferry along the Eikesdalsvatn.

The route continues along the Eresfjord as far as **Eidsvåg** — a village with lovely old houses. Leaving the fjord, it then crosses the ridge on Road 62 to Eidsøra, where it meets the great Sunndalsfjord. It runs along the shore, passing through the Merraberget Tunnel. At the radio mast just after Øksendal, there is a wonderful view back along the fjord. The road climbs to Vetamyra, providing yet another lovely view of the Sunndalsfjord. Then it drops down into **Sunndalsøra** (see route 2e), where it comes into Road 16 from **Oppdal**.

The route now follows Road 16 in the direction of **Kristiansund** (see route 2e), but near Ålvundfoss it turns right along Road 670. There is then a ferry from Røkkum to Kvanne, from which the road goes on to Surnadalsøra and Skei. Here the route turns right, onto Road 65, which runs along Surnadal, with its river full of fish. The long, wooded valley is richly cultivated and full of old farms. At Røv, a bridge crosses the Surna to Mo, with its Y-shaped church built in 1726. Next comes the power station at Harang. The highest point (310m) of the valley forms the boundary between the counties of Møre og Romsdal and Sør Trøndelag.

At **Storås** a road goes off to **Berkåk** on the E6 (see route 4a). Road 65 carries on along the course of the Orkla, and near Forve passes a turning for Road 71 to Kristiansund. At **Orkanger** the river empties into the Orkdalfjord. This town manufactures plastics and shipping equipment, and the one-time manor house of Bårdshaug is a fine building in the style typical of the Trøndelag. The nearby small port of Thamshamn exports pyrites, which is brought down by railway from Løkken.

Road 65 continues along the shore of the fjord through Børsøra, with its medieval church, and Buvik; then at Klett it comes into the E6, which leads directly into **Trondheim** (see the section on towns and cities). At this point the route connects with routes 2a and 4a.

2 (c) The Ottadal route

(cross-route between routes 2a and 2b)

Lom ● Grotli ● Geiranger (about 82km)

What the route has to offer:

The journey from **Lom** through the Ottadal, and via Grotli and Dalsnibba to Geiranger, is probably the most attractive stretch of road in central Norway. From a lovely valley full of woods and fields, the road climbs steeply to over 1,000m. It crosses the plateau past lakes and mighty mountains, where the snow lies even in high summer. It winds on past some wonderful views of Dalsnibba and down to Flydalsjuvet, from which the famous 'postcard view' of the Geirangerfjord has so often been photographed. It is possible to make a short detour along the old road (258) to Videseter, and then back along the new road to Langevatn. Road 258 is not suitable for caravans, but is even more exciting than the new Road 15.

Road 258 is closed from 15 October to about 10 June — likewise Road 58 to Geiranger and the road up to Dalsnibba.

The route:

Road 15 goes from **Lom** up through Ottadal (see route 2a), and at first runs parallel to the Ottavatn. The valley is unusually dry, so that the fields have to be artificially irrigated. Many old farms along here have been preserved as national monuments. The road crosses the river several times, and then gradually becomes steeper. It climbs out of the valley, and the scenery becomes bare and rocky. The landscape is soon dominated by high mountains and vast areas of scree. The road has reached 870m by the time it arrives at **Grotli**.

Detour via Videseter

Road 258 goes off at **Grotli**, following the original track of the road before the new Road 15 was built. This route is unsuitable for caravans, and is closed from mid-October to mid-June. The road is unmade in places as it runs through the bare mountains, often with snow either side. The top of the pass is at 1,139m, with a marvellous view south to the Tystig Glacier. There is a large summer skiing centre here, which stages an international race event at the end of June. **Videseter** offers a wonderful view across Videdal. The road winds down to meet Road 15, which goes left via Hellje to **Stryn** (see route 2b). But the route back goes right along the Helårsvei, climbing through several long tunnels to a maximum height of 943m. It rejoins the main route at **Langevatn**, where Road 58 goes left for Geiranger.

The new Road 15 continues through the mountains from **Grotli**, passing alongside Breidalsvatn. There are views across to the snowy peaks further south, where the glaciers from the mighty Jostedalsbre peep through. At **Langevatn**, the present route turns right along Road 58 for **Dalsnibba**, while Road 15 continues on its way to the North Sea coast.

A short way beyond the junction, past the Djupvatn, the road reaches the top of the pass (1,038m), where from the Djupvasshytte a tollroad winds up to the top of Dalsnibba. The 5km long climb is a very difficult one, but it is worth the effort. It is of course closed in the winter. The summit of the mountain (1,476m) offers breathtaking views of the mountains and the Geirangerfjord.

As the road drops steeply down to the Geirangerfjord, one's eyes keep straying to the wonderful views of the fjord. The best viewpoint is probably the Flydalsjuvet, from which most of the famous Geirangerfjord pictures are taken. There are a few more hairpins to go before the road reaches sea level at **Geiranger**, where it connects with route 2b.

Åndalsnes

2 (d) The Romsdal route

(cross-route between routes 2a and 2b)

Dombås ● Åndalsnes (about 106km)

What the route has to offer:

This cross-route can be used as part of a tour which does not include northern Norway. Although such a tour misses Trondheim, it still includes all the most important elements of a tour of central Norway, provided that one then follows route 2b southwards from Åndalsnes.

The scenery of Romsdal is a complete contrast to the gentler landscape of Gudbrandsdal. The bare, wild valley is surrounded by high mountains and numerous waterfalls. The last part of the journey is particularly exciting as the valley cuts through the mountains of Romsdal. The valley falls gently throughout the route from the high point at Dombås.

The route:

The route leaves Dombås along the E69 parallel to the Rauma Railway and the River Lågen, and goes past a number of lakes. The pretty church at **Lesja** was built in 1784 and has a beautifully carved interior. 20km further on is the Lesjaskogvatn, which has numerous streams running into it. This lake is quite extraordinary in having two outlets, one at each end. There is a hut on the shore called the Lesjaverk, which is the last remains of some old eighteenth-century iron workings. The old church at the opposite end of the lake was built in 1695.

The railway remains close to the road, which runs along an old mail route. Near **Stuguflåten** is an old mail coach station, which is now at the bottom of an old ski-lift. The valley now becomes narrower and the mountains much steeper, with numerous waterfalls on either side. The road crosses the railway and the river. The bridge near **Bjønnakleiv** provides a beautiful view of the mountains of Romsdal, which reach a height of about 1,650m. About 6km further on at **Verma**, the railway goes over a 56m high bridge called the Kylling bru, which is sometimes known as the 'Tiger's Leap'. The waterfall at Verma has been harnessed for a power station; but the other waterfalls which follow have lost none of their beauty to technology, and have names such as Slettafoss, Brudesløret ('The Bridal Veil') and Mongefoss.

The church at **Kors** was built in 1910 using the remains from other churches nearby. It thus contains some much older treasures, such as Jakob Klukstad's altarpiece from 1769. The next part of the valley is so deep and narrow that it has no sun at all for 5 months of the year. Near **Horgheim** there is an impressive view of the surrounding peaks, including the **Romsdalshorn** (1,550m) and **Trolltindane** (1,797m), which is much feared by mountaineers for its vertical rock faces.

The road soon arrives at **Sogge bru** near Åndalsnes, where route 2b comes in from the left down the famous Trollstigveien.

2 (e) The Drivadal route

(cross-route between routes 2a and 2b)

Oppdal ● Sunndalsøra ● Kristiansund (164km)

What the route has to offer:
Road 16 goes from Oppdal through the valley of the rushing **Driva**, with its many salmon. Near **Sunndalsøra** there are two possible excursions: one into **Litledal**, with the 1650m high vertical wall of Kalken; the other into **Innerdal**, with its 'sugarloaf'. The route continues via **Tingvoll** along the fjord of the same name to the lovely fishing port of **Kristiansund** on the North Sea coast.

The section between Oppdal and Sunndalsøra connects routes 2a and 4a with route 2b.

The route:
Road 16 leaves **Oppdal** (see route 4a) in the direction of Sunndalsøra. The

Driva is still fairly small at this stage, and runs in a torrent through a deep ravine, parallel to the road. A number of roads (some of them toll roads) lead off into the mountains of Trollheimen, where walking and climbing expeditions can be undertaken from the various mountain huts. Road 16 climbs quickly; it reaches 600m near Festa bru, and a side road climbs away past Gjevilvatn to the Gjevilvasshytte. Near a small village with a sawmill called Lønset, another road turns right and goes to Storli past the Vindøla rapids.

From Gråura, the road winds steeply down to Gjøra in the depths of the valley. From here another side road winds steeply up to Jenstadjuvet, which lies in an impressive setting at the meeting point of five valleys. The valley is subject to avalanches, and the old farms which can be seen have been dug into the mountainside for protection.

Road 16 carries on via Romfo, where the church (dating from 1820) has a statue of St Olav, to Fale, which is a popular meeting point for salmon anglers. The large farms on the slopes are typical of the locality. The road crosses the famous salmon river a number of times. The Leikvin Museum at Elverhøy bru is very much worth a visit. It is housed within the manor of Lady Arbuthnott of Scotland, who lived here in the middle of the last century, and who became known as the 'Queen of Sunndal'. Part of the museum is devoted to salmon fishing.

The road soon arrives at the little industrial town of **Sunndalsøra** (population 5,500) at the end of the Sunndalsfjord. There is an aluminium plant here, and the power station at Aura is one of the largest in Norway. The road past this power station leads to **Litledal**, which is very much worth a short excursion. Not far along it is the 1,650m vertical wall of the mighty Kalken.

At Sunndalsøra, Road 62 comes in from Eidsvåg. This is also the route for Åndalsnes, the Trollstigveien and the Geirangerfjord (see route 2b). The present route continues via three tunnels along the side of the fjord, which it leaves at Oppdøl. It crosses the ridge of a moraine near the church at Ålvundeid, where a side road goes off into **Innerdal**.

Excursion into Innerdal

Innerdal offers some glorious scenery, with luscious meadows farmed by the smallholders along the way. The road has a good surface but crosses numerous cattle grids as it winds slowly along beside a babbling brook. The surrounding mountains are unusual in shape, some resembling a sugarloaf, while others look like giant pointed trolls' hats. The road ends in a car park, with an old farm ringed by barns built in the traditional style. Numerous paths fan out from here into the surrounding conservation area. Mountaineering expeditions are organised from nearby mountain huts into the 1,800m high mountains round about.

Tourist lodge in the Norwegian mountains

At **Ålvundfoss**, Road 670 goes off for Surnadalsøra and Trondheim (see route 2b). Road 16 goes alongside the Ålvundfjord via Sandnes to Meisingset, from which a side road continues along the fjord and then crosses the peninsula to **Tingvoll**. Road 16 follows the direct route to **Tingvoll**. This industrial village has an unusual garrison church built in 1120, and a district museum. There is also a ferry to the opposite side of the Tingvollfjord.

The road continues along the side of the fjord through a number of

tunnels. Soon after leaving the fjord, it comes to a junction at Breiteråsen.
Here Road 65 goes off over a ferry, and meets Road 71; both roads lead
eventually to Trondheim. Road 16 carries on to yet another shore at
Kvisvik, where a ferry crosses the Freifjord to Kvalvåg on the island of
Frei.

The road crosses this island to where a bridge leads over the Omsund to
the island of Nordlandet. Nordlandet is one of the three islands on which
Kristiansund (population 19,000) is located, the other two being Innelandet
and Kirkelandet.

Kristiansund is traditionally a fishing port, and its chief occupation used
to be the production of stockfish. But nowadays the port has become

increasingly involved in drilling for oil off the coast. The old town was mostly destroyed by German bombers during World War II, but it has not lost its charm, thanks to an idyllic setting among the islands and waterways that give the town its distinctive atmosphere.

Kristiansund is one of the ports on the Hurtigrute line (see page 203). A 3-hour boat trip can be made to the lovely little island of Grip (population 70), with its old fishermen's cottages and fifteenth-century stave church. There is also a lighthouse to warn ships of the dangers from surrounding islands and rocks.

There are two main routes back from Kristiansund: the first goes back along the same route to Sunndalsøra, while the second takes the direct route to Trondheim along Road 65 and/or Road 71.

3 OSLO TO SOGNEFJORD

3 (a)   The Begnadal route

Oslo ● Hønefoss ● Nes ● Fagernes ● Borgund ● Revsnes (about 350km)

What the route has to offer:
The E68 is one of Norway's most important traffic routes. In combination with the E76 it is an ideal route for a tour of southern Norway. It passes through varied scenery, from more populous regions through lush valleys and dense forests, past many old farms, storehouses and stave churches. Then the valleys become narrower, the rivers faster and the mountains higher, as the road follows Lærdal from the famous Borgund stave church to the shores of the Sognefjord. From Revsnes, the traveller has two options: either to take the ferry to Gudvangen, follow the E68 to Bergen and return via the E76 (route 1a); or else to cross to Kaupanger and continue north through central Norway on route 2a or 2b.

The route:
The route leaves Oslo on the E68, which is a dual carriageway as it crosses the outlying suburb of Sandvika. The first towns along the route are all popular resorts, especially at weekends, when the traffic can be very heavy. Immediately outside the city boundary, the ski-lifts and the ski-jumping platforms appear. The side branches of the Tyrifjord Lake are popular weekend resorts in the summer for the people of Oslo. The road is a very good one to Sundvollen, where a toll road goes off to Kleivstua (4km). From here it is a 20-minute walk to the Kongensutsikt (King's View), which at 483m provides a superb view of the lake and the Hole Peninisula. At the top of the hill is the eleventh-century church of **Bønsnes** — an ancient settlement where the ancestors of Olav the Holy and Harald Hårdråda are supposed to have lived.

The E68 crosses the Hole Peninsula and the Ringerike conurbation (population 27,000), which is centred on **Hønefoss**. The chief industries are wood processing and electrical power. The town lies on the confluence of the Begna and the Randselva; it is divided by a large waterfall, which also supplies the power station. The Riddergården Museum is also worth visiting, having fourteenth-century buildings with original interiors. Hønefoss is a station on the Oslo-Bergen railway.

From Hønefoss, Road 7 goes left for **Hallingdal** and **Gol** (see routes 1c and 3b). A right turn along Road 35 provides an interesting excursion (12km) to Jevnaker, with its glass-blowing factories and museum. The present route, however, continues along the E68, following the course of the Begna.

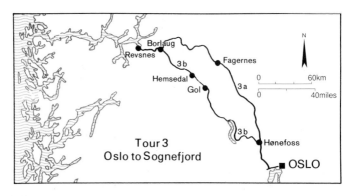

Tour 3
Oslo to Sognefjord

The road passes Hallingby and numerous small villages, then runs alongside Lake Sperillen. At **Nes** at the top end of the lake, there is a turning (Road 243) for **Hedal**, with its medieval stave church (not to be confused with the one at Heddal near Notodden on the E76). Though converted in 1738, it still retains an invaluable collection of original carvings and paintings, making it very much worth the 30km detour. A small road to the right just before Hedal leads back to the E68.

The next town, **Bagn**, has some industry and a power station by a reservoir. Its church was built in 1735. A side road goes off parallel to the E68, past the early medieval stave church of **Reinli**, with its valuable interior. At Bjørgo, Road 35 comes back into the E68 from the glass town of Jevnaker via the Randsfjord and Dokka. The road passes **Aurdal**, where Knut Hamsun wrote his novel *Victoria*, and the school centre of **Leira** (several schools and colleges are situated here), where Road 49 turns left for **Gol** in **Hallingdal** (see routes 1c and 3b).

Fagernes (population 2,800) is the railway terminus and centre of the Valdres region. Its open-air museum includes fifty buildings of historical interest, and there are regular folklore festivals during the summer. Road 51 goes off to the high mountains of Jotunheimen, where it connects with route 2a.

The E68 continues past two long lakes called the Strondafjord and Slidrefjord, and the landscape becomes increasingly mountainous. Between the two lakes are an impressive waterfall near Fossheim and a medieval church at **Ulnes** with typical rose motifs. A small toll road leads off from Ulnes across a mountain pass (950m) to Nøsen and Hemsedal (see route 3b).

The E68 passes some old storehouses, and the churches of Røn (eighteenth century), Slidre (cathedral, 1150) and Lomen (stave church, 1170). Not far from the road are a graveyard near Volden, a ruined church near Neste and a fourth-century runestone at Einang. A turning just past Lomen leads to the early medieval stave church of Hurum with its strange carvings. The little road goes on past the old mills of Kvie to Hensås —

Lomen stave church

where a chapel on the hillside commands a beautiful view — and returns to the E68 just before Lake Vangsmjøsa.

The E68 goes along the shore at the foot of the Grindane massif (1,724m). Near the church at Grindane stands the Vang Stone, a runestone from about AD 1000. Several side roads lead to ski-lifts in the nearby mountains. The stave church at **Øye** has been reconstructed from historical remains. At the popular winter resort of Hugostua, Road 53 turns off right across the mountains. It climbs to 1,000m, then drops steeply to Årdalstangen at the end of the Sognefjord, where a ferry crosses to **Kaupanger** (route 2a).

The E68 becomes steeper as it enters the Fillefjell, reaching its highest point (1,004m) at Nystuen. The road runs past lovely mountain lakes to the historic staging post of Marienstuen (first recorded in 1300), and then winds downhill towards **Borlaug**, where Road 52 comes in from **Gol** (see route 3b).

A little further along, at the entrance to Lærdal, is the **Borgund stave church**. This is the best-preserved and most original stave church in Norway, having remained almost unchanged since it was built in about 1150. The black, pitch-covered roofs are placed one on top of another. These, together with the dragons' heads, the runes and other carvings, make the building feel more like a heathen temple than a Christian church. The roofs come right down over the aisle that goes all the way round the church, protecting the wood and any visitors from the weather. Three sides of the church have a gabled porch with an entrance door. The doors are richly carved, especially the west door, with intricate scrollwork and dragonlike animal motifs. The windowless interior is dark and mostly bare of decoration, apart from a few carvings at the tops of the weight-bearing columns (staves) and around the altar. The yellow-brown pinewood gives out a certain amount of heat. The belfry stands across the churchyard. There is the usual kiosk at the entrance, selling entry tickets, together with the inevitable souvenirs and a brochure in three languages.

Not far from the church is a deep gorge with rapids at the bottom. There is a nice walk from here along the old post trail. A winding path leads up to the Sjurhaugsfoss, where a salmon ladder has been provided to help the salmon leap to the top. The waters beneath the waterfall are particularly good for fishing.

At **Lærdalsøyri**, the road reaches the Lærdalsfjord — a branch of the Sognefjord — and runs along the shore to **Revnes**. From here a ferry crosses frequently to **Kaupanger** (15 minutes), while five ferries a day go to **Gudvangen** and **Årdalstangen** respectively. From Gudvangen, the E68 goes on to **Bergen** (see routes 2a and 2b). The Kaupanger ferry connects to route 2a for **Jotunheimen** and (via Hella and Dragsvik) to route 2b for the **Geirangerfjord**.

3 (b) The Hallingdal route

Oslo ● Hønefoss ● Gol ● Borgund ● Revsnes (about 320km)

What the route has to offer:

Route 3b is mostly a combination of routes 1c and 3a. The route through Hallingdal from **Oslo** to **Gol** is described on pages 63 and 64 as part of route

The Lærdal river is renowned for salmon

1c. The route from Gol is through the mountainous Hemsedalfjell to **Borlaug** and the famous stave church at **Borgund** in Lærdal. The route then joins route 3a from Borlaug onwards.

The route:
See route 1c for the section from **Oslo** on the E68 to Hønefoss and on Road 7 through **Hallingdal** to **Gol**. Road 7 goes left at **Gol** towards the **Hardangervidda** and **Kinsarvik** on the Hardangerfjord (see routes 1b and 1c). Road 49 goes right towards **Leira** and **Fagernes**, forming a cross-route to route 3a.

The present route leaves **Gol** along Road 52 through Hemsedal, and at first rises gently through an undulating landscape of woods and meadows. A few side roads run parallel or into the mountains nearby. One road, for example, goes to a viewing point at Ulsåk, and continues along a beautiful scenic route past Storevatn and the Skogshorn (1,728m).

The town of **Hemsedal** is a busy tourist centre with a large variety of facilities. The area has some good fishing rivers and marvellous winter skiing centres such as Holde bru. Many of the ski-lifts are still used as chair-lifts during the summer.

The road keeps on climbing, and at **Tuv** the scenery becomes much more mountainous with some marvellous views. A side road goes off into the skiing area of Grøndalen. A little further on is the beautiful Rjukande

103

The mountains of Hemsedal

Waterfall. The road climbs over the Hemsedalfjell, reaching a maximum height of 1,137m at Eldrevatn. With luck, it is possible to see a few reindeer wandering across the fjell. Over to the north east is the 2,000m peak of Jukleegga.

The road winds down steeply, and at Bergstølen passes a 40m waterfall before meeting the E68 road at **Borlaug**. Here the route joins route 3a, which goes left along the E68 via **Borgund** and Lærdal to Revsnes, or else right and back to Oslo via Fagernes.

4 THE ARCTIC TOUR

4 (a) Oslo to the North Cape

Oslo ● Eidsvoll ● Hamar ● Lillehammer ● Otta ● Dombås ● Oppdal ● Trondheim ● Grong ● Mosjøen ● Mo (Arctic Circle) ● Fauske (Bodø) ● Bognes ● Narvik ● Moen ● Nordkjosbotn (Tromsø) ● Skibotn ● Alta (Kautokeino) ● Skaidi (Hammerfest) ● Olderfjord (North Cape) ● Lakselv

What the route has to offer:

The Arctic Road (E6) to the North Cape is not only the longest road in Europe, but also the oldest and most important traffic route in Norway. Even as early as the Bronze Age, Germanic tribes were moving and settling along this route. And it is mentioned again and again in Norwegian mythology, literature and song.

The route covers vast distances to arrive at the northernmost tip of Europe. Starting from Oslo, it runs through the beautiful Gudbrandsdal, famous for its rich folk culture, and past the Dovrefjell plateau to Trondheim. It continues over high tundra, with its bogs and mosquitoes, and through deep forests that become continually sparser. It passes through busy modern ports, fishing villages and Lapp settlements. Beyond the Arctic Circle the remarkable phenomenon of the midnight sun can be seen. This only occurs over a short period, so the trip must be timed carefully (see page 40). Finally, the northernmost point of the journey — the North Cape — provides an unforgettable glimpse of the blue-green waters of the Arctic Ocean.

Length and timing:

A trip to the far end of Europe is not something to be undertaken lightly. Even the shortest route to the North Cape covers about 5,000km. If interesting places are to be included on the way, it can be as long as 6,000km or more. So careful planning is absolutely essential.

The journey is relatively fast as far as Lillehammer, but it becomes slower from upper Gudbrandsdal onwards: the road is often steep, and the scenery is too good to pass through in haste. The roads after Trondheim are often narrow and twisty, especially along the fjords; so the average speed will not be very great. In addition, the ferry connections require a certain amount of waiting time.

The roads through Lapland and the Arctic are still unmade in places, though not in bad condition. High daily mileages cannot therefore be counted on, especially in view of the conditions and style of the roads and the delays caused by Ferries. On the other hand, the summer daylight is long — effectively all night in places above the Arctic Circle — so one can

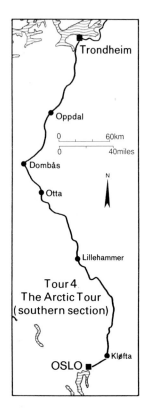

Tour 4
The Arctic Tour
(southern section)

always do an extra hour's driving.

Four weeks is the minimum time to allow for the journey to the North Cape, bearing in mind that this does not allow for much stopping time on the way. The trip can admittedly be fitted into a rather shorter time, but it will not then be very enjoyable. It is better to allow five or six weeks altogether. If the weather is bad at a vital stage of the journey, one can then wait a little extra time for it to clear. Or one might include a short break for bathing on the way, or preferably on the way back — on the south coast of Norway, or by a Finnish or Swedish lake.

The best time to travel:

The most favourable time of year is during the long days of summer. From mid-June to mid-August is when the weather is most likely to be good, and when the passes through Gudbrandsdal and Dovrefjell are least liable to a sudden fall of snow. (Gudbrandsdal has a decidedly continental climate instead of the warmer though damper climate of coastal regions.)

The Skibladner, paddle-steamer on Mjøsa

September and the last ten days of August are likely to have high rainfall in these northerly climes, especially between Bergen and Trondheim.

The coastal route is quite passable from early June onwards, because it is warmed by the Gulf Stream. But the same is not true of the return journey through polar continental regions, where the ground can remain frozen well into June. The sun shines at midnight above the Arctic Circle from 1 to 25 June, and at the North Cape from 14 May to 29 July. July would seem to be the best month to travel, since it is also the driest period of the year. Autumn in Scandinavia begins to make itself felt within the last part of August.

The route:
The E6 leaves Oslo along the Bispegata and the Strømsveien, and is signposted to Hamar and Trondheim. Being a motorway at this stage, Kløfta can be quickly reached, where Road 2 goes off via Kongsvinger to Sweden. The E6 continues via Jessheim and Dal to **Eidsvoll Verk**, which is where the Norwegian constitution was first passed in 1814, in the administrative building of the then ironworks. The building has now been converted into a museum. Also by the E6 is the Eidsvoll District Museum, which includes fifteen old houses.

Near Minnesund the road crosses the Vorma, and the bridge affords a wide vista of Lake Mjøsa, which is the largest lake in Norway (366 sq km in

Twelfth-century Hamar Cathedral

area; up to 400m deep). In summer a paddle steamer plies the century-old route along the whole length of the lake from Minnesund to Lillehammer.

The road runs along the side of the lake into Hedmark, which is an agricultural region with large, wealthy farms. The village of **Stange** is typical. Just off the E6, it is surrounded by large estates, some of which are kept as national monuments. Also worth mentioning is the medieval church. Built in 1250, it is one of the most beautiful in the area.

A little further on is the town of **Hamar**, which with a population of 16,000 is one of the largest inland towns in Norway. It is the industrial and commercial centre for the surrounding area, and the administrative centre for the county. It became a bishopric in 1152, as the ruins of the cathedral bear witness. Not far from these ruins is the Hedmark Museum — an open-air museum exhibiting items of local interest. The Railway Museum, also an open-air site, presents a historical survey of railways, including different types of track and several old station buildings with original interiors from the last century; there is also a model railway.

The road continues along the shore via Brumunddal, with its clothing factory which has opened its doors to the public as a museum. It crosses a neck of land, and returns to the lake shore just before **Ringsaker**. The twelfth-century church here has a 70m high tower and a beautifully carved sixteenth-century altar, with frescos depicting scenes from the life of St

The Railway Museum, Hamar

Olav. 2km further on at Stein is another historical site — the Steinholmen, or the ruins of Håkonsson's fortress — and nearby are some Bronze Age rock paintings. Another 4km further on, next to Smestadsletta, a ring of stones indicates a prehistoric burial site.

The E6 keeps to the shore of the lake, which becomes narrow and fjord-like, until it arrives at **Lillehammer** (population 22,000), the provincial capital of Oppland. Lillehammer is picturesquely situated among the hills at the entrance to Gudbrandsdal, and is a popular resort all the year round. The main thing to see in Lillehammer is the open-air museum at **Maihaugen**, which is second only to Bygdøy in Oslo. It all started in 1887, when a dentist called Anders Sandvig began a comprehensive collection of antique furniture and traditional farm tools. These he exhibited in an old farm hut which he had bought and re-erected in his garden. It was gradually expanded into a large museum showing the historical development of Norwegian architecture and customs. The museum was eventually taken over by the town, who transferred it to an extensive park site at Maihaugen. The museum presents a lasting memorial of the past, including ancient storehouses, farmhouses, stables, workshops, a parsonage, a dairy, and a stave church from Garmo near Lom. The town also possesses an art gallery, containing works mostly by Norwegian painters. On the edge of the town is the Bjerkebæck House, home of the feminist writer and Nobel

109

prizewinner Sigrid Undset.

The E6 leads from Lillehammer into **Gudbrandsdal**, the 'valley of valleys'. The valley is fairly broad, and is dotted with centuries-old farms. The route along the River Lågen has been an important north-south link from time immemorial, and the numerous old *Stuen* (huts) and inns have a tradition going back centuries.

Roughly parallel to Gudbrandsdal is the famous **Peer Gynt Way**, which branches left off the E6 at **Tretten**. It consists partly of tollroads, and runs along the top of the plateau past numerous mountain hotels, which form good bases for walking and skiing expeditions. It comes back into the E6 at **Hundorp**.

The main road meanwhile keeps to the course of the river, which after Tretten turns into Lake Losna, and passes two stave churches at Kirkestuen and **Ringebu**, both of which were heavily restored in the seventeenth century.

Detour via Rondane

At **Ringebu** a road goes off to the right known as the **Rondane Road**. It begins as Road 220, becomes Road 27 as far as Folldal, and Road 29 to **Hjerkinn**, where it returns to the E6. The route is closed until 15 June, but runs through some lovely mountain scenery. It twists and climbs a lot, and is unmade in places. It reaches a maximum height of 1,060m. The section

Ski-touring at Lillehammer

The open-air museum at Maihaugen

along Lake Atna (fully surfaced) is one of the most impressive in Norway. The boggy moorlands are a nature reserve with a research station. At Folldal there is an old pyrites mine. The route comes back into the E6 at **Hjerkinn.**

Around Hundorp the valley becomes narrower. The village has some interesting old houses, an octagonal church built in 1787, and some monuments and mound graves. This is the point where the Peer Gynt Way comes back into the E6.

The main road carries on past the power station at Harpefoss to **Vinstra**, the chief tourist centre of Gudbrandsdal. Nearby are Hågå — the Peer Gynt estate — and Peer Gynt's grave across the river in the chapel at Sødorp. Round a bend in the river is **Kvam**, where the British and the Germans fought for possession of Gudbrandsdal in 1940. A church was built here in 1952 to commemorate the British soldiers who fell.

9km further on at Sjoa, Road 51 goes left for **Randsverk**. It goes through the beautiful Heidal, passing Bjølstad — the best-preserved traditional farmstead in Gudbrandsdal. A short way further along the E6 is the village of Kringen. A monument here commemorates the time in 1612 when the local peasants fought off a band of Scotsmen who were on their way to Sweden.

Soon after that is an important road junction at **Otta**, where Road 15 goes left via Vågåmo to **Lom**, and eventually to the Nordfjord. There are further turnings: at Lom for Road 55 through **Jotunheimen** (see route 2a), and at Langevatn for Road 58 to the Geirangerfjord (see route 2c).

A little way further along the E6 is Selsverket — a village full of tradition, which was the setting for Sigrid Undset's novel *Kristin Lavransdatter*. A small private toll road goes off to the right to **Mysuseter**, and carries on into the **Rondane National Park** past the unusual Kvitskruprestinn — a gravel mound left behind by an ice-age glacier.

The Gudbrandsdal becomes narrower and the scenery more romantic. Just past the mountain resort of Dovre, on the right-hand slope of the valley, is the old royal palace of **Tofte**, which is one of the largest and most beautiful estates in Gudbrandsdal; it is now a national monument.

The next place is **Dombås** (659m, population 1,200), which is the centre of the Dovre mountain region and an important road and rail junction. The E69 goes left from here towards Åndalsnes and **Ålesund** (see routes 2d and 2b), while the **Rauma Railway** branches off towards Åndalsnes. Dombås is the training and instruction centre for the Norwegian Sports Federation (Dombåshaugen). The **Dovrefjell** stretches across to the north east of Dombås, with several peaks over 2,000m, the highest being Snøhetta at 2,286m.

The E6 turns right here, and climbs out of the valley. There is a view of Snøhetta from near Fokstua; the peat-bog area to the left of here — the Fokstumyrene — is a nature reserve, with many interesting plant and animal species. It is closed to visitors from the end of April to the beginning of June. By the railway station at **Vålåsjø** is Dovregubbens Hall. The hall of the troll of the Dovrefjell, it has a restaurant and souvenir shop.

10km further on is **Hjerkinn** (956m), which is the driest place in Norway, with an average annual rainfall of only 220mm (Bergen has almost ten times as much). The Eystein Church was built here as a memorial to King

Oppdal, Norway's leading alpine resort

Eystein, who had the first mountain hut built here in the twelfth century. A stone indicates the path of the Kongevei (Royal Road), which has been used by more than forty monarchs on their way over the Dovrefjell.

At Hjerkinn, Road 29 goes right towards Folldal (see page 110). Just after Hjerkinn, the E6 reaches the top of the pass at 1,026m. The road passes close to an area for military exercises, and a pyrites mine and enrichment plant.

The route goes high past the peat bogs of **Dovrefjell**, which form a nature reserve and are very good for walking expeditions. The Kongsvoll bru Hotel provides a resting point on the way. With its old-fashioned utensils and traditional interior, it recalls the old hut where the twelfth-century kings dismounted. A stone's throw away is a lovely railway station, with a small botanical garden displaying typical mountain plants.

The road has now entered the valley of the Driva. Running parallel to the road is an ancient footpath called the Vårstig, offering a magnificent view of Drivdal. It begins just past Kongsvoll, and comes back into the E6 near Nestavoll. In the area west of Nestavoll, called Stølådal, it is possible, with a great deal of luck and patience, to see a few of the musk oxen that have been reintroduced there.

The Driva can often be glimpsed at the bottom of a deep gorge. It runs in a roaring torrent, eroding the rocks into strange, cylindrical shapes. Typical of such gorges is the Magalaupet, which is reached by turning left

Mo i Rana on the edge of the Arctic Circle

along a stretch of the old road. The river is mostly glacial in origin; it has brought down numerous large boulders, which it has spun round like a pestle in a mortar, making them circular in shape.

Just before **Oppdal**, there is an open-air museum to the left of the road, which includes twenty old farmhouses, stables and storehouses. The small town of Oppdal has a pleasant camping site and a good hotel, and there are ski-lifts into the surrounding mountains. From Oppdal, Road 16 goes left, continuing along the course of the Driva and through Sunndal to **Sunndalsøra** (see routes 2e and 2b).

The present route stays with the E6, which at this stage has been made into a wide, modern highway as it goes on to Berkåk, where Road 700 makes a detour via Løkken to Trondheim — pleasant, but not absolutely necessary.

The E6 continues to Støren (66m), which is a popular centre for anglers. It has an octagonal church built in 1817, and a quarry where granite is hewn out of the rock. At Støren, Road 30 turns off right into Gauldalen. After 100km it comes to Røros, where it enters Road 31 going towards the Swedish border.

The next place is Høvin, which is best known for a massive landslide that took place in 1345, killing 250 people. Just beyond Høvin, the river plunges over a waterfall. This has also produced some strange boulders, though

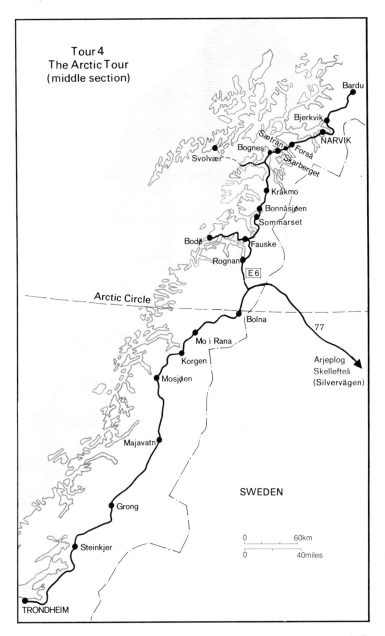

Tour 4
The Arctic Tour
(middle section)

Bardu

Bjerkvik

NARVIK

Sætran Forså

Bognes Skarberget

Svolvær

Kråkmo

Bonnåsjøen

Sommarset

Bodø Fauske

Rognan

E6

Arctic Circle

Bolna

77

Mo i Rana

Arjeplog
Skellefteå
(Silvervägen)

Korgen

Mosjøen

Majavatn

SWEDEN

Grong

0   60km
0   40miles

Steinkjer

TRONDHEIM

115

they can only be seen when the water is low.

At Heimdal the road enters the outskirts of **Trondheim**, and soon comes right into the city. Trondheim is described in detail in the section on towns and cities. This completes the first third of the route from Oslo to the North Cape. The second third goes as far as the Arctic Circle.

The E6 leaves Trondheim along the shore of the fjord, and continues via Melvik to **Hell**, which is the railway junction for the line to Sweden. Just before Hell, the road passes some rock drawings from the early Stone Age. They are known in Norwegian as *helleristninger* — a word which appears again on signposts along the next part of the route. Just beyond Hell is the famous medieval church of Værnes, which is interesting for its architecture, its fine baroque pulpit and its intricate carvings.

At **Stjørdal**, the E75 goes off east towards Sweden. Then at Tiller a small road goes left towards Flosjøen. Opposite Flosjøen on an island in the fjord is the ruined castle of Steinviksholm, which was built in about 1525. At low tide it is possible to walk over to the island. The island and the castle can be seen from the E6 just beyond Tiller.

The E6 comes to Åsen, where a road goes left along the **Frosta Peninsula**. This is an area full of history, with its ancient lawcourts, ruined monastery, medieval church, and Stone Age rock drawings. More such *helleristninger* can be seen near Skjerve. Skogn is a centre for wood carving, and the church at Alstadhauget has its unique medieval frescos. The E6 carries on to the small trading port of **Levanger**, which has handled goods for Sweden since the middle of the fifteenth century.

The next place is Verdalsøra, where the wharf for building oil platforms is quite clearly visible. Just a little further on is a turning for Stiklestad, where King Olav the Holy met his death in 1030. A century later, a church was built in his memory on this historic battlefield.

From Røra, a small detour is recommended onto the **Inderøy Peninsula**. There are some interesting birds to be seen here, and the two medieval churches of Sakshaug and Hustad are also worth a visit. The road returns to the E6 at Vist.

A side road from Mære leads to a site at Mærehaugen, which in ancient times was used for heathen sacrificial rites. A church was built over it in the twelfth century; the grotesquely carved animal heads are original. Some Viking finds have also been discovered in this area.

The E6 continues via Vist to **Steinkjer** (population 20,000). Two thirds of the town was destroyed during air raids in 1940. The newly-built modern town lives from the processing and export of wood. The area around Steinkjer is full of rock drawings. At the exit of the town, a road turns off to the left towards Egge kirke and Bardal (11km from the E6), where a number of colourful Stone Age motifs are to be found on a large slab of rock. There are also a number of grave mounds in the area.

Excursion to the Reindeer of Bøla

The most famous rock drawing in Norway is the amazing **Reindeer of Bøla**, which is to be found to the north east of Steinkjer on the eastern shore of the Snåsavatn. The route to Bøla leaves the E6 at Steinkjer on Road 763, which goes via Stod to the east bank of the lake. The road is in poor condition, and is unmade in places. The rock drawing is just past the railway station at ⌘ Valøy, on the shore of the lake and at the end of a 200m footpath signposted *Bølaristningen*. The road returns to the E6 beyond Snåsa at Vegset, at the far end of the 40km long lake.

7km after Steinkjer, at the village of **Asp**, Road 17 goes left in the direction of **Namsos**. Those wishing to make a detour to this town, which offers water sports and a marvellous salmon river, should afterwards leave Namsos on Road 17, turning at Skogmo onto Road 760, which re-enters the E6 at Grong.

The Arctic Road continues along the western shore of the Snåsavatn. At Vegset it leaves the lake, and goes via Heia to **Formofoss**, which is near a 30m high waterfall. Road 74 goes off at Formofoss towards the Swedish border.

Soon after Formofoss, Road 760 comes in at **Grong** from Namsos. The E6 now enters the valley of the Namsen, which is an outstanding river for salmon. One of the most famous salmon ladders is at Fiskumfoss — a waterfall that has partly been harnessed by a power station. The road becomes narrower, and repeatedly crosses the railway over single-track bridges. It passes over a bridge called the Grøndalsbru and under the cable car to the Skorovass Mine. Near Flåtådalen, the Namsen drops 15m as it roars down over the rapids at Trongfoss. 13km further on, near Brekkvasselv, a road leads off to the right towards the Grong copper mines at Ornes. The E6 continues northwards, and soon crosses the county boundary from Nord Trøndelag into Nordland.

The next village is **Majavatn** (364m). During World War II this was a centre of the resistance, where twenty partisans were sentenced to death and executed by a firing squad. The village is surrounded by lakes which are excellent for fishing. A little further on, at Kappfjelli, the road reaches its highest point (375m), and then begins to descend through the rocky, wooded valley of Svenningdal.

At **Trofors**, Road 73 goes off via Hjattfjelldal, with its Lapp school, towards the Swedish border. At **Fellingfors** there was once a silver mine. A short way further on, a small road is signposted off for Laksfoss, where the Vefsnaelv plunges over a 16m high waterfall. The leaping salmon are able to bypass the waterfall by means of a salmon ladder.

The E6 continues along the course of the Vefsnaelv until it enters the Vefsnefjord at the port of **Mosjøen** (population 13,000), whose chief activities are wood shipment and aluminium smelting. The E6 leaves the shore of the fjord, and climbs through an area of hills and forests. It crosses the Fusta — another popular salmon river — and runs along the shore of the Fustavatn. On the right is the Smedsengfjell (1,058m). The road climbs again to Osen on the Luktvatn, and continues to climb as it crosses a ridge

Crystal Grotto near Mo

(550m). It then winds steeply down the hillside to the Korgen Power Station, which is one of Norway's largest power stations, with an output of about a quarter of a million kilowatts.

The road passes the southern shore of the Sørfjord and goes through some gorgeous scenery as it runs along the bank of the Finneidfjord to the new industrial town of **Mo i Rana** (population 26,000). Mo has Norway's only steelworks. The iron ores are brought down from Dunderlandsdal to be smelted at Mo. The town has thus become an important industrial centre, with the world's largest smelting furnace. Worth visiting are the Rana District Museum, which has a Lapp section, and the Steinneset Museum, which is an open-air village museum. A cable car goes to the top of the Mofjell, where there are marvellous views over the Rana and across to the **Svartisen**.

At Mo, there is a right turn along the E79 (Blåvägen), which crosses Sweden to Umeå on the Gulf of Bothnia.

Excursions from Mo i Rana

There are several very interesting places in the Mo area. Nesna on the coast, for example, can be reached via Road 805 from Selfors bru. From Nesa there are some wonderful views of the Sjofjell, and boat trips to neighbouring fishing villages and bird islands.

Another excursion leaves the E6 near Røssvoll on the road to Mo Airport, and continues via Røvassdalen to Grønli, where a turning is signposted to **Grønli Cave** (22km). The last part of the journey is on foot (25 minutes). There are guided tours of the cave, for which wellington boots and a raincoat are needed. This stalactite cavern is 1.5km long and was discovered in 1965.

Another road from Grønli is signposted to the Svartisvatn (32km), where an hourly boat service takes visitors to the Osterdalsisen — the most impressive outlet of the **Svartisen**. It is an hour's walk from the boat to the foot of the glacier (sturdy footwear required). Those wishing to climb the glacier itself should inquire at the tourist office in Mo. The Svartisen is the second-largest glacier in Norway, and is divided into a western and an eastern section. The Arctic Circle runs a few kilometres north of the Østerdalsisen, which forms the southernmost outlet of the Svartisen.

The E6 goes from Mo via Storforshei into Dunderlandsdal, where the Rana is fed by numerous underground rivers. The road climbs out of the coniferous forests, and the birchwoods which follow become gradually sparser, until the road passes the treeline near **Bolna** at a height of 550m. The road here is only about 5km west of the Swedish border. About 8km further on, there is a monument on the left overlooking the road. It commemorates the place where the Germans set up a Yugoslav prison camp during World War II.

Soon after that, the road crosses the **Arctic Circle**, which is marked by a

Bodø, looking east

boundary stone on the right-hand side of the new road. The old road leads from the car park to a 'Lapp camp' for tourists and a coffee bar. A souvenir shop sells postcards, stamps and the usual tourist junk, much of which has nothing to do with the Arctic Circle. The road has now entered the Land of the Midnight Sun, where the sun never rises in midwinter and never sets in midsummer.

From this point onwards, it is interesting to note how the railway is protected from snow by a series of shelters built over it. At Stødi Station, 2km beyond the Arctic Circle, there are some interesting Lapp stone altars. The area to the right of the road is a nature reserve. The road soon reaches its highest point (707m), and begins to drop into Lønsdal, which is not far from a Lapp settlement.

Excursion into Junkerdalen

At Hestbrinken, Road 77 (Graddisveien) goes right into the wild and romantic valley of **Junkerdalen**. After 24km, it crosses the Swedish border, where it continues as Road 375 (Silvervägen) and goes all the way across Sweden to Skellefteå on the Gulf of Bothnia. But Junkerdalen is worth an excursion on its own. This nature reserve is incredibly beautiful and contains a number of rare plants. With luck, a few wandering reindeer may come into view. About 6km before the Swedish border (which is marked by a boundary stone), there is a tourist centre to the right of the road, which includes a restaurant, a petrol station and a play area.

The E6 carries on to **Storjord**, where there are plant nurseries and a state institute for research into growing vegetables north of the Arctic Circle. The road then drops gently through the forests of Saltdal until it eventually arrives at **Rognan** (population 1,600), which is at the top end of the beautiful Saltdalsfjord. The E6 runs along the shore of the fjord. At Botn, 3km after Rognan, there is a military cemetery just over the railway, where 2,700 Germans and 1,700 Yugoslavs lie buried. The road carries on via **Finneid** to **Fauske**.

Excursion to Bodø
Road 80 to Bodø leaves the E6 at Fauske. Near Vågan, it passes a rock drawing of an elk, which is 4,000 years old.

At Tverrlandet there is a right turn along Road 813 for the **Saltstraumen** (13km). The Saltstraumen is a strait only 3km long and 150m wide. Large volumes of water are forced through it by the tides, reaching speeds of up to 50km/h to form the fastest tidal current in the world. The current is especially strong at full and new moon, and numerous fish are attracted by the large number of algae, plankton and krill that are released by the current. The Saltstraumen is thus very popular with anglers.

The route returns to Road 80 and turns left for **Bodø** (population 30,000). The town was almost completely destroyed by air raids in 1940, and has been rebuilt in the modern style. The town has no special industry of its own, the harbour being its chief employer and the main source of income. The country's naval and air force headquarters are also located here.

The harbour remains ice-free throughout the winter, and is a focal point for fisheries and sea transport to the islands off the coast. There are daily trips to the two fascinating bird islands of **Værøy** and **Røst**, and a 2-day excursion to the Lofoten Islands. Ships on the Hurtigrute also stop here daily.

The Nordland Museum in Bodø is very much worth a visit, with sections on the history of fishing, the Vikings and other local items of interest.

Detour via Nordfold
Near Vargåsen, 8km along the E6 from Fauske, there is a left turn along

Vedøy bird-rock at Røst

Road 81 for Røsvik, where a ferry crosses to Nordfold. Road 81 then continues to Bogøy, where another ferry crosses to Skutvik on the island of Hamarøy (see below). Road 81 returns to the E6 at Ulsvåg.

This alternative route offers a chance to savour the delights of the coastal islands and to glimpse the Lofotens. It is no longer than the direct route via the mainland, but the ferry crossings may well cause delays.

The E6 crosses the Tørrfjord over a 179m long bridge called the Trengselbru. It carries on through a series of tunnels, the longest of which is nearly 3km long, and arrives at Sommarset, where a ferry crosses another fjord to Bonnåsjøen. The crossing takes a quarter of an hour, and passes near to the Starfoss. This is one of the narrowest parts of Norway. The Swedish border runs just east of here through the Rago National Park, and at one point is only 15km from the head of the fjord, and hence from the coast.

From Bonnåsjøen, the E6 climbs quickly, reaching a maximum height of 390m at the Tennvatnet. It continues to **Kråkmo** through an area of lakes grouped round a mountain called the Kråkmotind (924m). The writer Knut Hamsun lived for some time at Kråkmo, and used seven of these lakes as the settings for some of his novels.

The road carries on past a whole complex of lakes until it comes down to the Sagfjord at Tømmerneset. A path leads off to some rock paintings of reindeer. At Innharvet the road enters an undulating region with yet more lakes and some beautiful views of the fjord. It then begins to climb, and from the ridge overlooking **Ulsvåg** there is an impressive view of the Vestfjord, and in clear weather of the **Lofoten Islands** beyond.

At Ulsvåg Road 81 comes in from Hamarøy (see above) — one of a lovely group of islands with magnificent mountain scenery. Knut Hamsun spent his childhood on Hamarøy. The name Hamsun was actually a pseudonym, which he derived from the place where he grew up. (His real name was Knut Pedersen.)

The E6 continues across this rugged and indented peninsula to **Bognes** on the Tysfjord. Just before Bognes, at Boghøgda, a small road goes off to the northern end of the fjord, where between Kornes and Leiknes there are a number of interesting Stone Age rock paintings. From Bognes there are ferries to Lødingen for the **Lofoten** and **Vesterålen Islands**. But the main route is by ferry across the Tysfjord to Skarberget, where the E6 resumes.

The many-branched Tysfjord is hemmed in by some incredibly bizarre mountain scenery. The Stetind (1,381m), which overlooks one of its eastern branches, is shaped like a gigantic obelisk. The Hellemofjord is the southernmost branch of the fjord, and goes so far inland that its far end is only 6.3km from the Swedish border — the narrowest point in Norway.

The road goes from Skarberget through some weird mountain scenery to Sætran, where the former ferry over the Elfjord to Forså has now been replaced by a series of three bridges. There is another rock painting here, this time depicting a fish.

The next place is Ballangen (population 1,000), from which pyrites from nearby Bjørkåsen used to be shipped. The road runs along the shore of the Ofotenfjord to Skjærvik, crossing the Skjomen over a 700m long suspension bridge. The blue waters of the Skjomen are supplied by

The Arctic Highway leading to Berlevåg

meltwater from the surrounding mountains and the nearby Frostisen Glacier (1,744m).

The road continues along the shore to Ankenes, from which Narvik can already be seen. It then crosses the Beisfjord Bridge into **Narvik** itself (see the section on towns and cities). Narvik is the beginning of the last third of the Arctic Road, which offers much of the beauty and variety of nature, from tundra and fast-flowing rivers to ice fields and many-branched fjords.

From Narvik, the road goes all the way round the Rombak, crossing the Rombaksfjord over the biggest suspension bridge in Norway. In 1940 there was heavy fighting here between the Germans and the British. At the small village of **Nygård**, a road goes off into Sweden, which was only completed in 1984. It becomes Road 98 from the Bjørnfjell border post, and follows the Ofot Railway to Kiruna.

At the small industrial town of Bjerkvik, Road 19 goes left to the Vesterålen and Lofoten Islands. The E6 climbs quickly to 330m, and crosses the county boundary from Nordland into Troms.

The tourist station near Gratangen affords a magnificent view of the surrounding area. The road runs on through birchwoods flanked by ice-covered peaks 1,200 to 1,400m high. Near Jordbruna, the road crosses the Spanselv, which at this point has eroded a tunnel through the limestone rock. There is a view along **Spansdal** — a wild and beautiful valley surrounded by mountains — and down to Lavangen.

Detour via Spansdal
Near Fossbakken, Road 84 leads off into Spansdal — a valley so delightful that it repays the short detour of some 30km. Road 84 follows the valley down to a fjord at Lavangen, then crosses a tongue of land to Salangen, which is gorgeously situated at the end of the Salangenfjord. From here, Road 851 leads back into the main E6 route at Brandvoll.

Just before Brandvoll, the E6 passes the Bardu District Museum, which has an interesting section on war weapons through the centuries. The Bardu-Setermoen area was first settled and farmed in the eighteenth century by a number of families from Gudbrandsdal and Østerdal.

A right turn at **Elverum** leads off along Road 87 towards the Målselvfoss — a beautiful waterfall with a lot of fish and a salmon ladder. Road 87 continues via Rundhaug, and eventually returns to the E6 at Øvergård beyond Nordkjosbotn. It is 15km shorter than the main road, but is not so well-made.

A side road leads quickly back from the Målselvfoss to the E6 at Andselv-Bardufoss, passing a museum and the Bardufoss, which has been harnessed for a power station. Andselv-Bardufoss has an airport with connections to Oslo and Kirkenes. The E6 continues to Olsborg, then leaves the Målselv and goes up Takelvdal to the Takvatn. The valley is again flanked by massive peaks such as the Blatind (1,380m) and the Hattavarre (1,408m).

The road comes down to the Balsfjord near Storsteinnes. A rock drawing was discovered by the shore near Balsfjord Church. The road carries on along the shore to **Nordkjosbotn**.

Excursion to Tromsø (about 73km each way)
The E78 goes left for Tromsø at Nordkjosbotn. This road has come from Kilpisjärvi in Finland via Skibotndal and the Storfjord. The Finns have for some reason named it the Road of the Four Winds.

The road runs beside the fjord to Slettmo, then through Lavangsdal, past a Lapp sacrificial stone, to Fagernes. Road 91 turns right here for the Breivikeidet-Svensby ferry, continuing to the Lyngseidet-Olderdalen ferry, which crosses the Lyngenfjord to meet the main route again. This is a possible alternative for those travelling on from Tromsø to the North Cape.

From the E78 between Sandvik and Tromsdalen there are views of the Rystraumen. These narrow straits have a strong tidal current, which causes problems for shipping. From Tromsdalen, a cable car goes up to the 420m high Storsteinen, where there is also a restaurant. The town has an

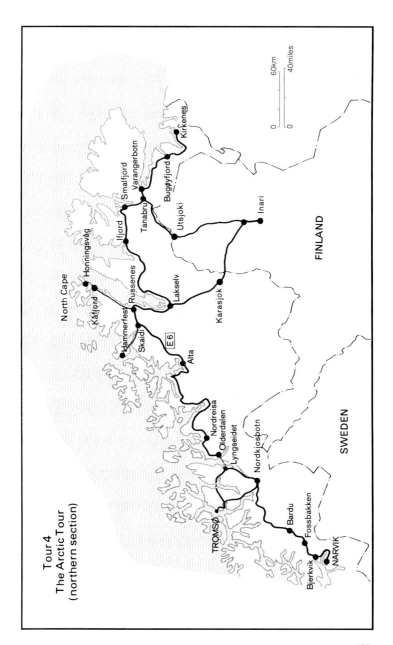

Tour 4
The Arctic Tour
(northern section)

North Cape
Honningsvåg
Kåfjord
Hammerfest
Skaidi
Russenes
Ifjord
Smalfjord
Varangerbotn
Kirkenes
Bugøyfjord
Tanabru
Utsjoki
Lakselv
Inari
Karasjok
E6
Alta
Nordreisa
Olderdalen
Lyngseidet
Nordkjosbotn
TROMSØ
Bardu
Fossbakken
Bjerkvik
NARVIK

FINLAND
SWEDEN

60km
40miles
0

127

Aerial view of Tromsø

intriguing modern church built in 1965. The roof is especially interesting architecturally, being made with glass to symbolise the power of natural forces — the ice, the long Arctic night and the midnight sun.

The road crosses the Tromsøysund via the 1.1 km long Tromsøbru — the longest bridge in Norway — to arrive at Tromsø (population 45,000). The city boundaries have been expanded to include the surrounding fishing villages, so that Tromsø, with an overall area of 2,400sq km, is the most extensive municipal authority in Norway. The original city centre is on the island of Troms, and still has some beautiful old wooden houses.

Tromsø is a major port for the shipment of fish products, animal skins and industrial goods. In spite of its northerly location, its harbour remains ice-free thanks to the Gulf Stream. It has been the base for many Arctic expeditions, some of which are commemorated by a monument to Roald Amundsen. Tromsø boasts the most northerly university in the world. An observatory has been set up to observe the behaviour of polar light together with other local phenomena. The midnight sun shines in Tromsø from 21 May to 23 July.

Also worth seeing in Tromsø are the old Tromsøya Church, with its medieval Madonna and seventeenth-century altarpiece, and the Tromsø Museum. This comprises collections of finds from the local area and from Spitzbergen, plus a geological and zoological survey of the Arctic, and a section on marine biology, which includes an aquarium. Tromsø's brewery is again the most northerly in the world. A pub is attached, inviting visitors to sample the beers.

Flåm, at the southern end of the Aurlandsfjord

Stone and Bronze Age rock carvings at Bardal, north of Trondheim

Sordalen scenery just south of Narvik

Excursion into Signaldalen

Near Kittdal bru between Oteren and Storfjord, a side road turns off the main route towards Paras in **Signaldalen**. This valley is ideal for a short excursion, being one of the most beautiful in Norway. 14km along it, at the bridge near Signalnes, there is a breathtaking view of pyramidal mountains such as Otertind (1,320m), Polvartind (1,250m), Mannfjellet (1,585m) and Parastind (1415m).

From Oteren a new section of the Arctic Road runs along the eastern shores of the Storfjord and the Lyngenfjord. From now on it is no longer the E6 but simply Road 6. At Olderbakken the E78 goes off towards Kilpisjärvi in Finland. Known as the Road of the Four Winds, it continues along the Swedish/Finnish border as far as the Gulf of Bothnia.

Near Diupvik at the end of the Lyngenfjord, the road climbs onto a plateau offering a marvellous view. During World War II the Germans built a strong fortification at this point. At Diupvik there is also a Lapp settlement.

At Sørkjosen there is a small airport, which is linked into the national air passenger network. The next village, **Nordreisa**, is at the mouth of the Reisa. This salmon-rich river comes down through a fertile valley, at the top of which are two magnificent waterfalls. A small road (865) leads off up Reisadalen as far as Bilto and Sarelv, from which a boat service runs up the river to the hut at Nedrefoss. The 3-hour boat journey goes past the mighty Mollesfoss (269m), which is one of the highest waterfalls in the country. The Imofoss is not far from the boat terminus.

The main road crosses a pass through an area frequented by Lapps, and then runs along the shore of a fjord called the Kvænangen. A new bridge over the Sorstraumen, with its strong tidal currents, shortens the journey to the North Cape by as much as 35km. The road climbs again to Baddereidet (240m), and returns to the shore of the fjord as far as Alteidet.

A side road on the left goes to the fishing village of Jøkelfjord, from which trips are possible to the Jøkelfjord Glacier. A side branch of the Øksfjordjøkul (1,204m), it is the only mainland glacier in Europe from which icebergs break off directly into the sea during the summer.

Road 6 continues along the side of the Langfjord and around a headland near Toften, where there are still the remains of a German fortification. The road carries on via Talvik to **Kåfjord**, where there was a copper mine in the last century. The reserves were exhausted and the mine abandoned. On the slopes of the Haldde, at about 900m, was the Northern Lights Observatory, which has similarly been abandoned.

The next place is **Alta** — a town made up from the parishes of Bossekop, Bukta, Elfebakken and Middbakken. A former whaling port, it has now become important for slate quarrying. The quarries themselves are owned by the state, but their quarrying rights are leased out to private individuals.

Fishing vessels in harbour, Tromsø

Throughout the long winter the Lapps hold big markets at Bossekop, which during the sixteenth century was a busy Dutch trading port.

The Alta River is one of the best salmon rivers in the world. In July and August its waters are rented out at exorbitant rates. Alta has an airport with direct flights to Oslo and Kirkenes. Norway's oldest known settlement was unearthed not far away at Komsafjell. It has been dated to between 5000 and 9000 BC.

The Lapp Road from Alta to Kautokeino (about 130km)
Road 93 goes from Alta to **Kautokeino** — an important Lapp centre only 30km from the Finnish border. The road is known as the Lapp Road because it goes through the largest Lapp district in Norway. Travellers will most likely meet Lapps with their reindeer herds.

Soon after Road 93 has left Alta, the old road goes off to the left towards the Gargia mountain hut. It is narrow and in very poor condition, but passes through some beautiful and dramatic scenery. It goes to Norway's deepest canyon, where the Alta River has carved out a gorge 500-600m deep. It also passes some impressive waterfalls, and a Lapp summer encampment on the Båskades Plateau. It meets the new road again at Suolovuobme.

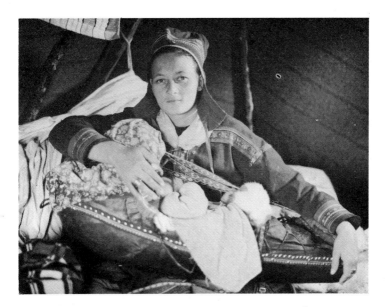

Lapp mother with baby in traditional komsa or carrying cradle

Meanwhile, the new road goes through Trangdalen up the only significant climb of the whole route. It passes rivers and lakes as it continues via Suolovuobme to the small Lapp settlement of **Masi**, with its modern Lapp church. The old church was founded in 1700 by Thomas, missionary to the Lapps. Masi is a good centre for walks across the nearby countryside, with its remarkable mountain flora. Boat trips are also possible from Masi.

The road continues along the valley of the Alta to Sornes, where Road 92 turns off for Karasjok and Tana bru (see routes 4b and 4c). 12km further on at Mieron, the old road from Suolovuobme again comes back into the new road, which after a further 18km arrives at **Kautokeino**.

Kautokeino is the administrative centre for the largest and most thinly populated district in Norway, with only 2,000 people but between 60,000 and 65,000 reindeer. It is the most important Lapp winter camp on Norwegian territory. There is a large reindeer market here both in the autumn and at Easter time. All the many festivals and celebrations revolve around the reindeer, be they Lapp weddings, Lapp baptisms or reindeer races. Kautokeino has the only technical college which is specifically intended for Lapps. There is also the Lapland Institute, plus an information centre on Lapp culture, a large and beautifully decorated silversmith's workshop and a village museum.

The Finnmark plateau

There are some delightful walks into the surrounding countryside, marred only by the innumerable midges that wait eagerly for the next human victim. It is vital to use an effective midge repellent before venturing forth.

The Finnish border is only 30km further along Road 93, which continues as Road 958 via Enontekio to Palojoensuu. Here it meets the E78, the Road of the Four Winds. The E78 runs along the Swedish/Finnish border to Haparanda on the Gulf of Bothnia. Road 93 is in fact the shortest route between Sweden and the North Cape.

Road 6 leaves Alta and runs along the shore as far as Rafsbotn, where it turns inland across a boggy plateau. This is where Finnmark proper begins — a bare wilderness that is nonetheless impressive. The Lapps frequently set up a summer encampment near Nipivatn, which is in a popular grazing area for reindeer. The highest point on this road is near Sennalandet (380m). 13km further on near another Lapp encampment is a Lapp chapel, which was built by Finnish missionaries. The road continues through Breidalen to the small village of **Skaidi**, which is good for salmon fishing. Skaidi is not far from the North Cape, but even those who are impatient to get there should not miss visiting **Hammerfest**.

Excursion to Hammerfest

Road 94 goes from Skaidi through Repparfjorddalen (it is still unmade in places). It crosses the Kvalsund via Norway's longest suspension bridge (714.5m) to the island of Kvaløy. There are views of the glaciers on the neighbouring island of Sailand. Luckier visitors will catch glimpses of itinerant reindeer. They are plentiful on Kvaløy, but often out of sight. The same applies to the native elk, which are depicted in rock paintings near Leirbukt. The massive Stallo Rock near Stallogarggo is supposed to be a Lapp sacrificial altar. There is a radio mast above Rypefjord on the 419m high summit of Tyven. 2km further on is **Hammerfest**, the most northerly town in the world. It is described in detail in the section on towns and cities.

Road 6 goes from Skaidi across the Porsanger Peninsula to **Olderfjord**, where it goes right for **Lakselv**. But the present route goes left along Road 95 for the **North Cape**. **Russenes** was formerly the ferry port for the North Cape, but there is now a good road along the shore of the Porsangerfjord (via a 3km long tunnel) to **Kåfjord** for the ferry to **Honnigsvåg**. The car ferry takes 45 minutes, the foot ferry only 20 minutes. In the peak season there may be a long waiting time for the car ferry, so it might be worth taking the foot ferry and then a tourist bus to the North Cape.

The ferry arrives at **Honnigsvåg** on the island of Magerøy where the North Cape is situated. Honnigsvåg is the biggest fishing port in Finnmark, with a large fish factory and a national school of fisheries. It is the last port of call for ships to Spitzbergen and Archangel, and is one of the ports on the Hurtigrute. The *Nordkapp–Båtservice* offers several boat services round the North Cape. A new boat called the *Solfuglen* (or Sunbird) runs on five different routes. It seats fifty-three passengers in comfortable armchairs with a good view. The jetty is graced by a modern statue which is commonly known as 'The Fish-hook'.

The most northerly point in Europe is now only 34km away along the North Cape Road. Soon after Honnigsvåg, the road crosses the seventy-first parallel. It twists and climbs past Nordmannset and the North Cape Camping Site (open in summer only — huts available) to the highest point on the route (312m). Straight ahead is the Duken, which is covered with a layer of white chalk like a cloth (*duken* means 'cloth'). Magerøy, with its typical Arctic landscape, has been a nature reserve for 50 years. In the early summer, many reindeer swim across the narrow Magerøysund from the mainland to breed here.

The road passes the Duken to the right. Then a small road goes off to **Skarsvåg**. The most northerly fishing village in the world, with barely 250 inhabitants, Skarsvåg is too nice to miss, and the North Cape is disappointing by comparison. Skarsvåg is full of old-fashioned fish-drying racks. Cruisers often anchor in the bay, and ships from the Hurtigrute take

Slettnes Lighthouse, Gamvik on the Nordkinn Peninsula

their North Cape visitors back on board. There is a Lapp encampment nearby. It is now only a few kilometres to the **North Cape**.

The North Cape or Nordkapp is a vast table of slate, 307m above the sea. At 71° 10′ 21″, it is supposed to be the most northerly point of Europe, but this is not strictly true. The nearby Knivskjellodden, which is inaccessible by road, is very slightly further north at 71° 11′ 8″. And since Magerøy is an island, the most northerly point of the actual mainland is the Nordkinn further east, which is at 71° 8′ 1″.

To be perfectly honest, this bare headland is rather disappointing. There is nothing but rock and sea — apart from a shop and restaurant selling the usual souvenirs and junk food. A rather dilapidated path leads to the most northerly point, where the cliff drops sheer into the sea. Visitors' reactions vary from deep meditation to a mere shrug of the shoulders. The only way now is southwards, after all.

The midnight sun is certainly very impressive from here, provided the weather is good. It is fully visible from 14 May to 30 July.

In front of the restaurant is a statue of Louis Philippe of Orleans, Citizen King of France, who gave it to the Norwegians on his visit to the North Cape in 1795. The original bust disappeared in the confusion of World War II, so the present one is a copy. There is also a memorial to the visit in 1873 of King Oscar II of Sweden. The North Cape was given its name by the

English explorer Richard Chancellor during his search for a north-east passage in the mid-sixteenth century. A British naval officer was given the name 'Lord of the North Cape' when he sank the German battleship *Scharnhorst* in the waters around the cape.

There is not much more to say about the North Cape. To avoid disappointment, expectations should not be set too high. Once the obligatory postcard has been filled in and dispatched (there are no more special stamps or postmarks), all that remains is to return to Olderfjord via the Honnigsvåg-Kåfjord ferry.

The Arctic Road continues from Olderfjord alongside the Porsangerfjord, which is the widest fjord in Norway. At Stabbursnes it crosses the Stabburselv. This river full of fish has come down through the Stabbursdalen National Park, which contains the most northerly pine forest in the world.

Lakselv (population 2,200) is at the end of the fjord. A small port situated by a salmon river of the same name, it is served by an airport. Road 6 goes east from Lakselv to Kirkenes (route 4c), while Road 96 goes south via Karasjok into Finland (route 4b). This is a much shorter route into Finland than to go east to Tana and then south via Utsjoki (route 4d).

4 (b) Lakselv via Karasjok to Inari

Return route into Finland

Road 96 goes southwards from Lakselv to Karasjok. The land rises gently as the road runs along the Lakselv (salmon river), which passes through a number of branching lakes. Just south of the town of Lakselv, the road passes a sign indicating the seventieth parallel. Greenland is roughly bisected by it and the north coast of Siberia is also at about 70°N. It is therefore all the more remarkable that this sign is surrounded by woodlands — a clear demonstration of how far the influence of the Gulf Stream penetrates.

The landscape becomes increasingly wild and bare as the road enters the Finnmarksvidda, where the reindeer rules supreme. There is a small tourist centre by a lake at Skoganvarre - a meeting place for anglers and walkers. There is a Lapp sacrificial altar on an island in the lake. The road passes one or two scattered settlements — mostly Lapp summer encampments — then enters a totally uninhabited area. At Nattvatn there is a lonely, midge-ridden tourist hut surrounded by bogs and lakes. The road descends to the valley of the Karasjokka, which runs into the Tana.

The road arrives at **Karasjok** — a modern township with a mainly Lapp population. Of cultural interest are the Lapp Museum and a library with the world's largest collection of Lapp literature. Looking after reindeer is one of the subjects taught at the Lapp schools. The small wooden church built in 1810 is supposed to be the oldest original church in Finnmark. Autumn in Karasjok is the time of the great 'Division of the Reindeer'. This

The Karasjokka river, Finnmark plateau

---

festival is an attraction for natives and tourists alike. The herds are driven down from the surrounding countryside, and the young animals are sorted and marked. In Karasjok it is worth stocking up with petrol, water and food, since it is a long way to the next township, and prices in northern Finland are high.

Road 92 goes left from Karasjok, and goes north along the west bank of the **Tana** (which forms the border with Finland) to Tana bru (see route 4c). There is no bridge across the river for the whole of the route from Karasjok to Tana bru. **Utsjoki** (route 4d) is only accessible via Road 895 along the east bank.

Road 96 crosses the Karasjokka, and carries on to **Karigasniemi** on the Finnish border, where it becomes Road 4. It continues in an endless straight line through increasingly dense, uninhabited forests. There is a good chance of running into elk or reindeer at this stage. Just before **Kaamanen**, Road 970 comes in from **Utsjoki** (route 4d), followed 6km later by a small road from **Neiden** (route 4c). Road 4 crosses the Kaamanenjoki, then turns sharply southwards to **Inari**. The road has now entered the typically Finnish countryside of endless forests and lakes.

4 (c) Lakselv to Kirkenes

This route goes from **Lakselv** via **Tana bru** to **Kirkenes**, crossing the vast, uninhabited wastes of eastern Finnmark almost to the Soviet border. Kirkenes is effectively the end of the road, having no road link with Finland apart from a tiny road from **Neiden** to **Kaamanen**. But travellers need not go all the way back to Lakselv. The new Road 92 goes along the west bank of the Tana to Karasjok (see route 4b), while Road 895 runs along the east bank to **Utsjoki** and **Inari** (route 4d). The road from Lakselv is unmade in places.

Road 6 leaves **Lakselv** along the east shore of the Porsangerfjord. The silver-grey stone along the coast is a kind of dolomite that forms a seam all the way through the sandstone of Finnmark. About half-way to Børselv, a raised beach can be seen, showing where the coastline ran during the Ice Age. **Børselv** is a Finnish settlement, and the languages spoken there are Finnish and Lapp.

Road 6 leaves the fjord and rises over the Børselvfjell. At the highest point of the road (200m), the Lapps from Karasjok have set up a summer encampment. The road then drops gently to the Laksefjord. The 38m waterfall at Adamsfjord was once very attractive, but has now been harnessed for a 40,000kW power station, which has robbed it of all its wild beauty. Nearby are the remains of some earth huts used by the lake Lapps.

The road leaves the fjord near Ifjord, and crosses the Ifjordfjell, which has the best rivers for salmon trout in Norway. Though only about 350m high, the fjell often has some snow cover even in summer. It is a good place for reindeer, though the herds are not always visible. The peninsula north of the Ifjordfjell leads to the **Nordkinn** (71° 8′ 1″), the most northerly point of the European mainland.

Road 6 winds itself around the many branches of the Tanafjord until at **Rustefjelbma** it meets the Tana, which is one of Norway's longest rivers, and certainly the richest in salmon. The newly surfaced road goes along the river to the suspension bridge at **Tana bru**. This is the only river crossing below Karasjok, now that the **Utsjoki** ferry has been closed down. So the choice has to be made before the bridge whether to take the new Road 92 along the west bank of the river to Karasjok (route 4b).

Over the bridge, Road 890 goes left for the two fishing ports of Berlevåg and Båtsfjord on the Varanger Peninsula. Road 6 goes right for **Skipagurra**, where Road 895 goes off up the east bank of the Tana via Polmark and Utsjoki to Inari in Finland (see route 4d). Road 6 then crosses the isthmus of the Varanger Peninsula to Varangerbotn on the Varangerfjord. **Varangerbotn** has an open-air museum of Lapp culture, with an interesting fifteenth-century earth hut, which was once used for official occasions. ⌘

Just off Road 6 at **Karlebotn**, a Stone Age settlement was found on the shore, with nearly ninety houses — similarly at Grasbakken, 14km further along. At Gandvik there is a turning for the picturesque fishing village and Finnish settlement of Bugøynes. The road continues via Bugøyfjord to

137

Adamsfoss Falls

Neiden, where the sixteenth-century chapel is Norway's oldest Eastern
Orthodox church. The last service was conducted here in 1917, and the
chapel is now closed; but a key can be obtained from the landlord in one of
the nearby huts. The interior is quite beautiful and full of icons.

A very rough little road goes from Neiden across the Finnish border. It continues along the side of Lake Inari to **Kaamanen**, where it meets Road 4 for Inari (see route 4b).

Road 6 goes round the Neidenfjord and Munkfjord, and passes Høybuktmoen Airport, which has flights to Oslo. There is a road junction at **Hesseng**, from which Road 885 goes south along Pasvikdal to the Finnish and Soviet border areas. A viewing tower near Skolvevatn affords a wide panorama of the Russian tundra and of the Soviet settlement of Nikel. Road 886 goes east to the border village of Grense-Jakobselv.

6km beyond Hesseng is the small town of **Kirkenes** (population 5,000). Kirkenes is an important centre for the export of metal ores. They are mined near Bjørnstad on the Soviet border by Syvaranger, Norway's largest mining company. Kirkenes is at the far end of the Hurtigrute, of the national air network, and of Road 6 (2,500km from Oslo). Its proximity to the Soviet border makes it important strategically. The area was the scene of fierce fighting during World War II, when the town was completely destroyed.

4 (d) Kirkenes via Utsjoki to Inari

Return route into Finland

The route goes back along Road 6 (see route 4c) as far as **Skipagurra**, where Road 895 goes left for **Polmark** on the Finnish border. It crosses the border to Nuorgam, and continues along the east bank of the Tana (in Finnish, Tenojoki) to **Utsjoki**, which at one time was served by a ferry from the Norwegian side.

At **Utsjoki** the route turns southward along Road 970, and goes along a river bank through birch and pine forests. Apart from a tourist station at Kevo, the area is virtually uninhabited (one person for every 6sq km). The road goes for nearly 100km before it meets Road 4 just before **Kaamanen**, where it goes left for **Inari**.

5 LOFOTEN AND VESTERÅLEN

The Lofoten island chain lies off the coast between Tromsø and Bodø. There are more than eighty islands in all, extending for 190km with some glorious scenery. Steep rocks and broken cliffs rise sheer from the waves like gigantic fortresses. Away from the cliffs and in areas facing the mainland, there are just one or two soft, green valleys.

The inhabitants have lived by fishing since the early Middle Ages. The fishing season in its heyday brought as many as 35,000 fishermen to the islands between January and April — practically the whole male population of Nordland. The number has since dwindled to about 5,500. The trawling begins when the cod shoals arrive, following the north-west winds of the New Year. Apart from cod, the main fish caught are red and pink salmon, mackerel and shrimps. The main industry outside the fishing season is tourism.

The islands have numerous small huts known as *rorbuer*, which house the migrant fishermen during the fishing season. In summer they are not needed by the fishermen, and are let to holidaymakers very cheaply.

Svolvær is the chief town of the **Lofoten Islands**. Its resident population of 4,200 is tripled during the fishing season. Mainly a fishing port, it has also become a meeting place for Scandinavian artists, several of whom work at the Kunstnerneshus or 'Artists' House'. The mountain above the town is called the Svolværgjeita, because it is supposed to be shaped like a

Svolvær, capital of Lofoten

goat. A boat trip is recommended to the beautiful Trollfjord, hemmed in by steep, rocky cliffs.

Road 19 goes south west from Svolvær to **Kabelvåg**, passing a large wooden church at Vågan. Nearby is a pre-Christian relic called the Trollstein. Kabelvåg is a fishing and tourist village, which at the time of the Vikings was the capital of the Lofotens. The Viking King Øystein built the first *rorbuer* here in 1100 as shelters for fishermen. The Lofoten Museum presents the history of fishing on the islands, while the aquarium next door provides an overview of the local marine fauna.

The road continues westwards via a 700m tunnel through the mountains. The old road over the pass, when it is open, affords a marvellous view, with the 942m high Vågekallen to the south. 2km further on is a turning for Festvåg, from which a ferry goes to **Henningsvær** (12 minutes). This lovely little fishing port, built on several islands, is typical of the Lofotens.

Road 19 crosses via successive bridges to the islands of Gimsøy and Vestvågøy respectively. Between Lyngvær, Smorten and Leknes, there are several ideal spots for viewing the midnight sun, though only between 26 May and 19 July. At Hol Church near Leknes are the remains of a Viking shipwreck. Just after Leknes, Road 818 goes south to Ballstad — another

141

Fishermen's huts may be rented in Lofoten

---

lovely little fishing village, with houses on stilts and *rorbuer* to let.

From Lilleeidet a ferry crosses the Nappstraumen to Napp on the island of Flakstad. (The main Lofoten Islands are otherwise linked by bridges.) There follows another stretch of road from which the midnight sun is particularly impressive. Ramberg has a gorgeous sandy beach. Hamnøy is one of the oldest fishing villages on the islands, with yet more of those typical houses on stilts. Road 19 ends at the picturesque village of Å, which has a train-oil distillery built in 1850.

South of Å is the notorious Moskenstraumen, immortalised by novelists Jules Verne and Edgar Allan Poe. It divides the main Lofoten group from the islands of **Værøy** and **Røst**, which together make up the world's largest bird colony. They have as many as 5 million sea birds, including kittiwakes, puffins, oystercatchers, razorbills, guillemots, fulmars, terns, eider-ducks, peregrine falcons, and even a few sea eagles. One zoological curiosity is the six-toed puffin hound. At one time every farm would have a troop of these dogs, which were used to hunt birds from inaccessible rocks and cliffs. Conservationists have banned the sport, but a few six-toed dogs have survived on these island fastnesses. They are poodle-sized and related to the Siberian wolf. Røst and Værøy can be reached by boat, either from ports on the main islands or from Bodø (see route 4a). In summer there is also a helicopter service from Bodø.

Road 19 goes north from **Svolvær** to Fiskebøl, where a ferry crosses to Melbu on the **Vesterålen Islands**. The small town of **Stokmarknes** (population 3,000) is the headquarters of the Vesterålen Shipping Company — one of the companies that run the Hurtigrute. It is also the location for a large hundred-year-old market. From the mountains near Sortland, there is a magnificent view of all the islands, and also of the midnight sun (from 26 May to 19 July), which bathes the mountains and sea in a glorious symphony of colour.

A bridge crosses the Sortlandsund to **Hinnøya**, which is the largest island in Norway. Road 19 goes across the island, passing numerous fishing villages with rows of houses on stilts and fish-drying racks. It runs along the Gullesfjord to Gullesfjordbotn at the southern end of the fjord, where there is a view of the snow-covered Vestpolltind (just under 1,000m).

Near Kåringen there is a right turn for **Lødingen**, from which a ferry to **Bognes** connects with the E6 (see route 4a). Lødingen is one of Norway's largest pilot stations. There is also a reindeer research station at Kåringen. Road 19 continues along the Tjeldsund, then turns right across the Tjeldsund Bridge to the mainland. It continues across the mainland to **Bjerkvik**, where it joins the E6 (see route 4a). At the point where it turns across the bridge, Road 83 carries straight on towards Harstad.

Henningsvær

Nusfjord, Flakstad Island

Historical drama at the Harstad Festival

Harstad (population 21,000) is one of Norway's largest parishes, and its economy is based on fishing and fish products. Attempts have recently been made from Harstad to open up the oilfields off the Lofoten Islands, so its future may well depend on the ups and downs of the oil boom. There is naturally fierce opposition from local fishermen. Harstad is also the port from which ships go to Spitzbergen. There are two important local festivals: a festival of music and theatre in June, and the International Deep-sea Fishing Festival in July. Just north of Harstad at Trondenes is a beautiful medieval church built in 1250.

There are several ways of reaching these islands:

(a) by road along Road 19 from Bjerkvik on the E6;

(b) by sea, from Bodø to Stramsund or Svolvær, from Skutvik on Hamarøy to Svolvær, or from Narvik to Svolvær;

(c) by aeroplane from Bodø or Narvik to Svolvær, or by helicopter from Bodø to the island of Røst.

Those travelling north up the coast are recommended to take the car ferry from Bodø, returning afterwards to the mainland via Hinnøya along Road 19 to Bjerkvik on the E6. This is the ideal route for an extended detour through these beautiful islands.

6 A ROUND TOUR

Oslo ● Kongsberg ● (Numedal) ● Geilo ● (Hardangervidda) ● Kinsarvik ● (Hardangerfjord) ● Bergen ● Dale ● Voss ● Vangsnes ● Dragsvik ● Moskog ● Hellesylt ● (Geirangerfjord) ● Dalsnibba ● (Ottadal) ● Lom ● (Jotunheimen) ● Kaupanger ● (Sognefjord) ● Revsnes ● (Lærdal) ● Borgund ● (Hemsedal) ● Gol ● (Hallingdal) ● Hønefoss ● Oslo (about 1,500km)

What the route has to offer:
This tour is a particularly good one because it includes a varied and representative selection of the very best that this fascinating country has to offer, and all within a distance of 1,500km.

It includes the country's two largest cities: the capital and metropolis of Oslo, with its many interesting museums, and the Hanseatic city of Bergen in beautiful surroundings. Wild, romantic valleys, such as Numedal and Hallingdal, alternate with the great fjords of Hardanger, Sogne and Geiranger. Then there are magnificent waterfalls such as the Vøringfoss, Tvindefoss and Brudeslør. All this, together with breathtaking passes, famous stave churches and the magnificent mountain scenery of Jotunheimen, make for an altogether unforgettable experience.

In short, this tour has everything in it, and should take anything from 10 days to 3 weeks, depending on how long is spent at each place. The tour is made up of sections of the following routes: 1b, 2a, 2b, 2c and 3b.

7 OSLO AND THE SURROUNDING AREA

The history of Oslo

One cannot be sure exactly how old Oslo is, since people are known to have lived here for thousands of years. The city was probably founded in 1048 by King Harald Hårdråde, who turned a small market town into one of the largest ports in the region. He had a church built of stone, which was unusual for those times, with the result that the foundations are still visible at **Gamleby**. Oslo soon became a bishopric and the country's religious centre.

The city began to flourish under King Håkon V (1280-1319). Up to that time, Bergen had been the capital. But Håkon V moved his residence to Oslo, where he was crowned in 1299. The next year he began to build the castle at **Akershus**.

The city's importance dwindled from then onwards. It was several times destroyed by fire and war, and in the mid-fourteenth century the population was decimated by the plague. At the end of that century, Norway was absorbed into the Union of Kalmar, and Oslo lost its political importance. Trade at this time was dominated by the Hanseatic League, and Oslo was overshadowed by the great Hansa ports. Oslo's churches were pulled down in the course of the Reformation in 1537, and the city was totally destroyed by fire in 1624, thus ending the first chapter in its history.

King Christian IV (1586-1648), the then ruler of Denmark, commissioned the reconstruction of the city beneath the castle on the west bank of the River Aker. This time it was rebuilt in stone, and was named Kristiania in honour of the king. The city grew again into a flourishing port, and in 1811 a university was built.

In 1814, Norway was united with Sweden. King Karl Johan XIV ordered the building of the **Royal Palace** and of a boulevard called **Karl Johans gate**. The city grew fast, from only 8,000 in 1800 to 20,000 in 1840, and only 15 years later the population numbered 42,000. In 1877, the name of the city was changed from Kristiania back to its original name of Oslo.

Sightseeing tours

Visitors will never have enough time to see everything, so it is necessary to select with care those places one most wishes to visit.

If only a few hours are available, there is not enough time to get to know Oslo properly, so one is left with a choice, either to get a general impression of the city, or else to visit just one place in particular. The first of these options is effectively limited to the city centre. The best place to park a car is by the harbour near the Town Hall. The suggested route starts from the **Town Hall** and goes along Roald Amundsens gate towards the city centre,

Christian IV Hall, Akershus Castle

Akershus Castle and Fortress

passing the **National Theatre** and the **West Underground Terminus**. It eventually comes to **Karl Johans gate**, with the **University** opposite. The route now turns right along Oslo's main boulevard, passing the Eidsvollplass with the **Parliament Building** on the right, and coming to the **Cathedral**. The route then goes right along the Kirkegata, and right again onto the Rådhusgata, which leads back to the Town Hall and the harbour at **Pipervika**. If there is still time available without making the tour into a marathon, then a left turn at the next crossroads leads down the Kongensgata to the castle at **Akershus**. Apart from this, there are many interesting shops and pleasant cafés to explore.

Those who prefer to visit just one place are recommended to visit the museum area of **Bygdøy**. A note of caution: time always goes quicker than expected, so it is best to decide first which museums to visit. The **Shipping Museum** and **Folk Museum** might take up a lot of time. So it is best to look at the **Viking ships** first, and then if there is a time one can choose between the **Kon Tiki Museum** and the **Fram Museum**. It is of course best to visit everything if time allows, and it is certainly well worth the effort. The quickest way to Bygdøy is by ferry from **Pipervika**.

If a whole day is available, then these two alternatives can be combined. For those with even more time, an excursion to **Holmenkollen** is recommended. But if time is short, one good way of getting a general impression of the city is to go by bus on one of the official city tours from the Town Hall.

There now follows a detailed description of the various parts of the city and the things to see there.

Things to see in Oslo

CITY CENTRE

The Town Hall (Rådhus)
Oslo is proud of its town hall. Begun in 1931, its construction was interrupted by the war, and it was not finished until 1950. It was designed by architects Arnstein Arneberg and Manus Poulsson.

It is a vast brick edifice, with two large square towers over 60m high. It fronts onto the Fridtjof Nansen plass and backs onto the harbour. The building is surrounded by numerous statues, such as those of Harald Hårdråde and St Hallvard, the city's patron saint. The enormous clock on the east tower is 8.5m across, and can be seen from the fjord. Every hour there is a peal of thirty-eight bells. The inside courtyard contains an astronomical clock, which gives the time and the date, plus details of the stars and the state of the sun and the moon.

The interior is decorated with paintings, frescos and wood carvings by some of Norway's leading artists. They depict scenes of everyday Norwegian life, from Norwegian folklore and mythology, and of the German wartime occupation.

Oslo City Hall

Karl Johans gate

Karl Johans gate forms the main boulevard through the centre of Oslo, and can be reached from the Town Hall along the Universitetsgata. It goes all the way from the East Station to the Royal Palace, and is well worth a stroll. There are shops, cafés, restaurants, street-side traders, buskers, bustling crowds and a lovely park with a pond and a fountain. The eastern half of the boulevard (right, coming from the Town Hall) is mostly taken up with shops, boutiques and department stores, while the western half goes past the National Theatre and the University to the Palace.

The University

This is Norway's oldest institution of higher education, and was founded by King Frederik VI in 1811. It is the country's leading university, with over 20,000 registered students. The building was designed by the famous German architect Karl-Friedrich Schinkel. The central portion was refurbished on the occasion of the University's centenary, and the great hall contains eleven paintings by Edvard Munch. The park in front of the University has a number of rune stones, some of which go back to the fifth century. The building is open to the public, except on official occasions.

The National Gallery

Further along the Universitetsgata is the National Gallery, which contains

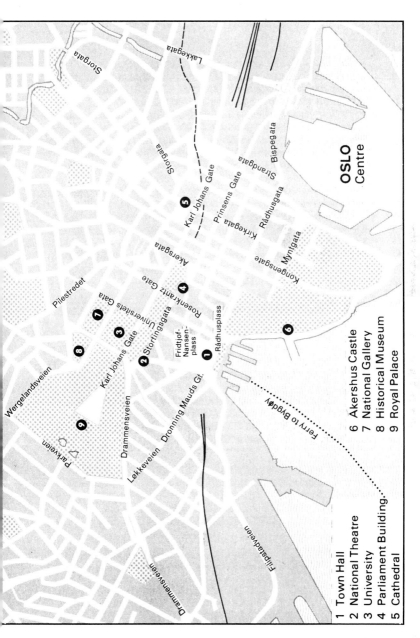

OSLO
Centre

1 Town Hall
2 National Theatre
3 University
4 Parliament Building
5 Cathedral

6 Åkershus Castle
7 National Gallery
8 Historical Museum
9 Royal Palace

151

works by a large number of European masters, plus a large collection of paintings by Norwegian artists. The Norwegian section includes works by Christian Dahl, Christian and Per Krohg, Harriet Backer, Jakob Weidemann and others. Edvard Munch is of course represented here too, though his life's work is exhibited more fully in the Munch Museum in the east of Oslo.

The various European sections display works by Rembrandt, Van Gogh, Cézanne, Gauguin, Renoir, Matisse, Manet, Picasso and others. Oslo is more interested in quality than in quantity, as is shown by the Långard Collection with its paintings by Goya and El Greco's 'Peter the Penitent'.

In addition, the gallery houses an icon collection, a large number of sculptures, and exhibitions of contemporary art.

Historical Museum
The Historical Museum is directy opposite the National Gallery in the Frederiksgata. It provides some wonderful insights into the life and art of the Vikings and of medieval Norway, and includes a large number of treasures from Viking ships.

Of particular interest is the ethnographic section, which displays the art and culture of many different peoples. A special section is devoted to Roald Amundsen, the polar explorer.

The University's coin collection is also housed here, and includes decorations, medals, seals and coins from all over the world.

The Royal Palace
The Royal Palace is in the middle of a large park at the top end of Karl Johans gate. It was built between 1823 and 1848 under King Karl Johan. It is in the classical style, but looks rather sober from outside, and subsequent modifications have done little to alter its unpretentious appearance. It is not open to the public, but the daily changing of the guard at half past one is very colourful, and is often accompanied by a band concert.

Karl Johans gate leads back to the University. Opposite here is the **National Theatre**, with the **Norwegian Theatre** next to it.

The Parliament Building (Storting)
This imposing if rather functional building is sited next to the Eidsvollplass towards the eastern end of Karl Johans gate. It was built between 1857 and 1866, but has been considerably extended and restored since then. The interior is decorated with wall hangings and frescos. A large wall painting by Vergeland commemorates the signing of the Norwegian constitution at Eidsvoll in 1814.

Oslo Cathedral
The cathedral stands almost at the eastern end of Karl Johans gate. It is thus very close to the **East Station** — Oslo's main international railway terminus.

The home of Norway's legislative assembly, Oslo

It was originally built in 1694 according to the plans of the French architect Châteauneuf. However, it was heavily restored in the middle of the last century, and only took on its present form in 1950 when the interior renovation was completed.

The altarpiece and the pulpit were created by a Dutch master in the seventeenth century. The impressive organ case was made by a Dane in the eighteenth century. The massive new organ was built in Ludwigsburg in 1930, and contains about 6,000 pipes. The stained glass windows in the choir were made in 1916. The bronze entrance doors were created by Dagfin Werenskiold in 1938, with motifs from the Sermon on the Mount. The newest features are the ceiling frescos depicting scenes from the Bible. The interior decorations are thus a varied collection of works by artists and craftsmen from all over Europe. The individual items are of outstanding artistry, but the overall impression is of a lack of harmony.

Akershus Castle
The castle is situated to the east of the harbour. It was built in about 1300 by King Håkon V as his official residence. It survived many sieges without ever being captured. As is so often the case, it was fire damage that forced Christian IV to renew the massive structure in 1527. He extended the

fortification, and had the residence rebuilt as a large Renaissance mansion. From the beginning of the nineteenth century, it was no longer lived in, and fell into disrepair. It was not restored to its original state until after World War II. There are now guided tours of the newly restored rooms, and some of the magnificent halls are used for official events.

The castle site also includes the **Norwegian Defence Museum** and **Home Front Museum**. The Defence Museum describes the whole history of the Norwegian armed forces, from the time of the Vikings down to the present day. The Home Front Museum, on the other hand, is concerned only with the period from 1940 to 1945, during which Norway was occupied by the Nazis. Having seen the museum, one can well understand the strong anti-German feelings that many older Norwegians still harbour. Immediately behind the building is a monument to those who fell while defending their country.

Pipervika

This is the name of the bay next to the Town Hall. It is the landing and embarkation point for boats round the fjord and for the harbour ferry, which is the quickest means of getting to the museum site on the Bygdøy Peninsula. The **West Station** is also nearby.

Other places of interest

There are several specialist museums which may be of interest to some visitors, such as the **Theatre Museum** (Slottsagata 1) east of the Town Hall, the **Architecture Museum** (Josefinegata 32) north of the castle, or the **Museum of Applied Art** (St Olavs gate 1) north-east of the National Gallery, which contains furniture, glass and china up to 700 years old. The **Postal Museum** at the main post office (Dronningensgate 15) presents the history of the Norwegian postal service, plus a complete collection of Norwegian stamps.

North of the great Cemetery of Our Saviour (Vår Freslers Gravlund), where Ibsen and Munch are buried, is the **Gamle Akers Kirke** (Old Akers Church), which is the oldest building in Oslo. It was built at the beginning of the twelfth century, and being of limestone it survived all the many fires. For those with extra time, the **Bergfjerdingen** quarter of the city is within walking distance of the centre. With its old houses and narrow streets (especially around St Margaret's Church), it gives an impression of what Oslo was like centuries ago.

BYGDØY

The museum site at Bygdøy is a must for all visitors to Oslo, even when time is limited. All of the city's most interesting and representative museums are located on this peninsula to the south west of Oslo. Bygdøy is most easily accessible by ferry from **Pipervika** by the Town Hall. There is a boat every few minutes from Pier 3, calling first at the Restaurant Dronningen and then directly by the Shipping Museum.

Norwegian Shipping Museum

Immediately in front of the museum is the *Gjøa*, the famous ship in which Amundsen was the first to sail through the north-west passage. The museum displays a large number of ships and models, presenting the whole of the long history of seafaring in Norway. Pictures, displays and accurate scale models provide a vivid picture of how sailors have lived through the ages and down to the present day. Scientific facts are presented by means of slide displays.

The Fram Museum

Immediately next to the Shipping Museum is a wooden structure shaped like a tent. It houses the *Fram* — the ship in which Fridtjof Nansen made his famous expedition to the North Pole. Nansen allowed the *Fram* to be carried by pack ice, and tried to use the ice drift to get him to the North Pole (1893-1896). Otto Sverdrup made a second attempt with the *Fram* (1898-1902), and this time he was successful. Amundsen used the ship for his expedition to the South Pole (1910-1912), and then it became a museum piece. The *Fram* can be boarded. Most of the original equipment has been left on board, so that one has the impression that the crew has only recently landed.

The Kon Tiki Museum

This building directly opposite the Shipping Museum was originally built to house the *Kon Tiki* — Thor Heyerdahl's famous balsa-wood raft. With five companions, he used it to sail 8,000km across the Pacific from Peru to Polynesia. He thus supported his theory that the Polynesians came over from South America and not from Asia. The raft has been carefully positioned so that the underside is visible through a clever plastic mock-up of the Pacific Ocean.

A second attraction is also on display. Thor Heyerdahl's 14m long papyrus boat *Ra II* is an accurate reconstruction of an ancient Egyptian papyrus boat, which he used successfully in 1970 in his second attempt to cross the Atlantic.

The museum also contains an underwater display, a mock-up of a burial chamber and a facsimile of a 9.5m high Easter Island head statue.

The Viking ships

Not far away from the Shipping Museum, along a well-signposted route, is one of the most fascinating museums of all. The building is in the form of a cross, and contains three Viking ships that were found in the Oslofjord. They were used as the graves for important Viking rulers, because it was thought that they had to cross the sea to get to Valhalla. Of the Tune Ship, found in 1867, only the keel remains. The Gokstad Ship, discovered in 1880, is the best-preserved and the most representative of the three. But the most beautiful of all is undoubtedly the magnificent Oseberg Ship. It probably belonged to Queen Åsa (about AD830). Its sleek, elegant form and its rich ornamentation bear ample witness to the skill of its builders.

The Oseberg ship at Bygdøy, Oslo

When it was discovered in 1904, it contained the body of the queen herself and another body, presumably that of one of her slaves. They were surrounded by rich grave goods, now known as the Oseberg Treasure, which are also exhibited in the museum. They have been quite remarkably preserved, and in some cases restored.

The Kon-Tiki balsa raft

Norwegian Folk Museum
Immediately behind the Viking ship museum is the vast open-air site of the Folk Museum. Plenty of time will be needed here. Indeed, there is quite enough to occupy a whole day. There are about 170 buildings in all, and they have been brought here from all over Norway. Houses, mills, whole farms, and even a stave church from Gol — all have been rebuilt on the museum site exactly as they were, and suitably landscaped. They are all open to the public. Most have their original interiors, and some are even places of work, where craftsmen can be seen producing hand-made goods in the traditional manner. Some of these goods are on sale, either on the spot or at a general store built in the style of the turn of the century. An English guide is available at the ticket office, giving detailed information about all the exhibits.

Oscarshall
North west of the Folk Museum, and directly by the fjord, is the Oscarshall.

Norwegian Folk Museum, Oslo

King Oscar I had it built between 1847 and 1852 as a 'pleasure house' in the style of the English Gothic Revival. It houses a collection of paintings.

WEST OSLO

Frogner Park and the Vigeland Sculptures

Frogner Park is north of the Bygdøy Peninsula, and its most notable feature is a garden containing about a hundred sculptures. They are all works by Gustav Vigeland (1869-1943), who bequeathed them to the City of Oslo. They are made of bronze, iron or stone, and represent combinations of human or animal figures. The central sculpture is a 17m high monolith called 'The Wheel of Life', which is covered with 121 intertwined human bodies. Opinions are varied as to the artistic merit of these works, but the collection is undoubtedly unique.

Frogner Park is worth a visit on its own, especially in the summer, with its fountains and its wonderful flower displays. There are many leisure activities on offer. It has swimming baths, tennis courts and two open-air restaurants.

The Vigeland Museum

Situated just south of Frogner Park, this was originally Gustav Vigeland's workshop. It was built for him by the City of Oslo, who also paid him a

Frognerseteren, Oslo

salary. Vigeland in return bequeathed all his unsold works to the city. His vastly prolific output (or maybe those works he was unable to sell?) is represented by 1,650 sculptures, 3,700 wood carvings and roughly 11,000 drawings. Together with the sculptures in the park, it gives a vivid impression of the extraordinary legacy that Vigeland has left. There are guided tours during the summer, plus occasional concerts.

The City Museum (Oslo Bymuseum)
The City Museum is housed in an eighteenth-century manor house on the edge of Frogner Park, just opposite the Vigeland Museum. It provides a pictorial history of the city. The furniture and interiors are a varied representation of the best styles to be found in Oslo.

The Henie-Onstad Art Centre
This is situated at Høvikodden, about 12km west of the city centre, along

Henie-Onstad Art Centre

the E18 past the exhibition halls. It was opened in 1968, and is the bequest of Sonja Henie and Niels Onstad. Sonja Henie became famous in the twenties as the world's top figure skater, with three Olympic golds and ten world championships to her name. Her husband Niels Onstad was a famous rower.

Fishing huts in the port of Hamnøy, Lofotens

Vaerøy, an island populated by millions of seabirds.

The mountains around the island of Straumøya

A peaceful evening, Sandhornøya

This museum is far from traditional in its outlook, being a cultural centre for the encouragement of art among the younger generation. It includes comprehensive collections of art from the twenties — abstract painting (Paul Klee and Hans Hartung), cubism (Braque and Picasso), surrealism (Max Ernst) and tachism. Apart from these permanent collections, there are temporary exhibitions, concerts, ballets and films.

NORTH-WEST OSLO

Bogstad
The manor house at Bogstad is one of the most beautiful in Norway. It is 10km north west of Oslo along the Sørkedalsveien from Frogner Park and the West Cemetery. The house was built in 1750, and the interior has been faithfully preserved.

Holmenkollen
Norway's best-known hill is only a few kilometres north west of Oslo. The easiest way to get there is on the Holmenkollen Line, which goes from the West Underground Terminus in the city centre (on the corner of Drammensveien, next to the National Theatre and opposite the University). Motorists should go north along the Bogstadsveien to the Valkyrjeplass, and then either keep straight on parallel to the railway along the Slemdalsveien, or else bear left along the Sørkedalsveien and turn right into the Holmenkollenveien. Both ways are well-signposted.

The Holmenkollen Ski-jump
The world-famous ski-jump is 371m above sea level. For ski-jumpers, a victory on Holmenkollen amounts to the same as an Olympic victory. The Holmenkollen International Ski-jumping Contest takes place in March. This great event brings not only the world's top ski-jumpers, but also the Norwegian king and up to 100,000 spectators.

Those with a good head for heights are recommended to go up to the starting point, which is 60m above ground level. A lift goes most of the way, but the last few metres must be negotiated on foot. The height of the starting point is adjustable, so that the skiers can achieve the maximum speed that the conditions allow, without being carried too far. Visitors will not only appreciate the courage of the competitors, but will also have a beautiful view over Oslo and the Oslofjord.

The landing area at the bottom consists partly of a pool, which is of course frozen over in the winter. Stunt skiers have set up a small ski-run there for practising their acrobatics during the summer.

The Skiing Museum
The museum is immediately next to the ski-jump, and has been beautifully landscaped. The first museum of its kind, it was opened in 1923. It traces the development of skis from the 2,500 year old Øvrebø Skis to the high-performance skis of today. Some of Nansen's and Amundsen's skiing equipment is also on display.

Holmenkollen ski-jump

Tryvannshøgda
The highest point in the Oslo area, Tryvannshøgda is a short distance north of Holmenkollen, and is only a quarter of an hour's walk from the terminus of the Holmenkollen Line. It is topped by the Tryvannstårnet, which is Norway's highest tower. The tower is 118.5m high, reaching an overall height of 650m above the water level of the fjord. In clear weather there is a magnificent view of the city and the fjord, extending far across lakes and forests and right into Sweden.

EAST OSLO

Natural History Museums
The Mineralogical, Palaeontological and Zoological Museums share a

Holmenkollen 50km ski race

single site in the Botanical Gardens to the east of the city. The three buildings have recently been restored. The displays are well-constructed and highly informative. The Zoological Museum is the most interesting of the three, especially for children. Animals from all over the world are shown in their natural environment, some of them in both summer and winter coats. Visitors who are about to return home without having seen a live elk or reindeer will at least have a last chance to see these animals, albeit stuffed.

Botanical Gardens

These gardens spread out to the south of the Natural History Museums. They contain some admirable displays of Scandinavian flora, plus a number of exhibits from countries further south.

The Munch Museum

Situated across a car park from the main entrance to the Botanical Gardens, this museum houses a vast collection of works by Edvard Munch. There are 23,864 items in all, including oil paintings, watercolours, graphic sketches and sculptures, and covering the entire span of the artist's career. There is so much that only a small proportion can be displayed at a time. But those wishing to see something not on display need only ask the curator. The building is modern, having been built in 1963, and contains a restaurant, a library and a children's playroom. The lecture theatre is used for lectures, films and concerts.

Oslo Ladegård

This recently restored building is situated on Bispegata, just beyond the point where the E6 road to Gothenburg turns southwards. It was originally the medieval bishop's palace, which in the thirteenth century was the religious centre of Oslo. In the seventeenth century it was turned into a Baroque mansion in which the mayor lived. This former stronghold of the church eventually came to be used as a brothel. Recently, however, the palace rooms and the medieval vaults have been beautifully restored. It now includes a scale model of Oslo before the great fire of 1624.

Gamleby (the old city)

Medieval Oslo was situated between the present East Station and the Gamleby Cemetery. Sadly, very little of it has survived the many wars and fires that have occurred. However, in 1917 the foundations of several churches and monasteries were discovered in Gamleby, including St Hallrod's Church, where King Håkon V was crowned in 1299.

Museum of Technology

This museum is in the eastern suburb of Etterstad along the E6 road to Trondheim. The development of Norwegian industry is described by means of numerous working models. A model railway is also included.

OSLO'S ENVIRONS

The beauty of the Oslofjord cannot be described adequately to someone who has not seen it. The fjord goes a long way inland, and because parts of it are so narrow, it often gives the impression of being an inland lake. It is a sight not be be missed. In the summer there are hourly boat trips round the fjord from the pier in front of the Town Hall. But the Oslofjord is not only beautiful from the water, it is also interesting from the shore.

The eastern shore of the Oslofjord

Oslo ● Moss ● Sarpsborg ● Frederikstad ● Svinesund (about 120km)

What the route has to offer:
The road along the Oslofjord runs through some glorious scenery and past some interesting historical sites, while the Skjeberg area has ancient rock drawings *(helleristninger)*, castles, classical manors, Viking graves and army fortifications. The undulating landscape is heavily cultivated. Sawmills, factories and Norway's first nuclear power station form a stark contrast to the beautiful beaches, holiday resorts, villas and marinas. The route goes as far as the Swedish border; a continuation to Göteborg (Gothenburg) is possible.

The route:
The route leaves Oslo along the E6 in a southerly direction. Immediately outside the city, there is a turning on the right along the Herregårdsveien for the beach at Ingierstrand. At **Vinterbru** there is a large game park with elk, reindeer, red deer, foxes and birds. The model village and model railway are also worth visiting. At Vinterbru the E18 turns off left for Askim, Mysen and the Swedish border (see page 171).

The present route continues along the E6. Left from the next crossroads at Korsegården is the Norwegian Agricultural College at **Ås**, while the road to the right goes to **Drøbak**. This picturesque little town by the fjord has a number of old timbered houses. Drøbak is popular with artists, and there are several galleries and exhibition halls. On the nearby bed of the fjord, 100m down, is the wreck of the *Blücher*, which was sunk from the Oscarsborg Fort in 1940. At Vestby there is another side road down to the fjord, this time to the holiday and beach resort of Hvitsen.

The main road continues via Hølen, with its eighteenth-century market place, to **Moss** (population 26,000), the provincial capital of Østfold. It is an industrial town, with activities ranging from shipbuilding to glass blowing, and has traditions going all the way back to the craftsmen of the Middle Ages. The town spreads out onto the Jeløy Peninsula, with its beautiful beach, its villas and its many leisure activities. At the edge of the town is an eighteenth-century manor house called the Konventionsgården, which is where the treaty uniting Norway with Sweden was signed in 1814. This treaty allowed Norway to have its own constitution, and paved the way for complete independence later on.

There is a ferry from Moss across the Oslofjord to **Horten** (see route 1f), from which the E18 returns via Drammen to Oslo along the west side of the fjord.

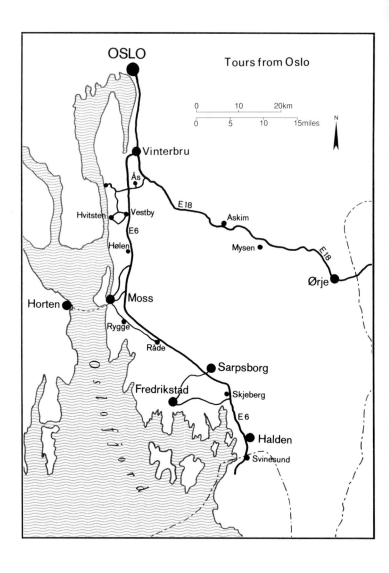

OSLO

Tours from Oslo

0   10   20km

0   5   10   15miles

N

Vinterbru

Ås

Hvitsten

Vestby

E18

Askim

E6

Hølen

Mysen

E18

Ørje

Horten

Moss

Rygge

Råde

Sarpsborg

Fredrikstad

Skjeberg

E6

Halden

Svinesund

Oslofjord

The E6 goes inland past the Rygge-Halmstad military aerodrome and a lake called the Vannsjø. Meanwhile, Road 118 runs parallel to the E6, passing a right turn for the popular beach at Larkollen, and going through **Rygge** and **Råde**. Both villages have medieval churches, and as the road leaves Råde it passes some Bronze Age grave mounds.

At the point where the E6 crosses Road 112, there is a beautiful view of the River Glomma where it widens to form the Visterflo. Just after Eidet, there is a left turn along a side road to **Kalnes**, which has some 3,000 year old rock drawings of animals and boats. There are several ancient burial sites and mound graves in this area, in particular by the shore of the Tunevatn.

Sarpsborg (population 13,500) is important for its wood-processing and electronics industries. The town is situated on the Glomma, which is Norway's longest river. The harbour is linked to the sea via the Glomma. Between the northern suburb of Borregård and Hafslund, the Glomma plunges over a massive waterfall, which provides power for two large factories. There have been foundries and smithies next to the waterfall since the Middle Ages.

Sarpsborg is said to have been founded by Olav the Holy in 1016. The fortification was later destroyed; the inhabitants fled to a new site down the river, and founded the neighbouring town of Fredrikstad. Nowadays the two towns have almost grown together.

The chief place of interest in Sarpsborg is the Borgarsyssel Museum, which contains numerous Bronze Age finds from all over Østfold. It also has

The Old Town in Fredrikstad

Halden, East Norway

an open-air site, which includes the remains of the twelfth-century church of St Nicholas, plus several houses between 200 and 400 years old.

A road along the bank of the Glomma goes directly from Sarpsborg to **Fredrikstad** (population 30,000), which is an important industrial port, specialising in the wood industries and in the import and export of goods. There is a ferry across the Oslofjord to **Tønsberg** (see route 1f). The islands nearby offer countless opportunities for bathing and various water sports. The king of Norway has a summer villa on the island of Hankø.

Fredrikstad was founded in 1567 by King Fredrik II and the inhabitants

of Sarpsborg (see above). The old town (Gamleby) is one of the few fortified towns to have been preserved. There are some interesting houses from the seventeenth and eighteenth centuries, in which artists and craftsmen have set up their studios. Fort Kongsten is also worth a visit - an impressive fortification at the top of a cliff.

Road 110 from Fredrikstad to **Skjeberg** goes through an area so steeped in history that it is known as the Road of the Sagas. At **Begby**, just outside Fredrikstad, a small side road leads off to some famous rock drawings of ships, huntsmen, animals and sun wheels. A large site on the opposite side of Road 110 contains yet more of these *helleristninger*, 3,000 years old.

Hunn has the largest archaeological site in the country, including stone circles, Viking grave mounds, 4,000 year old Stone Age remains, and clear

Svinesund Bridge linking Norway and Sweden

---

signs of ancient cultivation methods. The path from the road to the grave mounds is dug out like a trench, and is nearly 2,000 years old. On a nearby hill is the ancient Ravneberget fortification. The walls that remain go back to the fourth or fifth century AD.

Between **Gunnarstorp, Hornes** and **Ullerøy**, there are yet more ancient sites, with standing stones and rock drawings of ships and animals. Again at **Solberg**, there are three sites with nearly 100 representations of ships with crews, sun wheels, huntsmen and carts. Like the others, these probably date back to the Bronze Age, which in Norway was around 1000 BC.

The Road of the Sagas ends at **Skjeberg**, where it goes into the E6, only 15km before the Swedish border at Svinesund.

Just before the border, Road 104 turns off left for the ancient garrison town of **Halden**. Its fortress of Frederiksten was built between 1644 and 1645. It was continually being attacked and besieged by the Swedes, but was never actually captured. King Karl XII of Sweden met his death during an attack on the fortress in 1718. Although the fortress withstood all attacks, the town itself was destroyed in the seventeenth century and at the beginning of the eighteenth. Halden is the site of Norway's oldest nuclear power station, which was built in 1959 to provide energy for the local wood-based industries.

The route from Halden to Bengtsfors in Sweden is via Roads 21 and 106. But the main border crossing is on the E6 at **Svinesund**, where the Iddefjord forms the border. The Svinesund Bridge crosses the fjord in a single span 450m long and 65m above the water.

Oslo to Askim and the Swedish border

The route for Stockholm

What the route has to offer:

The E18 from Oslo crosses the border at Ørje, and goes on past Lake Vånern to Stockholm. It is a good link route for those wishing to tour Sweden as well.

The route goes via **Askim** and Mysen through a heavily cultivated region, and past the beautiful **Lake Rødenes** to the Swedish border. The landscape then becomes flatter, with lakes and vast forests, as the road continues via Årjäng, Sillerud and Grums to **Lake Vänern**. The quickest route to **Stockholm** is then via **Örebrö** and Eskilstuna, past **Gripsholm Castle**, and then by motorway to the Swedish capital.

The route:

The route first goes south from Oslo along the E6. At **Vinterbru** there is a large game park with elk, reindeer, red deer, foxes and birds, and also a model village and model railway. The E6 goes straight on for Moss, Sarpsborg and Svinesund (see page 165).

But the E18 goes left towards **Askim** (population 9,500), which is on the River Glomma, Norway's longest river. The largest industrial concern is a factory producing rubber goods. The Glomma supplies three power stations, and is also used for transporting wood. Askim has a small local museum.

Just after Slitu, the road crosses a ridge, offering a marvellous view of the Glomma and of the town of **Mysen**. In August and September there is a fair in Mysen, which is very popular. There is a small museum in Mysen at the Folkenborg, which was the birthplace of King Håkon Håkonsson. From Mysen, Road 22 goes north to Lake Øyeren and the eastern suburbs of Oslo. The same road goes south to **Halden** (see page 170).

The E18 carries on towards the border town of **Ørje** (26km). Ørje is situated at the point where Lake Rødenes empties into Lake Øymark via an interesting lock. The ruined castle provides a lovely view of both lakes. 6km further on, the E18 crosses the border. The rest of the route is described in *The Visitor's Guide to Sweden.*

8 BERGEN

With a population of about 210,000, Bergen is Norway's second-largest city; it is also one of the most beautiful. It is often said of Bergen that it has a southern feel to it and therefore appeals to people from countries further south.

Bergen is the wettest town in Norway. It rains here three or four times as often as in any other part of the country. It is often said unkindly that Bergen children are born with their raincoats on, and it has also been claimed that at one time horses on the streets would shy at anyone without an umbrella. But it is the same mild, wet maritime climate that gives the nearby mountains their lush, green vegetation.

Bergen has a marvellous natural harbour, and is cut off from its hinterland by mountains and fjords. This means that the people's livelihood and traditions have always depended on the sea. Bergen's fish market is world famous, and some of its old commercial buildings bear witness to its glorious past as a Hansa port. The museums also include many treasures from the sea.

A short history

Bergen was founded by Olav Kyrre (the Peaceful) in 1070 on the site of an even older market town. Few Norwegian towns go back so far. Because of its favourable position, Bergen grew quickly as a fishing and trading port, and was the capital of Norway until the end of the twelfth century. King Håkon was a champion of maritime trade; in 1217 he made a trade agreement with England, which was the beginning of a long association between the two countries.

The Hanseatic League brought Bergen its greatest prosperity in the fourteenth century. The merchants became so powerful and influential that eventually the Norwegian kings moved their capital to Oslo. In 1350 the Hanseatic League opened its counting houses at Bryggen, the part of the city overlooking the harbour. The city thus became the gateway to the European continent, with trade and fisheries under its control. Magnificent churches, monasteries and other buildings grew up all over the city. Sadly, very few of them have survived the many fires that have ravaged the city.

The decline of the Hanseatic League allowed the Norwegian merchants to take trading into their own hands. Norwegian stockfish in particular became very popular in Europe as a food for Lent. The wealth of the city grew until it overtook all the other great trading ports such as Copenhagen.

In 1702, however, the city was almost completely destroyed by fire; a second conflagration in 1916 finished off the last remnants of its glorious past, and it had to be rebuilt from scratch. However, when they restored the

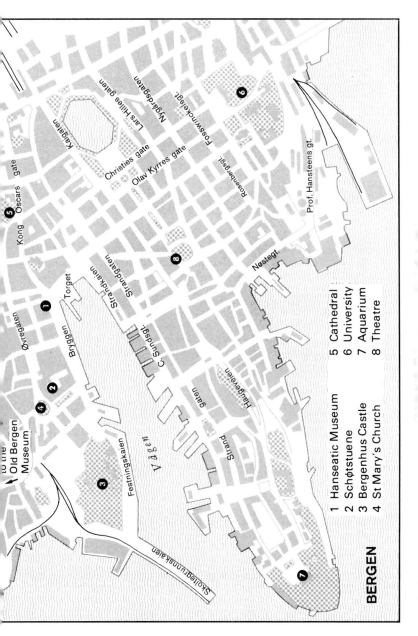

BERGEN

1 Hanseatic Museum
2 Schøtstuene
3 Bergenhus Castle
4 St Mary's Church
5 Cathedral
6 University
7 Aquarium
8 Theatre

to the
Old Bergen
Museum

Øvregaten
Bryggen
Torget
Strandkaien
Øvregaten
Kong Oscars gate
Kaigaten
Christies gate
Lars Hilles gaten
Nygårdsgaten
Olav Kyrres gate
Fosswinckelsgt.
Rosenberggt.
Prof. Hansteens gt.
Nøstegt.
C. Sundsgt.
Haugeveien
Strand gaten
Vågen
Festningskaien
Skoltegrunnskaien

'Bryggen' in Bergen

---

old city centre at Bryggen, they followed the old style as faithfully as possible.

Things to see in Bergen

City centre tour

Bergen is centred around Vågen, the main harbour, at the top end of which is Bergen's famous fish market or **Torget**. Trading is on weekdays from morning to early afternoon. Apart from every conceivable kind of seafood, it also sells fruit, vegetables and flowers. In fine weather it presents a colourful scene of bustling activity. But take care over the price of the fish! On Finnegård, immediately next to the Torget and overlooking the harbour, is the **Hanseatic Museum**. Built in the style of the sixteenth century, it describes the everyday customs and activities of the Hanseatic merchants.

Rosenkrantz Tower and Håkonshallen, Bergen

The road from here along the harbour is called **Bryggen**. It was originally named Tyske Bryggen or 'German Bridge' after the German Hansa merchants who at one time owned half of Bergen. Bryggen was where they built their counting houses, warehouses and shops. The buildings have been successfully restored to some of their former glory. The narrow lanes between the wooden houses lead into courtyards surrounded by modern shops, high-class boutiques, cosy taverns, and craft shops selling everything from paintings to jewellery.

At the far end of Bryggen is another old Hansa building, called the **Schøtstuene**. None of the other warehouses were allowed to be heated in the winter for fear of fire. So it was used by the merchants as a refectory and assembly hall.

Further out along the quay is the great thirteenth-century fortress of **Bergenhus**, inside which is King Håkon's palace, known as **Håkonshallen**. This is the sole model for all Norwegian palaces. Its great hall is where the kings were crowned. On the site of King Håkon's ancient defence tower is the sixteenth-century **Rosenkrantz Tower**, which Erik Rosenkrantz used as his lordly residence. The tower and the fortress were destroyed by a heavy explosion in the harbour in 1940, but both were beautifully restored between 1961 and 1964.

Above the Schøtstuene is Bergen's oldest building. **St Mary's Church**

'Troldhaugen' Edvard Grieg's residence for 22 years

(Mariakirke) was built in the early twelfth century in the Romanesque style. Its construction was mostly financed by the German Hansa merchants. Thus the altar, for example, was made by craftsmen from Lübeck, and many of the wall paintings have German inscriptions. The magnificent pulpit is from the Baroque period. The churchyard contains many beautiful old gravestones.

Opposite St Mary's is the **Bryggen Museum**, which displays all the treasures unearthed during the restoration of Bryggen. They include collections of tools, china and other medieval finds, plus an invaluable collection of runic texts.

At the far end of Øvregate from St Mary's Church is **Bergen Cathedral** (Domkirke). This was built over the remains of a twelfth-century church, and has been extended and rebuilt through the centuries in a number of different styles. The neo-gothic choir and tower entrance are a hundred years old. Kong Oscars gate leads from the cathedral back to the starting point at the Torget.

Other things to see

The open-air museum of **Old Bergen** (Gamle Bergen) is in Sandviken, and can be reached by car or by bus along the Nye Sandviksveien from St Mary's Church. It is a collection of nineteenth-century wooden houses, beautifully laid out in streets. Besides a chapel, a mill and a restaurant, there are craft shops, boutiques and period studios. The adjoining park affords some lovely views of Bergen.

On a hill between the Puddefjord Bridge and Christies gate is the university complex, which houses three very interesting museums. The **Historical Museum** includes finds from the Viking, medieval and renaissance periods, plus an ethnographic collection. The **Natural History Museum** presents the fauna and flora of Norway. Of particular interest are the extinct Lofoten Horse, a whale skeleton and the magnificent rhododendron bushes in the Botanical Gardens. The **Shipping Museum** shows the development of ships from the Viking period down to the present day.

Also off Christies gate is a pretty little lake called Lille Lungegårds vatn, around which are several more museums. The **Fisheries Museum** covers the history of Norwegian sea fishing. The **Museum of Applied Art** (Vestlandske Kunstindustrimuseum) includes antique exhibits from China and Europe, and a collection of Bergen silver. The **Leprosy Museum** is housed in the restored medieval building of St Jørgen's Hospital near the station, and documents the researches of Dr Hansen of Bergen who discovered the leprosy virus. Finally, the **Rasmus Meyer Collection** is a private collection of furniture and paintings by various Norwegian masters, including Edvard Munch.

Apart from the museums, the **Aquarium** is also very well worth a visit. It is situated in Nordnes Park, at the tip of the tongue of land between Vågen and the Puddefjord. One of Europe's largest and most comprehensive aquariums, it is housed in a beautiful modern building. Most of the sea creatures on display are from northern waters.

Bergen's environs

The best view of Bergen is from **Fløyen** (320m), which can be reached by funicular from a small station on the corner of Lille Øvregate and Vetrlidsalmenning. The service is half-hourly in the summer. Apart from the panorama of Bergen and its surroundings, there are some lovely walks through the woods.

Bergen's other local mountain is **Ulriken** (640m), which provides an even more breathtaking view of Bergen and the neighbouring fjords and mountains. It is also well-provided with footpaths. Ulriken can be reached by cable car or bus, or by a combination of the two.

South of the city towards Nesttun are the suburbs of Fjøsanger, Fantoft and Hop. The **Gamlehaugen** at Fjøsanger is where the king always stays when visiting Bergen. It originally belonged to Michelsen, Norway's first prime minister (1905).

A road off the E68 at Paradis leads to the **Fantoft stave church**. This was originally built in the twelfth century at Fortun near the Sognefjord, but was rebuilt here in 1880 on the instigation of a private individual.

A short way further on at Hop is an estate called the **Troldhaugen**, which belonged to Edvard Grieg of *Peer Gynt* fame. Idyllically situated beside Lake Nordås it now houses the **Grieg Museum**, with numerous mementoes and Victorian furniture. The composer and his wife Nina lived at Troldhaugen for 22 years, and both of them are buried here. It is also used for chamber concerts during the Bergen Festival.

Outside Bergen on Road 553 is the village of **Fana**, where folklore evenings are held four times a week during July and August, with dancing, folk music, feasting and local costumes. Transport to these events is organised by the tourist office in Bergen.

Out beyond **Fana** are the ruins of the Cistercian monastery of **Lyse**. Founded by English monks in 1146, it was the country's largest monastery until the Reformation.

Excursions from Bergen

There is a wide choice of excursions available from Bergen to the local fjords. Best known of these is the voyage of the *White Lady* — a tour of the local fjords lasting between 1 and 4 hours. There are also boat trips to the Hardangerfjord, Sognefjord and Nordfjord, and numerous combined ship and bus excursions. Most of these trips go from the Torget or from the quays along the Vågen harbour basin. Details of timetables, itineraries and bookings are available from Bergen's tourist information centre or from travel agents.

9 TRONDHEIM

With a total population of 135,000, Trondheim is Norway's third-largest city, and the one with the most history. It has a bishopric, a university and a number of industries. It is the administrative centre of the province of Trøndelag and a major port. It is a traditional centre for the import and export of wood and fish products and shipping equipment. Its harbour is nicely sheltered, and is kept ice-free by the Gulf Stream. The Trondheimfjord protects it from storms and high seas, but at the same time provides good access to the North Sea. Agriculture flourishes in the gently undulating region around Trondheim, which includes Norway's largest strawberry-growing area.

Trondheim is known as the gateway to the north, and many of the landmarks from its thousand-year history have managed to survive the ravages of fire — Nidaros Cathedral, the Archbishop's Palace, the Stiftsgården and the Kristiansten Fortress, to name but a few.

A short history

In 995 a young Viking prince called Olav Tryggvasson returned to the land of his ancestors to claim his right to the throne, having spent his youth raiding and pillaging in true Viking fashion. The centre of jurisdiction was a small market town sandwiched between the Nidelva and the fjord and sheltered from the sea. It was also the place from which the great Viking rulers set off on their voyages to Britain, Iceland and France, and was an important centre for trade. Once his predecessor was dead, Olav, who had been recently converted to Christianity, had a fortress and a monastery built on the island of Nidholm (now Munkholm) at the mouth of the river. In 997 he had a church built in the market town, and founded the city of Nidaros. But King Olav I died in battle only 3 years later.

He was succeeded by Olav II, who later became known as Olav the Holy. By the time Olav the Holy died in 1030, Nidaros (Trondheim) had grown considerably as Norway's then capital, religious and commercial centre, and large numbers of craftsmen, merchants and clerics had come in to settle. St Clement's Church, which Olav I had built out of wood when he had founded the city, was replaced by a stone structure. A shrine was built there to Olav the Holy, on the spot where a well is supposed to have sprung up from his tomb — a miracle for which he was made a saint.

In 1152 Nidaros became an archbishopric, and the Archbishop of Norway was given jurisdiction over seven dioceses, including Greenland and Iceland. As a result of this the church was turned into a Gothic cathedral.

Nidaros continued to grow in importance until 1350, when the plague

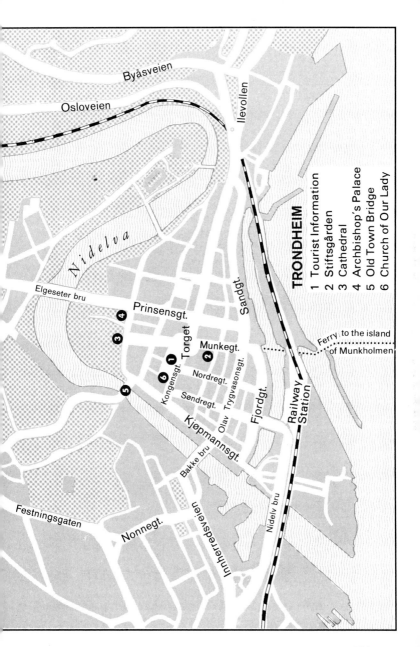

TRONDHEIM

1 Tourist Information
2 Stiftsgården
3 Cathedral
4 Archbishop's Palace
5 Old Town Bridge
6 Church of Our Lady

Ferry to the island
of Munkholmen

Byåsveien

Osloveien

Ilevollen

Nidelva

Elgeseter bru

Prinsensgt.

Sandgt.

Munkegt.

Torget

Nordregt.

Kongensgt.

Olav Trygvasonsgt.

Søndregt.

Fjordgt.

Railway Station

Kjøpmannsgt.

Bakke bru

Nidelv bru

Festningsgaten

Nonnegt.

Innherredsveien

181

Trondheim's picturesque centre

killed off nearly all the population. On top of that, the Hanseatic League took all the trade southwards to Bergen. The harbour thus fell into disuse. A great fire in 1531 reduced Nidaros to little more than a village.

In about 1600, the downfall of the Hanseatic League brought the trade back into the hands of the Norwegian merchants, many of whom returned to this sheltered harbour further north. The village was renamed Trondhjem, and quickly grew up again into a wealthy trading port. Magnificent wooden palaces, warehouses and counting houses appeared, only to be destroyed in the great fire of 1681.

The town was once more rebuilt at great cost, this time in a well-planned grid of wide streets, from which the modern town still benefits. By the early eighteenth century the town numbered about 8,000 inhabitants, and its fleet amounted to some 150 ships.

The intellectual community also flourished. In 1760 Norway's Royal Scientific Society founded Trondheim University, and in 1900 the local technical school was turned into a technical college.

Trondheim came back into the political limelight when Håkon VII, Norway's first independent king, was crowned in Nidaros Cathedral. In the course of spelling reform, Trondhjem was changed to Trondheim.

Things to see in Trondheim

The city centre

The focal point of the city is the **Torget** or market place, which is dominated by a statue of Olav I Tryggvasson, founder of the city. Next to the Torget is the information bureau, where maps, brochures and details of excursions can be obtained. The two streets which cross at the market place are Kongensgate and Munkegate.

Munkegate goes north from the Torget to the harbour, and passes the **Stiftsgården**. A large wooden mansion built in 1770, it is typical of the lavish architecture of the period. It is said to be the largest wooden structure in Norway. The Stiftsgården is used today by the Norwegian royal family whenever they visit Trondheim. Nearby is the beautiful house of the Swan Apothecary.

From the opposite end of the Torget, Munkegate leads straight to the cathedral. Just before that it passes the **Museum of Applied Art** (Nordenfjeldske Kunstindustrimuseum) — a modern building displaying handicrafts and applied art from both older and more recent times. There is a particularly valuable collection of European period furniture.

Nidaros Cathedral is at the southern end of Munkegate. It is the largest of the medieval buildings, and has an unusual history. The first church on the site was a wooden one. It was replaced by a stone structure, which was built over the tomb of King Olav the Holy. During subsequent centuries it has been enlarged, extended and converted. It was several times ravaged by fire, and was almost totally destroyed in 1531. When restoration was begun in 1869, it was more a question of reconstruction. Thus most of this apparently medieval building is actually of more recent origin. Indeed, the work is not yet finished, and discussions are still going on as to the form and design of the towers. The stone sculptures on the west front and the stained glass windows have been created by modern artists. Seven Norwegian kings have been buried in the cathedral, and the Norwegian kings are still crowned here in accordance with tradition. There are guided tours around the cathedral, and visitors may also go up the tower. On the way up there is an impressive view of the cathedral interior, and the roof and towers provide a marvellous panoramic view of Trondheim.

Next to the cathedral is the **Archbishop's Palace** (Erkebispegården). Built in 1160, it was the archbishop's residence until the Reformation. After 1537 it served as the residence of the feudal lord of Trondheim. Since the seventeenth century it has been used as an armoury. The building has now been restored, and houses the council chambers, the historical armoury with its collections of weapons, and the Museum of the Resistance, which documents the German occupation during World War II.

On Bispegate near the cathedral is the **Art Gallery** (Trondhjems Kunstforening), where the city's Art Union exhibits a collection of works by modern artists and Norwegian masters.

Bispegate goes down past the pleasantly laid-out cathedral cemetery to

Nidaros Cathedral and quayside, Trondheim

the banks of the Nidelva and the **Gamle Bybrua**, the old city bridge. The banks along from the bridge are lined with old buildings on piers, which were the warehouses and counting houses of the merchants and shipowners. Kjøpmannsgate runs behind them parallel to the river bank, and gives a vivid impression of the centuries-old mercantile traditions of Trondheim.

Kongensgate goes from here back to the Torget. It is one of the main shopping streets. Beside it is the **Vår Frue kirke** (Church of Our Lady). Originally a Gothic building, it was extended in the seventeenth century.

From the Torget, Munkegate goes down to the harbour and to the **Ravnkloa**, which was once the old fish market. There are some more old merchants' houses nearby. The boats to the island of **Munkholmen** go from here (see below).

On the corner of Kjøpmannsgate and Fjordgate is the **Shipping Museum**, which is housed in the former penitentiary (Gamle Slaveri), and describes Trondheim's seafaring history.

Outside the city centre

The **Museum of the Royal Scientific Society** (Det Kongelige Norske Vitenskabers Selskap — DKNVS) is out along Erling Skakkes gate. It included sections on zoology, church history, geology, ethnology (both Eskimo and Lapp) and archaeology (Stone, Bronze and Iron Age, and also medieval).

To the east of the city above Bakklandet is the **Kristiansen Fortress**. This was built by Cicignon following the great fire of 1681, and was of strategic importance during the time of the Swedish attacks at the beginning of the eighteenth century.

Further out to the north east, in the suburb of Lade, is the beautiful manor house of Ringve Gård, which houses the **Museum of Musical History**. Nearly 2,000 valuable musical instruments are kept here in tasteful surroundings. The instruments are placed amid furniture and decor from the appropriate periods in rooms such as the Chopin Room, the Mozart Hall and the Tchaikovsky Lounge. They include a harpsichord from Versailles and an Amati violin. Concerts also take place here. The information office in the Torget provides details of times when the instruments are played and when guided tours in English are given.

Out to the west of the city are the **Aquarium** and **Biological Research Station**. On a hill to the west of the centre are the remains of the old castle of Sverresborg, which now forms the site of the **Trøndelag Folk Museum**. It includes several old houses typical of Trøndelag, and also a stave church.

The island of **Munkholmen** is situated out in the fjord opposite the city. It is now a popular seaside resort, and is served by a half-hourly ferry from the Ravnkloa (the old fish market — see above). It was formerly called Nidholm, and was used by the Vikings for public executions. In 995 Olav I Tryggvasson erected a fort on the island, together with what was probably Norway's first abbey. Although the Benedictine abbey was destroyed while the fort remained, the island was later renamed Munkholm (or 'Monk Island'). Remains of the old abbey were unearthed in 1967. The fort was too far out from Trondheim to be of any strategic importance, so for a long time it was used as a prison.

Excursions from Trondheim

Some of the local travel agents organise excursions and guided tours of the city. Brochures and full details of these can be obtained from the tourist information office in the Torget.

10 STAVANGER

Nowadays the name Stavanger is usually associated with oil. No longer is the harbour full of trawlers and great cargo ships, and no longer is the city full of warehouses; for oil reigns supreme. The harbour is full of tanks, tankers and drilling platform docks, while the city is dominated by the oil magnates' skyscrapers — massive glass palaces that dwarf the cosy little wooden houses, sheds and shops in the old part of the city.

Stavanger has succumbed to the oil boom that began in the seventies off the Norwegian coast. In the last 10 years, the population has increased by about 10,000 to 90,000, and Norway's fourth-largest town is also its oil capital. For in 1972 the Norwegian Parliament (Storting) decided that the Norwegian oil programme should be directed and coordinated from Stavanger.

All has not been plain sailing. In 1980 the oil platform *Alexander L. Kielland*, which had been built in Stavanger, capsized in a storm, killing 123 workers. All attempts to raise the rig have so far failed, owing to the incredibly high costs and the massive technical problems. But in spite of technical and environmental setbacks, the oil boom is not quite over yet.

Old Stavanger

Bredevann Lake, Stavanger

The giant new *Statfjord C* oil platform has recently been finished. It weighs 600,000 tonnes, and at a height of 175m is half as tall again as Salisbury Cathedral.

However, in spite of all this — or maybe even because of it — the citizens of Stavanger have been able to preserve some of the city's old-world charm and traditions. The harbour is still graced by picturesque little shops in lopsided wooden buildings, and the old town is still quite delightful with its narrow streets and alleyways.

History

Stavanger was founded as early as the eighth century, making it one of Norway's oldest towns. In the twelfth century, an English bishop built a church here and made Stavanger a bishopric. The ever-increasing trade also made Stavanger more important. During the period of Danish rule, the queen of Denmark had her Norwegian residence in Stavanger. The city has always been mainly concerned with fisheries, shipping and trade, both with Europe and overseas — that is, until oil was found off the coast.

Things to see

Stavanger Cathedral is next to the Torget (market place). It is dedicated to

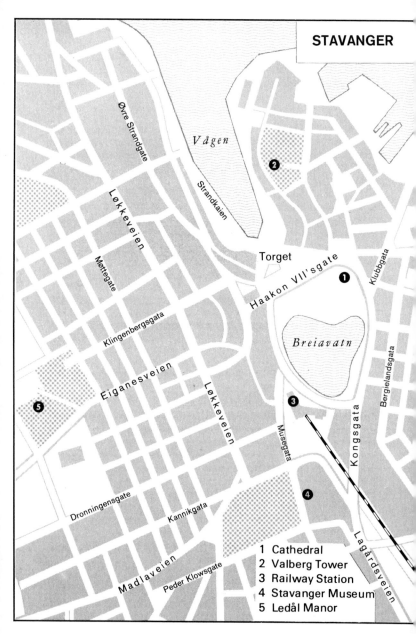

STAVANGER

Vågen

Øvre Strandgate

Strandkaien

Løkkeveien

Mortegata

Torget

Haakon VII'sgate

❶

Klubbgata

Klingenbergsgata

Breiavatn

Eiganesveien

Løkkeveien

Bergelandsgata

❺

❸

Musegata

Kongsgata

Dronningensgate

Kannikgata

❹

Madlaveien

Peder Klowsgate

Lagårdsveien

1 Cathedral
2 Valberg Tower
3 Railway Station
4 Stavanger Museum
5 Ledål Manor

'The Pulpit' in Rogaland

St Svithun, and was founded in 1125 by the Bishop of Winchester. The original building is Romanesque. After a fire in 1300, a Gothic extension was added, and much of the interior is Baroque (the pulpit, for example). However, in spite of restoration work, the cathedral is mainly in its original form.

Immediately behind the cathedral, and next to the Breiavatn, is the

Kongsgård (Royal Palace). This wooden building was originally the bishop's residence, and afterwards became that of the Danish monarch. A small bishop's chapel was added, now known as the Mauke Chapel. The whole of the structure was built in the thirteenth century.

In a pretty little park to the north of the Torget is the **Valberg Tower**. This was at one time used as a watch tower, and now gives visitors a lovely view of the city.

Muségate goes from the Torget past the Breiavatn, the railway station and the tourist office, and eventually comes to the **Stavanger Museum**. This houses a local history collection, including archaeological finds from the area, plus sections on zoology, ethnology and the history of shipping.

Ledål Manor is a museum of an entirely different kind. It stands in a park next to the Eiganesveien, and contains numerous mementoes of Stavanger's famous patrician family, the Kiellands. It was built by them in about 1800, and is still furnished in the style of that period. The king of Norway always resides here when visiting Stavanger. The Kielland family has exerted an enormous influence on the development of Stavanger. Its members have included consuls, chamberlains, captains, mayors, merchants, museum directors and, last but not least, the famous author Alexander Kielland. Their presence is everywhere, not only on the monuments and gravestones in the family cemetery near the manor, but also in the history and development of the city.

Excursions from Stavanger

Many different excursions are available from Stavanger, details of which can be found at local travel agents or at the tourist information office by the station in Muségate.

One can, for example, go on a boat trip to the island of **Møsterøy,** where the abbey of Utstein is still well preserved. Also popular is a much longer excursion along the Lysefjord to the **Prekestolen** (Pulpit). This much-photographed phenomenon consists of a vast table of rock with a flat top and vertical cliff faces nearly 600m high. The summit can be reached overland by means of a difficult climb on foot.

Stavanger's local beach is at Sola.

11 KRISTIANSAND

Kristiansand (population 60,000) is the largest town in Sørland and the administrative centre of the county of Vest-Agder. It is situated on the Skaggerak at the mouth of the Otra, and is a good ferry port from which to begin a Norwegian tour.

At one time the town's economy was based on shipping and shipbuilding, but nowadays it has a variety of important industries, such as electronics, aluminium and nickel.

Kristiansand has good road connections, both inland and along the coast to Oslo and Stavanger. It is also on the Sørland railway line from Oslo to Stavanger. It has ferry connections with Harwich and Newcastle in England and Hanstholm and Hirtshals in Denmark. The airport at Kjevik has flights to other parts of Norway.

History

The city was built in 1641 according to plans laid down by King Christian IV of Denmark. At that time there was a fashion for building towns in a square grid of broad streets. The same chessboard plan has been preserved to this day. The streets were made wide to prevent fires spreading, but in spite of that the city was several times burned to the ground. The old wooden houses have now mostly been replaced by stone buildings.

Things to see

The city centre still preserves the **Kvadraturen** (square grid pattern) in which Christian IV planned it, and consists of a set of ten parallel streets crossed at right angles by another set of seven parallel streets. Elvegate (along the bank of the Otra) has a slight bend in it, but preserves more of the original buildings than any of the other streets. Some of the wooden buildings have been burned down and replaced with stone ones.

The **Torget** (market place) and the area around the **Town Hall** (Rådhuset) have also retained some of the original wooden houses. The **cathedral** is the third-largest in Norway, and was built in 1885 to replace the old cathedral, which had been destroyed by fire.

Christiansholm Fort stands next to the East Harbour (Østre havn). Built in 1674, it has walls 5 metres thick and a set of old cannons. These have only been used once, at the beginning of the nineteenth century. The East Harbour is divided from the West Harbour (Vestre havn) by the **fish market** (Fyskebryggen), where fish is sold daily. Nearby are the **Europakai**, where the ferries dock, and the tourist information office in Vestre Strandgate.

Towards Kjevik Airport on the north-eastern edge of the city is **Oddernes Church**. Built in 1040, it has a seventeenth-century Baroque

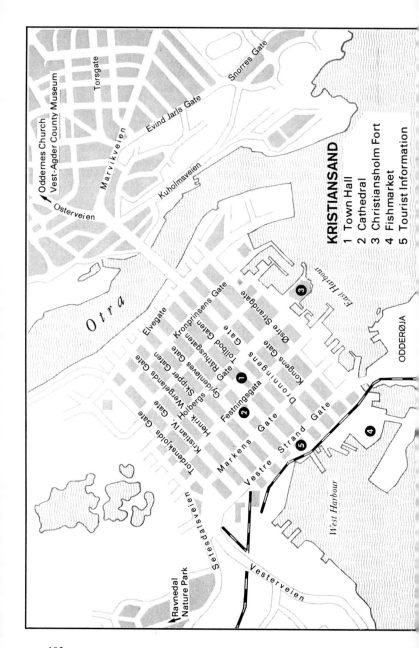

KRISTIANSAND

1 Town Hall
2 Cathedral
3 Christiansholm Fort
4 Fishmarket
5 Tourist Information

ODDERØJA

East Harbour

Oddernes Church
Vest-Agder County Museum

Osterveien

Torsgate

Snorres Gate

Eivind Jarls Gate

Marvikveien

Kuholmsveien

O t r a

Elvegate

Kronprinsens Gate

Tollbod Gaten

Gate

Østre Strandgate

Kongens Gate

Dronningens Gate

Rådhusgaten

Gyldenløves Gate

Skipper Gaten

Festningsgata

Wergelands Gate

Holbergs Gate

Henrik Wergelands Gate

Kristian IV. Gate

Tordenskiolds Gate

Markens Gate

Vestre Strand Gate

West Harbour

Setesdalsveien

Ravnedal
Nature Park

Vesterveien

192

Kristiansand, one of Norway's major communication ports

pulpit and several runestones. This is not far from the **Vest-Agder County Museum** — an open-air museum with old houses and farms from Setesdal, Vest-Agder and the old city of Kristiansand. It also includes collections of costumes, folklore, furniture and ecclesiastical objects, plus a section for temporary exhibitions.

North west of the city are the **Ravnedal Nature Park** and another **Baneheia**, with a viewing point. East of the city along the E18 is **Kristiansand Zoo**, which is reached via the 600m long **Varrod Bridge** — one of the longest in Scandinavia.

Excursions from Kristiansand

The **Setesdal Railway** runs on Sundays from **Grovane**, which is 15km north of Kristiansand along the main Sørland railway line. Steam trains ply the 5km long section of the old railway. A railway museum is attached.

There is a choice of several boat trips along the coast. Details of these are available from the tourist information office in Vestre Strandgate.

12 NARVIK

Originally no more than a small fishing village, Narvik suddenly grew in importance at the turn of the century with the building of the famous iron-ore railway. This was built through from Kiruna in Sweden, its purpose being to bring new ore supplies to the nearest point on the Norwegian coast, which unlike the Swedish coast is ice-free. The line was constructed under the most appalling conditions across an inhospitable plateau riddled with ice and snow, scree and steep precipices. The railway builders (*raller*) have become legendary like the cowboys of the Wild West, and the event lives on in many stories and traditions.

One such tradition is the Festival of the Black She-Bear in March. Every year a black-haired maiden is chosen as the 'Black She-Bear' in memory of Anna Hofstad, who lost her life while helping to build the railway. There is a monument to Anna Hofstad in the railway builders' cemetery at Tornehamn across the Swedish border, which has its own railway station.

The building of the railway has enabled Narvik to grow into a town of some 20,000 inhabitants. The large modern piers are equipped with automatic loading gear to speed the iron ore on its way to all parts of the world. All this technological wizardry has made its mark upon the town and upon the life of its inhabitants. The recent slump in the steel industry has been disastrous for Narvik, and the port is no longer used to capacity. During the summer there are guided tours of the automatic loading machinery.

There is another, much sadder chapter in the history of Narvik. In 1940 there was long and bitter fighting here between the Germans and the Allies, and much of Narvik was destroyed. The course of these campaigns is described in the displays in the Rød Kors Krigsmuseum (Red Cross War Museum). Thousands of soldiers are buried in the nearby military cemetery.

The midnight sun shines in Narvik from 26 May to 19 July.

Excursions from Narvik

Narvik is a good base from which to visit the Lofoten Islands. The famous Northern Arrow carries passengers 2,000km from Narvik to Stockholm along the iron-ore railway, passing through some breathtaking scenery. The road connecting Narvik with Kiruna was at last finished in 1984.

13 HAMMERFEST

This most northerly town in the world lies at a latitude of 70° 39′ 48″, which is as far north as the northernmost tip of Alaska. The small port was made a town in 1789, and its forty inhabitants were freed from tax liabilities to encourage the settlement to grow. Only 23 years later the population had grown to 350, and its present population of 8,000 is augmented during the week by workers who travel in from outside.

In 1891, Hammerfest was the first town in Europe to be given electric street lighting. For Hammerfest is plunged into darkness from 21 November to 23 January. The midnight sun shines here from 17 May to 28 July.

Hammerfest is situated by a well-sheltered harbour, which remains mostly ice-free during the winter. It has thus been a useful trading port for centuries. Fishing and its associated industries are the most important

Hammerfest, the world's most northerly town

occupations. It is the base for the Arctic fishing fleet, and its biggest employer is a frozen-food firm. It also acts as the port for supplies to the hinterland.

Tourism has also played its part, since Hammerfest is an important stopping-off point on the way to the North Cape. The town is not especially attractive to look at, since all its older buildings have been destroyed, either in the great fire of 1890, or during World War II.

Of most interest are the modern church (1958), with its enormous stained-glass window, and the **Meridianstøtte** on Fuglen Peninsula. This is a column topped by a stylised bronze globe, which was erected here to commemorate the work of the Norwegian, Swedish and Russian scientists who made measurements in the period between 1816 and 1852 in order to determine the size of the earth.

There is also the Royal and Ancient Society of Polar Bears. Anyone can become a member, and a certificate is given in return for a contribution to the society. In the small exhibition room is the skin of the largest known polar bear to have been shot. The society exists to promote the Arctic way of life, including both hunting and survival.

Hammerfest must be the only town in the world to be regularly overrun with reindeer during the autumn. They come in from their bare summer pastures and eat their way through the vegetables in people's gardens, often holding up the traffic in the streets.

During the period of the midnight sun, there are organised excursions from Hammerfest to the North Cape and to the tundras of Finnmark.

Not far away from Hammerfest is the most northerly wood in the world — a birch wood.

14 ADVICE TO TOURISTS

1. Travel preparations

Car drivers

A national driving licence is quite sufficient for driving on holiday in Norway. The Green Card, which at one time was compulsory in all Scandinavian countries, is now only optional; but all visitors are recommended to take one. In the case of an accident, it provides immediate proof of insurance cover.

It is worth noting that diesel vehicles seating over nine passengers or weighing more than 3.5 tonnes are required to pay an extra charge for using the roads. Information on this is available from the relevant customs authority. Caravans or trailers must not be wider than 2.5m or longer than 12.4m. Caravans over 2.3m wide must always be towed by a vehicle at least as wide. All British vehicles must display a national identity sticker.

For advice on travelling in Norway, turn to page 200.

Ferry crossings

The prices of these are always fluctuating, so it is important to find out the latest information. Exact details can be obtained from the shipping companies themselves, or else from travel agents.

Ferries from Britain

From	To	Shipping Company	Frequency in summer
Newcastle	Bergen	Norway Line	3 per week
Newcastle	Stavanger	Norway Line	2 per week
Newcastle	Kristiansand	Norway Line	weekly
Newcastle	Oslo	Norway Line	weekly
		DFDS Seaways	twice weekly
Harwich	Kristiansand	Fred Olsen Lines	weekly
Harwich	Oslo	Fred Olsen Lines	weekly

Travelling by plane

The main airports for international connections are Fornebu and Gardermoen near Oslo, and Bergen and Stavanger. Flights from Britain go to these airports and British Airways, Dan Air Services and Scandinavian Airlines all run regular services. Airlines such as Pan Am operate daily flights from the US to Norway. Details of flights may be obtained from the airlines themselves or from travel agents.

Arrival in Norway

Passports

A passport without a visa and inocculation certificates is sufficient for British subjects staying in the country for not more than 3 months. Other nationals are advised to contact their consulate for information.

Customs

There is not usually any difficulty with customs. A verbal declaration is sufficient in most cases, and hand luggage seldom needs to be opened. One is normally only asked to declare anything on arrival in the first Scandinavian country. Crossing boundaries within Scandinavia is very much easier, and the frontier posts are often unmanned.

Customs officers tend to concentrate mostly on tobacco and alcohol. Normal quantities of equipment and tools may be brought into the country. There is no import duty on vehicles for use in water sports or on items to be mounted on them such as outboard motors. Fuel totalling 200 litres may be imported with a motorvehicle or motorboat.

Visitors to Norway over 16 years of age and who are resident in Europe may bring in (per person) 200 cigarettes or 250g of other tobacco goods. Visitors not resident in Europe are allowed to bring in 400 cigarettes or 500g of tobacco. Visitors over 20 years of age may bring in 1 litre of alcoholic drinks above 23 per cent alcohol (40 per cent proof) or 2 litres of drinks under 23 per cent.

Regulations on food are rather complicated, but in general fresh meat, eggs, cream, milk and potatoes should be left at home. Other goods may be brought in up to a total value of 1200nkr.

Many customs areas have separate doors marked red and green. Those who have items to declare or are not sure should go through the door marked red. Those with nothing to declare should go through the green door.

Sickness or accident

There are reciprocal health arrangements between Norway and Britain entitling citizens to receive free or partly free medical care. British subjects should apply to the DHSS to see what forms are required. American visitors should take out short-term, full cover medical insurance before leaving home.

Animals and plants

It is virtually impossible to bring pets into Norway. Not only is a special permit required from the Ministry of Agriculture, but there is also a compulsory four-month quarantine period. These strict regulations are to prevent rabies and other animal diseases from entering the country.

As with food, there are strict limits on bringing plants into Norway. Apart from potted plants for personal use, or posies of flowers such as roses or carnations, it is best to avoid taking plants into the country.

CB radios

A permit is required for these. An application must be made at least four weeks in advance to the Norwegian Telecommunications Administration, Postboks 6701, N Oslo 1.

Currency and exchange

The Norwegian unit of currency is the Norwegian crown or krone (nkr, Nkr or NOK), which is made up of 100 øre. The exchange rate is usually around ten or eleven krone to the pound and seven or eight to the dollar. The Norwegian coins are 5, 10, 25 and 50 øre, 1nkr and 5nkr, and the notes are 10, 50, 100, 500, and 1,000nkr. The 1 and 2 øre coins have been taken out of circulation, and prices are rounded up or down.

There is no limit to the amount of currency one can take into Norway, but not more than 5,000nkr may be brought out again.

General information

Maps

Good maps are essential when travelling in Norway. Car drivers are recommended to take a general map to a scale of about 1:1,500,000 together with more detailed maps to a scale of between 1:300,000 and 1:400,000.

National holidays

School holidays in Norway are between mid-June and mid-August. Since all employees are given a statutory month's holiday, many firms will close down for part of this period.

Some of the statutory holidays are the same as in Britain: Christmas Day, Boxing Day, New Year's Day, Good Friday and Easter Monday. Maundy Thursday, Ascension Day and Whit Monday are also holidays. May Day is always on 1 May; National Day is on 17 May.

Electricity

Norway has the highest per capita consumption of electricity in the world. No house is without electricity, right down to the smallest mountain hamlet. Electricity is also very cheap, and is always available in places such as camping sites. Although the supply is 220V AC everywhere, normal three-pin 13A plugs do not usually fit, though two-pin electric razor plugs do. Many hotels have suitable adaptors available. It is also possible to make up one's own adaptor by taking an extension lead and replacing the plug with a Norwegian one.

A word of warning: passenger boats and ferries often have 220V direct current (DC), which will damage electric razors, hairdriers, radios, cassette recorders and other electronic devices.

Post

There are post offices in all Norwegian towns. Opening hours in the larger towns are normally Monday to Saturday from 8am to 5.30pm, though in small towns they are usually much shorter. Most villages along the main roads have small sub-branches that are usually part-time. Letters sent poste restante are usually kept at the nearest main post office. Such letters should always be addressed with the surname underlined so that they can be correctly sorted. All that is needed apart from the destination address is the phrase 'poste restante'. The normal postal rates to other European countries are 3.50nkr for postcards and letters (20g). Airmail (20g) outside Europe is approximately 4nkr.

Telephones
It is possible to make a telephone call to Great Britain from an ordinary red call-box in Norway. From Norway the international code for Great Britain is 095–44, for the US, this is 095–1. This should be followed by the national dialling code for the exchange (minus the first 0) and then the number. A call from Norway to Britain costs about 5.80nkr per minute, to the US, 15.10nkr per minute. Since 5nkr is the biggest coin that can be used, a large supply of these will be needed. With Norwegian call-boxes, the coins are placed ready in the machine before dialling. When looking up numbers in a Norwegian telephone book, it is worth noting that the letters æ, ø and å (in that order) come after z at the end of the alphabet. The international code for Norway from Great Britain is 010–47, from the US, 011–47.

Banks
Norwegian banks are usually open to the public from 8.15am to 3.30pm, and until 6pm on Thursdays. They are closed on Saturdays, and in the country they are sometimes closed in the afternoons. There are *bureaux de change* at airports, ferry ports and frontier posts, and at most of the main city stations. These usually have longer opening times.

Eurocheques are valid in Norway, and British visitors with a current National Girobank account may draw money at some Norwegian post offices. Credit cards are becoming increasingly accepted in Norway. The most frequent cards to be accepted are American Express, Diners Club, Eurocard and VISA.

Shopping in Norway
Norway is not a very good country to shop in for visitors from EEC countries. The only food items that are cheap are certain basic foodstuffs that are produced in Norway - fish products, for example. All other food items are expensive, in spite of the devaluation of the Norwegian krone.

Shop opening times vary enormously in Norway. Shops usually open at 8.30am, but may close as early as 4.30pm, or even at 1.00pm on Saturdays. They are usually open until 7.pm on one evening a week.

2. Travelling in Norway

Apart from the usual maps and hotel guides, the Norwegian National

Tourist Office provides booklets with details of routes, prices and times of all the boat, rail, bus and air services which operate within the country.

Driving in Norway

Norway was for many years notorious among car drivers on account of its many unmade roads, steep passes and narrow lanes. A car tour of Norway required as much extra equipment as a safari, with spare windscreens, cans of petrol and specially protected headlamps. But these are mostly a thing of the past. There are admittedly still problems with a few mountain roads, and with some of the roads in the far north, for which a spare plastic windscreen would not go amiss. However, most of the road network has now been made up to a high standard.

Motorways are only to be found in the neighbourhood of Oslo. Most of the traffic — lorries in particular — is concentrated on the main arterial routes, which should therefore be avoided in the peak season. But away from the main routes, the traffic is remarkably light in comparison with other parts of Europe.

A few of the mountain passes are closed in winter, and some roads are unsuitable for caravans or trailers. Such roads are indicated, both in the relevant sections of this book and on most good maps.

The breathtakingly beautiful scenery is a good reason in itself for not travelling too fast. An average of between 150km and 250km per day is quite sufficient if one is to avoid the stress of driving for too long at a stretch.

Traffic regulations

The traffic signs and regulations are much the same as those in Great Britain, except that, as in all continental countries of Europe, traffic coming in from the right has priority at junctions, intersections and even roundabouts. Trams also have priority. Seat belts are compulsory.

The speed limit on ordinary country roads is 80km/hr (50mph); on motorways and on some major roads (indicated by signs) it is 90km/hr (56mph); in built-up areas it is 50km/hr (31mph).

Parking is strictly regulated. It is forbidden on main roads, on bends and in concealed positions. Overnight parking of caravans or dormobiles is forbidden on the public highway and frowned on even in parking places.

There are a few additional signs in Norwegian:

FERIST	—	cattle grid
VEIARBEIDE	—	roadworks
KJØR SAKTE	—	drive slowly
LØS GRUS	—	loose gravel or chippings
OMKJØRING	—	diversion
SVAKE KANTER	—	soft verges

Passing places on narrow roads are indicated by a white M (for Møtepass)

Winter voyaging from the Lofotens to Kirkenes

on a blue background. Elk warning signs should be taken seriously, especially at dusk. Finally a black ⌘ on a white background indicates a place of cultural or historical interest.

In view of the Norwegian authorities' strict views on alcohol consumption, and rigid laws relating to driving and drinking, it is very strongly advised that you do not drink and drive.

Petrol stations

Petrol stations are not thick on the ground and opening times are very variable, so it is best not to let the tank get too low. It is safest to have at least enough petrol for the next 100km. Petrol prices are variable.

Emergencies

The Norwegian Automobile Association (NAF) has patrols on all the main routes, plus an emergency telephone network on mountain roads. Besides which, lorry-drivers are usually willing to help out when a car breaks down.

Vehicles for hire

Hiring a car, a dormobile or a caravan should present no more problems in Norway than in Britain and all you generally require is a current drivers licence. There are plenty of car-hire firms. Caravans and dormobiles can be hired from the Norway Travel Association.

Ship and ferry connections

In Norway, ships are much more important than railways. Norway has a long coastline, and the land area is fragmented by long fjords and lakes. It is therefore not surprising that there are so many liner and ferry connections. Only the most important are given here. A fuller and more detailed list of all daily services is available from the Norwegian National Tourist Office.

Seat reservations are required for all ships on the Hurtigrute, and for all journeys lasting several days. Bookings are also available on the many ferry crossings over fjords, but they are not absolutely necessary. It is often difficult to estimate arrival times at the ferry ports, and the frequency of the service often varies depending on the number of ships available. But it is rare to have to wait a long time.

Hardangerfjord:
Kinsarvik—Kvanndal: Thirty-six departures a day between 5am and 12.40am; journey time 40min.

Sognefjord:
Vangsnes—Hella: Twenty departures a day between 6am and 11pm; journey time 15min.
Gudvangen—Revsnes—Kaupanger: Four departures a day between 9am and 6pm; journey time 2hr 20min.

Geirangerfjord:
Hellesylt—Geiranger: Five departures a day between 9am and 10pm; journey time 1hr.

This is only an approximate guide to the main ferry services on the routes described in this book. More accurate details are given in the official timetables.

The Hurtigrute
The famous Hurtigrute is a post and passenger service that runs along the Norwegian coast between Bergen and Kirkenes. The ships have plied this route day and night, summer and winter, since 1893. It is more than just a means of transport, for during the winter it is often the only means of communication that remains open to outlying coastal regions. Apart from goods, foodstuffs and post, the ships also carry passengers. A few simply furnished cabins are available for passengers who wish to make longer journeys. Only the really modern ships have any of the modern comforts, and a trip on a post steamer is nothing like a cruise on a luxury liner — but it is still an unforgettable experience.

It is possible to book a trip from Bergen to Kirkenes and back. The journey takes eleven days to cover a distance of some 2,500 seamiles, and the ships embark from Bergen at 11pm every night. Overland excursions can be included, such as a visit to Trondheim or a bus trip to the North Cape, and longer stops on the way are also possible. The ships call at thirty-five ports altogether, and parts of the route can be combined with bus, railway or aeroplane. The possibilities are infinite. However, the enormous popularity of the Hurtigrute means that bookings must be made a long time in advance. There are reductions for senior citizens, and the prices vary from season to season. The Hurtigrute is run by four different shipping companies.

Railways

The many special tickets and reductions that are now available internationally have made railway travel a particularly attractive option these days. Apart from *Interrail*, there is a special *Northern Tourist* roundabout ticket available, which is valid in the whole of Scandinavia for 3 or 4 weeks. On long-distance routes, it is advisable to make reservations in advance. This can be done from major railway stations or travel agents in this country.

Most of the lines radiate from Oslo, though they are connected by bus services. Every line has its own individual charm, be it the beautiful scenery, the strangeness of the landscape, or merely the number of superlatives involved — the highest, the steepest or the most northerly line. The most important lines are as follows:

1. The Sørland line
The southernmost line in Norway, the Sørland line runs along the coast from Oslo via Kristiansand to Stavanger. Several loops and branch lines lead to popular coastal resorts.

2. The Numedal line
This line goes from Oslo along Numedal as far as Rødberg, from which there are bus connections to Geilo.

3. The Bergen line
The Oslo—Bergen line is one of Norway's classic rail links. It runs through mountainous regions via tunnels and high passes, reaching a maximum height of 1,301m. Its branch line to Flåm provides yet further excitement.

4. The Flåm line
This short branch line drops 865m in only 20km. The gradient is incredible, reaching a maximum of 55 per cent — the steepest in Norway. The line plunges down through a narrow defile from the high plateau of the Hardangervidda to a branch of Norway's largest fjord, the Sognefjord. It must be one of the most exciting stretches of railway in the world.

5. The Valdres line
This line runs parallel to the E68 along Begnadal as far as Fagernes.

6. The Dovre line
The most important line in Norway, the Dovre line connects Oslo with Trondheim. It runs along the glorious Gudbrandsdal as far as Dombås, then climbs over the Dovrefjell, reaching a maximum height of 1,025m.

7. The Rauma line
A branch of the Dovre line, the Rauma line runs from Dombås to Åndalsnes, passing through beautiful scenery of a most unusual character.

8. The Røros line
This line runs mostly parallel to the Dovre line, passing through Østerdal along the banks of the Glomma, and via the mining town of Røros to Trondheim.

9. The Nordland line
This line may not go to the North Cape, but it at least makes it over the Arctic Circle to Bodø. It runs mostly parallel to the E6 through the typical fjell landscape of Nordland. The track often runs through so-called snow tunnels, which prevent the snow from blocking it during the winter.

10. The Ofot line
The Northern Arrow plies this line from Narvik via Kiruna to Stockholm, running along the track of the famous iron-ore railway. The building of this line has gone down in history (see the section on Narvik, page 194). This most northerly line in the world wraps itself round the mountainside past bizarre rock formations, and then plunges through tunnels as it crosses the Swedish border; it continues across the plateau of Swedish Lapland, past the Abisko National Park and the ore mines of Kiruna, and eventually arrives at the metropolis of Stockholm.

Airlines

Air travel is very popular in Norway for covering long distances. The national network is served by three companies: SAS, Braathens SAFE, and Widerøes Flyveselskap. A dense network of routes connects Oslo with all the larger towns and with the North Cape. In addition there are air shuttles, round-trip flights and helicopter services such as the one to Røst in the Lofoten Islands. Details of flight times, fares and special reductions are available from the flight companies themselves, from travel agents or from the Norwegian National Tourist Office.

3. Accommodation in Norway

Hotels
All parts of Norway offer a wide range of medium-price, first-class and luxury hotels to suit all needs. Detailed alphabetical lists of what is available can be obtained from the Norwegian National Tourist Office. Many of the hotels belong to country-wide chains, offering overnight reductions on the presentation of hotel vouchers or passes such as the 'Bonus Pass', 'Fjord Pass' or 'Hotel Cheque'. These are essential for hotel visitors who wish to travel around Norway, since they ensure a 25 per cent average reduction on overnight stays. They can again be obtained via

travel agents or via the Norwegian National Tourist Office.

Youth hostels
Norway has about 80 youth hostels, offering cheap overnight accommodation. They are housed not only in purpose-built hostels, but also (during the summer) in schools, farms or other suitable buildings. The only requirement for an overnight stay is membership of the Youth Hostel Association, either of Norway or of one's own country. This can be arranged at any of the hostels. Youth hostels cater for people of all ages. Some hostels even provide family rooms. The Norwegian National Tourist Office provides a list of youth hostels and camping sites. Other detailed information can be obtained from the Landeslaget for Norske Ungdom-sherberger (NUH), Dronningensgata 26, N Oslo 1.

Huts
Holiday huts are a Norwegian speciality. Signposts to *hytter* can be seen every few kilometres. They vary enormously, from nicely furnished bungalows with heating, WC, shower, hot and cold water, kitchen etc, to a simple overnight hut for which one has to provide one's own bedclothes, water and lighting. Some are for overnight stays only, while others can be rented on a weekly basis. Some of them belong to camping sites, while others are part of a large hotel complex. Some huts stand on their own in the middle of nowhere, and may actually be converted farmsteads. Longer stays will need to be booked via a travel agent, but no reservations are required for a simple overnight stay. More details of what is available can be obtained from the Norwegian National Tourist Office.

Similar to *hytter* are the *rorbuer* — fishermen's huts that are let out to holidaymakers outside the fishing season. They are mostly to be found in the Lofoten Islands.

Camping
There are over 1,400 camping sites in Norway, which are classified with one, two or three stars according to the facilities provided. Drivers with tents, caravans or dormobiles may stay overnight or for longer periods. A list of available sites can be obtained from the Norwegian National Tourist Office.

Rights of way and the countryside code
There is no exact English equivalent for the Norwegian term *allemannsretten* (literally 'everyman's right'), since it is a peculiarly Scandinavian concept. It signifies that, in principle, everyone has a right to enjoy what nature has to offer, even when it is on private or state land. The only condition of this is that one should respect other people, especially the owners of the land, and of course nature itself. One can bathe in the sea, pick fruit in the forest or camp in a beautiful spot. One is of course expected to ask for the owner's permission if one is staying for any period of time, and it goes without saying that no litter whatsoever should be left lying around. Indeed, it is

Country chalet at Golå in Gudbrandsdal

part of the Scandinavian countryside code that litter should always be picked up, even if it has been dropped by someone else. Environmental conservation became part of the Scandinavian philosophy long before it had even been heard of elsewhere.

Top-category camp with beach near Trondheim

Rural camp only 10 minutes from Oslo

4. Opportunities for sport

Angling
Norway's many rivers, lakes and fjords make it a real angler's paradise. The salmon rivers are particularly tempting from an angler's point of view. But it is not just a question of getting out a fishing rod and trying one's luck. There are numerous regulations that must be strictly observed.

Apart from an annual angler's licence, a special permit is also required for the particular waters to be fished, since the majority of them are privately owned or leased out. Anyone intending to fish for salmon, sea trout, sea char or freshwater fish must also pay a small fishing insurance fee. All angling equipment must be disinfected, including waders and wellington boots. Each species of fish may only be caught during the appropriate fishing season. Exact information on all these regulations can be obtained from the Hunting and Fishing Society, Prinsengate 21, Oslo.

Sea-fishing trips are also possible from many of the towns and villages along the coast, often with experienced fishermen. Details of these can be found at local tourist offices. Some of the *rorbuer* are let for special angling holidays.

Hill walking and mountaineering
The mountains of Norway offer countless opportunities for a great variety of activities, ranging from a stroll along forest paths to a mountaineering tour or a climb up a glacier. Most of the best areas are in the south of the country: the high plateaux of the Hardangervidda and the Dovrefjell, and the mighty Jotunheimen massif.

The best address to write to is that of the DNT: Den Norske Turistforening, Stortingsgate 28, N Oslo 1. This organisation not only produces detailed information, maps and route suggestions, but also provides hut and hostel accommodation. There are organised mountain hikes and year-round training courses. It also produces its own booklet giving vital information on equipment, accommodation, routes and area descriptions.

For those who prefer to join a hiking party, there are several all-inclusive holidays of this kind available from various travel organisations.

Water sports
Norway provides a vast range of rivers, lakes, fjords and coastal waters. It is thus an ideal setting for all kinds of water activities, from sailing and motorboat holidays to rowing and windsurfing. The variety is tremendous: beautiful harbours alternate with isolated bays and quiet inlets, while high mountain lakes empty into fast canoeing rivers. There are not many formalities involved in bringing boats and equipment into Norway, and boats and windsurfing boards can be hired on the spot.

Skiing
Modern skiing was invented in Norway by Sondre Nordheim, so it is not

Tourist Offices can arrange fishing trips in summer

surprising that the Norwegians love skiing. The area around Lillehammer is the best for cross-country skiing, while alpine skiing is good in the areas of Rondane, Geilo and Jotunheimen. The long, cold winter is guaranteed to provide a marvellous skiing holiday, whether in a hotel or in a hut. Some of the travel operators organise skiing package holidays.

There are even opportunities for skiing in summer. The summer skiing centre at Jyvashytta in Jotunheimen is open from mid-June to late September, while those on the Haukelifjell in Telemark and in the Stryn area are open from May to August.

5.　Food and drink

Norwegian cuisine can be described in a few words. It lacks the refinement of Danish and Swedish cooking, but is nonetheless solid and satisfying. Whatever the catering establishment, the meals are lavishly served, which is certainly necessary in the cold months when plenty of calories are required.

Certain establishments in Norway as elsewhere provide so-called international cuisine, but these need not concern us here. It is the local fare that is of particular interest.

Angler's paradise, Saltstraumen eddy, near Bodø

The day begins with an enormous breakfast (*Norsk frokost*), which may include not only smoked fish, continental sausage, cold meats and salads, but also cornflakes and porridge. There is also an interesting goat's-milk cheese that tastes rather like marzipan! A large jug of milk is provided, and coffee or a superior variety of tea are usually served. It is also possible to order a continental breakfast, for those who prefer to make do with a cup of tea or coffee and a slice of bread and jam. But this is not recommended.

After such a large breakfast, one can afford to be sparing at lunchtime. Lunch in Norway is usually little more than a second breakfast, in which the same cold table may possibly be varied to include the odd hot dish. Norwegians rarely eat out at lunchtime, and if they do they usually limit themselves to cold dishes or open sandwiches.

The main meal of the day is the *middagmat*, which the Norwegians usually eat after work between five and seven in the evening — and they usually take their time over it. In hotels and guesthouses this meal usually comes in several courses: cold hors d'œuvre, soup, main dish, dessert. All meals are lavish. However, vegetables in Norway are expensive and in short supply, and this should be noted when eating à la carte.

Fish is naturally the most important item on the Norwegian menu. The quality is always excellent, since the fish never has to travel far. Plaice and sole are great delicacies, while in the summer trout and especially salmon are a gourmet's delight. Salmon is the best fish in the world, in whatever form it comes — whether boiled, grilled or smoked, or served with a gorgeous horseradish sauce. And nowhere outside Norway is it so fresh and plentiful. Even the beautiful late-summer delicacies such as crayfish, lobster and prawns pale by comparison.

There are several specialities peculiar to the far north — ptarmigan, for instance, either fresh or smoked. These are new flavours which one can quickly become fond of. Another northern speciality is reindeer, which in

Norway is ideal holiday-country for children

flavour is somewhere between venison and veal. It comes in many different guises, and often in the form of tasty meatballs called *reinsdierboller*. It is usually served with stewed cranberries or the white and rather sharp-flavoured snowberries.

Alcohol was banned in Norway for some years (between 1920 and 1927), because alcoholism was proving so dangerous to people's health. Nowadays alcoholic drinks are sold by a state monopoly and are very highly taxed. The only shops selling alcohol are in the larger towns, and these are difficult for foreigners to find because advertising is forbidden.

The most popular beer — the so-called Pilsner or Bayer — has a very low alcohol content. It is often the only alcoholic drink available in restaurants during the day, and is also sold in shops outside the state monopoly. The so-called export beer is rather stronger. Imported beers and wines are extremely expensive.

Hotels and larger restaurants are licensed to sell alcohol during the day, though spirits are not normally allowed until after 3pm on weekdays, and are often banned altogether at weekends. Only larger establishments are licensed to sell wine, while smaller concerns are often limited to beer.

In the shops which are specially licensed to sell alcohol, there is in theory no restriction on how much one can buy. But the prices are sufficiently high to limit what one can afford. Most Scandinavian countries limit the consumption of alcohol in this way, though in Finland it is controlled by means of ration cards.

Most hotels and restaurants include a service charge in their prices, though an additional tip of between 10 per cent and 15 per cent is usually expected.

6. The language

Norway is a country with two official languages: *Riksmål* or *Bokmål* and *Landsmål* or *Nynorsk*. The reasons for these two Norwegian standards are fairly complicated, and are partly related to the fact that Norway did not have its own official language until the nineteenth century.

Up to then, Norwegian had mostly consisted of a large variety of spoken dialects, which were regarded as no more than aberrant varieties of Danish or Swedish. This was due in large measure to the political superiority of the Danes and Swedes, whose written languages had a strong influence on the many Norwegian dialects. The other main influence was the Hanseatic League, which brought in a number of German loan-words. It is very difficult to make a clear classification, since all Scandinavian languages (with the exception of Finnish and Lapp) are closely related.

In about 1300 the bishopric of Trondheim introduced its own official language — the first attempt to produce a uniform Norwegian standard. But in the sixteenth century this form, known as Middle Norwegian, was replaced first by Swedish and then by Danish as the official written language.

Up until 1850 Danish was the language taught in schools, though the Norwegians held on to their own spoken dialects. Their Danish took on a strong Norwegian flavour, and the written and spoken forms diverged considerably.

By now the nationalists, reformers and radicals were seeking to create a truly Norwegian standard. The problem was that the Norwegian dialects varied so enormously among themselves, and considerable disagreement resulted.

The Norwegian philologist Ivar Aasen published a Norwegian dictionary in 1850. He combined a variety of dialects, in particular those spoken in the west of Norway, which preserved many of the archaic features of the ancient Viking tongue (Old Norse). The resulting standard was known as *Landsmål* or *Nynorsk*.

Meanwhile the reformers introduced a different standard, which merely adapted the existing Danish standard to the Norwegian that was spoken. The result was much closer to the dialects of south-eastern Norway, which were of course the nearest to Danish. Known as *Riksmål* or *Bokmål*, this was the standard adopted by Ibsen and several other poets, while the lyric poets preferred the more pleasant-sounding *Landsmål* or *Nynorsk*.

The dispute was resolved in 1885 by the government, which granted equal status to the two written standards. School lessons were to be conducted in whichever of them was closest to the local dialect.

Nowadays educated Norwegians are expected to be fluent in both forms. They have no difficulty in understanding them both, since the differences are not great and are mostly divergences of spelling. This is why names on maps are often spelled differently — for example, Revsnes versus Refsnes, Håkon versus Haakon, or Torget versus Torvet. Other more significant differences are a matter for linguists, and need not be considered here.

One important feature of Norwegian is something which is also true of Danish and Swedish: the definite article — 'the' — is tagged onto the end of a word instead of coming before it. Thus Hardangerfjord**en** means **the** Hardangerfjord, while Jotunheim**en** means **the** Jotunheim.

Useful words and phrases

Pronunciation

æ is like *a* in 'cake'; *ø* is like *u* in 'urge'; *å* has the vowel sound of the word 'ore' and the vowel *y* is pronounced like the French *u* in 'lune'; *o* is frequently pronounced *oo*; *d* is usually silent before *s* and after *n* and *l* and when in the final position after *r*; *g* is usually hard as in 'get' but when before *j* and *y* has the sound of the consonant *y*; in the word *jeg* ('I') the *g* forms a dipthong pronounced somewhere between the dipthongs in 'pay' and 'pie'; *j* sounds like the English *y*, either consonantal or, after a vowel, vocalic; *k* before *j*, *i* or *y* is softened to sound like the German *ch* in *'ich'*.

English — Norwegian

Welcome — Velkommen
Hello — God dag
Good morning — God morgen
Good evening — God kveld
Good night — Got natt
Goodbye — Adjø
Hi! — Hei!
Have a good journey — God tur!
I am called ... — Jeg heter ...
I come from ... — Jeg kommer fra ...
Great Britain — Storbritannia
England, Wales — England, Wales
Scotland, Ireland — Skottland, Irland
the United States — de Forente Stater
How are you? — Hvordan står det til?
Very well, thank you — Takk, bare bra
Please ... — Vær så snill ...
yes, no — ja, nei
Do you speak English? — Taler De engelsk?
I understand a little Norwegian — Jeg forstår litt norsk
I don't understand — Jeg forstår ikke
I speak English — Jeg taler engelsk
I speak French and German — Jeg taler fransk og tysk
What did you say? — Hva behager?
Would you please ... — Vær så snill ...
... talk a little more slowly — ... å tale litt saktigere
... write that down — ... å skrive det opp
Many thanks — Mange takk
Not at all — Ingen årsak
I have to go now — Jeg må gå nå
What a shame! — Det var synd
What is the time? — Hvor mye er klokken?

It is **one** o'clock — Klokken er **ett**
It is a quarter to **two** — Klokken er kvart over **to**
...half past two — ...half tre (lit. 'half three')
...a quarter past **three** — ...kvart på **tre**
four, five, six, — fire, fem, seks,
seven, eight, nine, — sju, åtte, ni,
ten, eleven, twelve — ti, elleve, tolv
yesterday, today, tomorrow — i går, i dag, i morgen
in the morning (am) — om formiddagen
in the afternoon (pm) — om ettermiddagen
Sunday, Monday, — søndag, mandag,
Tuesday, Wednesday, — tirsdag, onsdag,
Thursday, Friday, — torsdag, fredag,
Saturday — lørdag
hotel, guest-house — hotell, pensjonat
Do you have a room free? — Har De et ledig værelse?
I am staying for one night — Jeg blir en natt
Where is the dining room? — Hvor er spisesalen?
What is the voltage here? — Hvor høy spenning er det her?
I wish to be woken at seven — Jeg vil gjerne vekkes klokken sju
Is camping allowed here? — Kan man slå opp telt her?
Is the water drinkable? — Kan en drikke vannet her?
restaurant — restaurant, gjestgiveri
breakfast, lunch — frokost, lunsj
dinner, supper — middag, aftens
coffee, tea — kaffe, te
milk, water — melk, vann
fruit juice — fruksaft
bread, butter — brød smør
jam, marmalade — marmelade
honey — honning
sugar, salt — sukker, salt
soup, broth — suppe, buljong
trout, salmon — ørret, laks
cod, herring — torsk, sild
veal, pork — kalv, flesk
meatballs, sausages — kjøttkaker, pølse
game — vilt og fugler
reindeer — rein
chicken — kylling
boiled egg, fried egg — kokte egg, speilegg
scrambled egg — eggerøre
potatoes, rice — poteter, ris
peas, runner beans — erter, snittebønner
strawberries, raspberries — jordbær, bringebær
cheese, ice-cream — ost, is
lemonade, beer — brus, øl

red wine, white wine — rødvin, hvitvin
Cheers! Your health! — Skål!
Where is the food good and cheap? — Hvor kan en spise godt og rimelig?
Is this table reserved? — Er dette bordet oppstatt?
May I have the menu, please? — Får jeg spisekortet, takk?
Do you serve a typical Norwegian dish — Kan De anbefale typisk norsk rett?
I would like fish, meat — Jeg ville gjerne ha fisk, kjøtt
May I have a cup of coffee? — Kan jeg få en kopp kaffe?
May I have the bill, please? — Får jeg regningen, takk?
Where are the toilets? — Hvor er toalettet?
gentlemen, ladies — herer, damer
Where can I buy bread? — Hvor kan jeg kjøper brød?
Where can I get ... ? — Hvor kan jeg få ...?
I need shoes — Jeg trenger sko
Do you have a jacket? — Har de en genser?
I don't like the colour — Jeg like ikke fargen
Can you show me something else? — Kan De vise meg noe annet?
I like that — Det liker jeg
How much does it cost? — Hvor mye koster det?
That is expensive — Det er for dyrt
Can you give me change? — Kan De veksle?
Where can I get change? — Hvor kan jeg veksle penger?
Where is the train for Oslo? — Hvor går toget til Oslo?
When is the connection for Flåm? — Når får jeg forbindelse til Flåm?
Is there a restaurant car? — Er det noen spisevogn?
No, only a buffet car — Nei, bare en kafévogn
Excuse me, ... — Unnskyld, ...
Is this seat taken? — Er denne plassen opptatt?
This is my seat — Dette er min plass
Which is the pier for the ship to Bergen — Ved hvilken kai ligger båten til Bergen?
When does the ferry depart? — Når går ferja?
Does this bus go to Voss? — Går det buss til Voss?
Where does the bus go from? — Hvor går bussen fra?
How do we get to Geilo? — Hvordan kommer vi til Geilo?
Which is the best way to Bygdøy? — Hva er den beste veien til Bygdøy?
Is this the right way to Mo? — Er dette den riktige veien til Mo?
Is it far? — Er det langt?
How long does it take? — Hvor lang tid tar det?
How many kilometres is it? — Hvor mange kilometer er det?
Can you show me it on the map? — Vil De vise meg det på kartet?
I'm afraid I'm a stranger here — Dessvere, jeg er fremmed her
Where is the nearest petrol station — Hvor er nærmeste bensinstasjon?
My car has broken down — Jeg har motorstopp
Can you help me? — Kan De hjelper meg?
right, left, straight on — høyre, venstre, rett fram

FURTHER INFORMATION

Admission charges have not been included as they are subject to change. Opening times also vary so it is advisable to check with the local information offices before setting out. Addresses and telephone numbers have been given where possible.

Armed Forces Museum
Akershus Fortress
Central Oslo
Tel: (02) 403582
Norway's involvement in the World Wars.
Open: all year, Tuesday and Thursday, 10am-8pm, Wednesday and Friday, 10am-3pm, Saturday, 10am-4pm and Sunday 11am-4pm.

Asker Museum
Kirkevn. 68
1364 Hvalstad (near Oslo)
Tel: (02) 781096
Collections relating to local rural history.
Open: May-September, Tuesday and Thursday, 4pm-7pm, Saturday, 11am-3pm, Sunday, 12.30pm-6pm.

Bryggens Museum
Bryggen
Bergen
Tel: (05) 316710
Tools, china and many archaeological finds.
Open: summer, Monday, Wednesday and Friday, 10am-4pm, Tuesday and Thursday, 10am-8pm, Saturday and Sunday, 11am-3pm.

City Museum
Frognervn. 67
0266 Oslo 2,
Tel: (02) 558600
Housed at Frogner Manor, pictorial history of Oslo.
Open: all year, May-September, Tuesday-Friday, 10am-7pm, Saturday and Sunday, 11am-5pm; January - April and October-December, Tuesday, Thursday and Friday, 10am-4pm, Wednesday, 10am-7pm, Saturday and Sunday, 11am-4pm.

Emanuel Vigeland Museum
Grimelundsvn. 8
0387 Oslo 3,
Tel: (02) 142328
Fresco painting, family portraits, sculpture.
Open: all year, Sundays only, 12noon-3pm.

Ethnographical Museum
Fredriksgt. 2
0164 Oslo 1
Tel: (02) 416300 ext. 935
Exhibitions portraying daily life in different cultures.
Open: all year, Tuesday-Sunday, 12noon-3pm.

Fishery Museum
'Permanenten',
Bergen
Tel: (05) 321249
History of Norwegian sea fishing.
Open: May-August, weekdays, 10am-3pm, Sunday, 12noon-3pm; off season, Wednesday and Sunday, 12noon-3pm.

Fram Museum
Bygdøynes,
0286 Oslo 2

Tel: (02) 438370
Houses polar exploration vessel
'Fram'.
Open: daily, pre-season, 11am-5pm;
summer, 10am-6pm; closed
November-14 April.

Grieg Museum
'Troldhaugen'
Hop
Near Bergen
Tel: (05) 135438
Home of Grieg for 22 years,
collections relating to the composer.
Open: daily, May-October,
10.30am-1.30pm, 2.30pm-5.30pm.

Hanseatic Museum
Bryggen
Bergen
Tel: (05) 314189
Customs and activities of Hanseatic
merchants.
Open: daily, summer, 10am-4pm; of
season, 11am-2pm.

Historical Museum
Sydneshaugen
Bergen
Tel: (05) 213116
Viking, medieval and renaissance finds.
Open: daily except Fridays, 11am-4pm.

Historical Museum
Frederiksgt. 2
0164 Oslo 1
Tel: (02) 416300 ext. 956
The life and art of Vikings and
medieval Norway.
Open: May-September, Tuesday-
Sunday, 11am-3pm; January-May,
September-December, Tuesday-
Sunday, 12noon-3pm.

Kautokeino Museum
Bygdetun,
Kautokeino
Tel: (084) 56303
Local Lapp culture.
Open: Monday-Friday, 12noon-3pm.

Kon-Tiki Museum
Bygdøynes
0286 Oslo 2
Tel: (02) 438050
Exhibition of the balsa raft Kon-Tiki,
papyrus boat Ra and archaeological
collections.
Open: daily, summer, 10am-6pm;
otherwise, 10.30pm-5pm.

Leprosy Museum
St George's Hospital
59 Kong Oscarsgate
Bergen
Documents research of Dr Hansen
who discovered Leprosy virus.
Open: daily mid-May to end of August,
11am-5pm.

Maihaugen
Lillehammer
Open-air museum, contains the
Sandvig Collection of over 100
buildings.

Maritime Museum
Sydneshaugen
Bergen
Tel: (05) 327980
Ships from Viking days to present.
Open: daily, except Saturdays,
11am-2pm.

Munch Museum
Tøyengt. 53
0578 Oslo 5
Tel: (02) 673774
Vast collection of works by the artist
Edvard Munch.
Open: Tuesday-Saturday, 10am-8pm,
Sunday, 12noon-8pm.

Museum of Applied Art
St Olavsgt 1
0165 Oslo 1
Tel: (02) 203578
Norwegian and foreign applied art.
Open: Tuesday-Sunday, 11am-3pm.

Natural History Museum
Muséplass 3
Bergen
Tel: (05) 213050
Fauna and flora of Norway.
Open: daily, except Thursdays,
11am-2pm.

Natural History Museum
Sarsgt. 1
Tøyen
0502 Oslo 5
Tel: (02) 686960
Mineralogical, palaeontological and
zoological museums share a site in
Botanical gardens.
Open: Tuesday-Sunday,
12noon-3pm.

Nordland County Museum
Prinsensgt. 113
Bodø
Tel: (081) 21640
History of fishing and the Vikings.
Open: Monday-Friday, 9am-3pm,
Saturday, 10am-3pm, Sunday,
12noon-3pm.

Norwegian Architecture Museum
Josefinesgt. 32/34
0351 Oslo 3
Tel: (02) 602290
Alternating exhibitions of
architecture.
Open: April-September, weekdays,
9am-3pm.

Norwegian Folk Museum
Museumsvn. 10
Bygdøy
0287 Oslo 2
Tel: (02) 437020
Open-air, 170 buildings from all over
Norway, dating from 1200.
Open: May-August, Monday-
Saturday, 10am-6pm, Sunday,
11am-6pm; rest of year, Monday-
Saturday, 11am-4pm, Sunday 12noon-
3pm.

Norwegian Maritime Museum
Bygdøynesveien 37
0287 Oslo 5
Tel: (02) 552700
Norwegian maritime traditions
through the ages.
Open: daily, summer, 10am-8pm;
winter, mostly 10.30pm-4pm.

Norwegian Museum of Science and Industry
Kjelsåsvn. 141
0491 Oslo 4
Industrial and technical developments
right into the space age.
Open: Tuesday-Sunday, 10am-8pm.

Old Bergen Museum
Elsesro
Sandviken
Bergen
Tel: (05) 256307
Open-air collection of eighteenth and
nineteenth-century wooden houses,
craft shops etc.
Open: daily, off-season, 12noon-6pm;
mid-June - mid-August, 12noon-7pm.

Post Museum
Dronningensgt. 151V
0152 Oslo 1
Tel: (02) 409050
Stamps, postal accessories etc,
development of communications.
Open: all year, Monday-Saturday,
10am-3pm.

Stavanger Museum
Muségt. 16
Stavanger
Tel: (04) 526035
Archaeological, historical, zoological,
nautical history.
Open: June and August, every day
except Monday, 11am-3pm; rest of
year, Saturday, 10am-1pm, Sunday,
11am-3pm.

Theatre Museum
Nedre Slottsgt. 1
0157 Oslo 1

Tel: (02) 418147
Oslo's theatre history from nineteenth century to 1940-50.
Open: all year, Thursday, 11am-3pm, Sunday, 12noon-2pm.

Vest-Agder County Museum
Vige
Kristiansand
Tel: (042) 90228
Open-air museum of old houses and farms; folklore and furniture.
Open: weekdays, 10am-6pm, Sundays 12noon-6pm.

Vigeland Museum
Nobelsgt. 32
0268 Oslo 2
Tel: (02) 442306
Gustav Vigeland's life work, sculptures in bronze, marble, granite, drawings etc.
Open: summer, Tuesday-Sunday, 12noon-7pm; winter, Tuesday-Sunday, 1pm-7pm.

Other museums, well worth seeing may be found at:

Ålesund
Ålesund Museum: relics of Ålesund old and new

Alta
Alta Museum: collections dealing with slate mining, home crafts, fishing, forestry.

Åsgårdstrand
Munch Museum: Edvard Munch lived here for several years.

Eidsborg
Open-air Museum: including a stave church, storehouses, farms, costumes and folklore.

Eidsvoll
Eidsvoll District Museum: fifteen ancient houses.

Elverhøy bru
Leikvin Museum: partly devoted to salmon fishing.

Fagernes
Valdres Folkemuseum: old buildings, domestic equipment, weapons, musical instruments.

Flateland
Setesdal Museum: old wooden houses.

Grimstad
Old Pharmacy (now a museum) in which Ibsen worked and wrote his first book.

Hamar
Hedmark Museum: old wooden buildings dating from 1583. A little way north is Norway's only Railway Museum.

Hønefoss
Riddergården Court Museum: ancient medieval buildings.

Horten
Naval Museum: Horten was the main base for the Norwegian Navy during World War II.

Jevnaker
District Museum: including two glass factories.

Kabelvåg
Fisheries Museum: showing the history of fishing on the Lofoten Islands.

Karasjok
The Sami Museum: devoted to Lapp culture.

Kaupanger
Heibergske Samlinger Museum: open-air.

Lade
Museum of Musical History.

Larvik
Municipal Museum: housed in the Herregård, a large wooden manor house, residence of Counts of Larvik from 1670-80.

Mandal
City Museum: including a large art gallery and monument to Gustav Vigeland.

Mo i Rana
Municipal Museum: history of the town, crafts, mining, geology.

Narvik
Rød Kors Krigsmuseum: much of Narvik was destroyed during the war and the campaign is described here.

Nesbyen
Hallingdal Folkemuseum: fourteen old buildings, clothing, tools, weapons.

Oppdal
District Museum: old houses, store-rooms etc.

Sandefjord
Whaling Museum and Seafaring Museum.

Sarpsborg
Borgarsyssel Museum: old houses, ruined twelfth-century church.

Slettebo
Dalane Folkemuseum: crafts and agricultural implements.

Tønsberg
Vestfold County Museum: with an Arctic section (whaling).

Tromsø
Tromsø Museum: N. Norway's largest; devoted to geology, botany, zoology, archaeology etc.

Trondheim
Museum of Applied Art
Museum of Resistance
Shipping Museum
Museum of the Royal Society of Sciences.

Voss
Voss Folkemuseum: old farm buildings.

ART GALLERIES AND CENTRES

Albin Upp
Briskebyvn 42
0259 Oslo 2
Tel: (02) 557192
Contemporary art, applied art, crafts. Opening times available from Oslo Tourist Information Centre.

Art Association of Oslo
Rådhusgt. 19
0158 Oslo 1
Tel: (02) 423265
Changing exhibitions of paintings, sculptures, prints, etchings.
Open: all year except July and August, Monday-Saturday, 11am-4pm, Sunday, 12noon-4pm.

Artist's Association
Kjeld Stubsgt. 3
0160 Oslo 1
Tel: (02) 414029/412532
Contemporary paintings, prints, sculptures, arts, crafts. Exhibition and sale.
Open: all year, Monday-Friday, 10am-5pm, Saturday, 10am-3pm.

Artist's Centre
Wergelanden 17
0167 Oslo 1
Tel: (02) 607423
Open: all year, Tuesday-Saturday, 10am-6pm, Sunday 12noon-6pm.

Galleri Haaken
Lille Frogner Allé. 6
0263 Oslo 2
Tel: (02) 559197
Gallery, sales.
Closed July. Opening times from
Oslo Tourist Information Centre.

Henie-Onstad Art Centre
1311 Høvikodden
West Oslo
Tel: (02) 543050
Twentieth-century paintings, modern
art, concerts, theatre, ballet, film shows.
Open: all year, Monday-Friday, 9am-
10pm, weekends, 11am-10pm

Mørchs Kunsthandel
Pilestredet 7
0180 Oslo 1
Tel: (02) 425561
Nineteenth and twentieth-century
pictorial art.
For opening times, contact Oslo Tourist
Information Centre.

National Gallery
Universitetsgt. 13
0164 Oslo 1
Tel: (02) 200404
Open: daily, Monday-Friday,
10am-4pm, Wednesday and Thursday,
6pm-8pm also, Saturday, 10am-3pm,
Sunday, 12noon-3pm.

Stavanger Art Gallery
Madlaveien 33
Stavanger
Tel: (04) 520463/527819
Changing exhibitions September-May.
Open: Monday-Friday, 9am-2pm and
6pm-8pm, Saturday, 12noon-3pm and
Sunday, 12noon-5pm.

Tromsø Kunstforening
Muségt. 2
9000 Tromsø
Tel: (083) 80979
Art Centre, exhibitions.
For opening times contact Tromsø
Tourist Information Centre.

Bergen
Mariakirken (St Mary's Church). The
oldest building in Bergen built in the
first half of the twelfth century.

Bergen Cathedral. This is a blend of
different styles and the oldest part
dates from the twelfth century.

Borgund (Lærdal)
Stave church, built 1150. Probably the
best-preserved and most original in
Norway.

Fantoft
Fantoft stave church, twelfth century.

Hamar
Ruins of twelfth-century cathedral.

Heddal
Heddal stave church, mid-thirteenth
century, largest of the old wooden
churches in Norway.

Hopperstad
Twelfth-century stave church.

Lom
One of the finest stave churches in the
country, built 800 years ago.

Oslo
Old Aker Church, built around 1100,
the oldest Scandinavian church still in
use.

Oslo Cathedral, consecrated in 1697.

Øye
Twelfth-century stave church, rebuilt
from parts found under a later church.

Reinli
Twelfth-century stave church.

Ringsaker
Twelfth-century church with carved
and painted Flemish altar.

Stange
Stange Kirke, founded c.1150.

Stavanger
Stavanger cathedral, dating from 1125,
largest after Trondheim.

Tingvoll
Interesting thirteenth-century church
containing runic stone and remains of
fresco.

Torpo
Thirteenth-century stave church with
fine medieval paintings and carvings.

Tromsø
Tromsøya church, containing medieval
Madonna and seventeenth-century
altarpiece.

Trondheim
Splendid cathedral, built 1066-1093.
Norwegian monarchs proclaimed here.

Urnes
Twelfth-century stave church, one of
the oldest in Norway, dating from 1100.

Vaernes
Thirteenth-century church with
interesting baroque pulpit and
carvings.

Voss
Voss church, one of the most remarkable
churches in S.W. Norway,
dating from 1270.

BUILDINGS, MONUMENTS AND OTHER
PLACES OF INTEREST

Akershus Castle and Fortress
Entrance from Festningspl.
Oslo
Tel: (02) 412521/402540

Medieval fortress, built about 1300.
Rebuilt as renaissance castle in
seventeenth century.
Open: May-September, Monday-
Saturday, 11am-4pm, Sunday,
12.30pm-4pm.

Alta Rock Carvings
Alta
Tel: (084) 35997
These carvings are about 2,500-6,200
years old and Alta has the largest
number in Europe.

Bjerkebæck House
Lillehammer
Home of feminist writer and Nobel
prize winner, Sigrid Undset.

Bogstad Manor
(Gård)
Sørkedalen
(5kms from Oslo)
Tel: (02) 504859
Dates from 1760, Norway's finest
landscaped garden.
Open: May-September, Thursday,
6pm-7pm, Sunday, 12noon-5pm.

Christiansholm Fortress
Strand Promenaden
Kristiansand
Built 1674 by Fredrik III

City Hall
Rådhusplassen
0037 Oslo 1
Tel: (02) 410090
Lavishly decorated by Norway's
leading painters and sculptors during
1930s and 40s.
Open: October-March, Monday-
Saturday, 11am-2pm, Sunday,
12noon-3pm; April-September,
Monday-Saturday, 10am-3pm,
Sunday, 12noon-3pm.

Finnesloftet
Finnesvegen Road
15 minutes walk west of Voss.
Tel: (05) 511100

Norway's oldest secular wooden building, built 1250.
Open: mid June-mid August.

Fred Hansen's House
Skagen 18
Stavanger
Merchant's residence, built in the beginning of the eighteenth century in Baroque style.

Gamlehaugen
Fjøsanger
Bergen
Tel: (05) 133620
Residence of King of Norway when visiting Bergen, home of late Prime Minister Chr Michelsen.
Open: June-September, Monday-Friday, 9am-12noon.

Grønli Cave
Grønli, near Mo i Rana
Famous stalactite caverns, 5km long.

Hadeland Glass Factory
Jevnaker
Guided tours of glass blowing works, museum, restaurant and shop.

Haraldshaugen
Near Haugesund
Granite Obelisk commemorating Harald the Fair-Haired's naval victory.

Iron Age Farm
Ullandhaug
Stavanger
Tel: (04) 534140
Reconstructed farmstead from the period approx AD350-550.
Open: May-September, Sunday, 12noon-3pm; June-August, daily 11am-3pm plus Tuesday and Wednesday, 6pm-8pm.

Juhls' Silver Gallery
Kautokeino
Scandinavian and Sami Arts and home crafts for sale.

Open: winter, daily 9am-8pm; summer, 8.30pm-10am

Kongsgruve Silvermines
Kongsberg
Pits partly open to the public, Silver Collections.

Konventionsgården
Moss
Østfold
Eighteenth-century manor house where treaty uniting Norway with Sweden was signed.

Kristiansand Zoo
Kristiansand
Tel: (042) 46200
Over 1000 different species.
Open: all year, 10am-4pm.

Ladegård Oslo
Oslogt. 13
0192 Oslo 1
Tel: (02) 557248
Built as private residence in 1725, erected on ruins of bishop's palace.
Open: May-September, Wednesday, 6pm-7pm, Sunday, 1pm-2pm.

Ledål
Eiganesveien 45
Stavanger
Tel: (04) 526035
Famous mansion built in 1800, now local royal residence.
Open: June-August, Monday-Saturday, 11am-1pm, Sunday all year except December and January, 11am-2pm.

Oscarshall
Oscarshallvn.
Bygdøy
0287 Oslo 2
Pleasure palace in English Gothic style, built 1847-52.

Parliament Building
Karl Johansgt.
Oslo
Tel: (02) 313050
Constructed 1861-66. Richly
decorated by Norwegian artists.
Open: all year, Monday-Saturday,
12noon-2pm.

Reindeer of Bøla
Bøla
Most famous rock drawings in
Norway.

Rosenkilde House
Rosenkildetorget 1
Stavanger
Built in 1811 in Neo-classical style.
Largest privately-owned wooden
house at that time.

Rosenkrantz Tower
Bergen
Tel: (05) 314380
Erected in 1560s as official fortified
residence of feudal lord.
Open: summer, daily, 10am-4pm.

Royal Palace
Drammensvn. 1
0010 Oslo
Constructed 1825-48. Residence of the
King. Public not admitted but the
changing of the guard is worth seeing
at 1.30pm daily.

Ruin Park, Old Town
Oslogt./Bispegt.
Oslo
Park with archaeological excavations.
Open: summer.

Schøtstuene
50 Øvregaten
Bergen
Tel: (05) 316020
Assembly rooms illustrating the social
life of the Hanseatic merchants.
Open: summer, daily, 10am-4pm.

NATIONAL PARKS

Ånderdalen, Troms

Børgefjell, Nordland

Dovrefjell, Oppland

Femundsmarka, Hedmark

Gressåmoen, Nord-Trøndelag

Gutulia, Hedmark

Ormtjernkampen, Oppland

Øvre Anarjåkka, Finnmark

Øvre Dividalen, Troms

Øvre Pasvik, Finnmark

Rondane, Oppland

Stabbursdalen, Finnmark

WINTER SPORT RESORTS

These resorts cater for most winter
sports including cross-country skiing,
downhill skiing and ski trekking.

Alta
Bardu
Grong
Gudbrandsdal and the Dovre railway
Hallingdal and the Bergen railway
Karasjok
Kautokeino
Kirkenes
Kongsberg and Numedal
Levajok
Lønsdal
Meråker
Narvik
Oppdal
Oslo and area
Østerdal
Røros

Skaidi
Skoganvarre
Svolvær
Telemark and Setesdal
Tromsø
Trondheim
Valdres
Vestoppland
Western Norway
(Voss, Oppheim, Utvikfjell,
Østa, Standa, Sykkylven, Seljestad,
Finse, Hjølfjeu, Vatnahalsen)

GEOGRAPHICAL TERMS

ås — hill ridge
berg, bjerg — hill, mountain
bre, bræ — plateau glacier
bru — bridge
by — town
dal — valley
elv — river
ferje — ferry
fjell — high mountain
fond, fonn — snowfield
foss — waterfall
gate — street
gjel — gorge
hammer — spur (of mountain)
have — garden/park
hø, høi — peak
jernbane — railway
jøkel — glacier
juv — gorge
kliev — rockface
klint — cliff
kirke — church
koll — low hill
li, lid — slope of hill
litenelv — small river
myr — moorland
nut — steep-sided peak
øy — island
skarv — rocky hill
skog — wood, forest
slott — castle
strand — beach
sump — bog, marsh
tårn — tower

tind — sharp peak
torg — square (market)
vann, vatn — water, lake
(lande) vei — road
vidda — high plateau

FESTIVALS AND ANNUAL EVENTS

January
Ekeberg
Boat Show

February
Kongsberg
Kongsberg Fair
Røros
Røros Fair
Vikersund
Ski-Flying week

March
Karasjok/Kautokeino
Reindeer races
Lillehammer
Ski Race
Oslo
Ski Festival
Narvik
Winter Festival

April
Kristiansand
Boat Show

May
Everywhere
Constitution Day

June
Eidskog
Eidskogadagene
(various entertainments)
Everywhere
Flag Day
Midsummer Eve (23 June
celebrations)
Lofthus
Grieg Festival
Harstad

North Norway Festival
Honningsvåg
The North Cape Festival

July
Kristiansand
Kristiansand Festival
Many places
St Olav's Day (29 July)

August
Oslo
Oslo Festival
Vinstra
Peer Gynt Festival

October
Oslo
Opening of Storting (first working day)

December
Many places
Christmas Fair

MOTORING IN NORWAY

Setting out
It has already been mentioned that it is
necessary to carry a full driver's
licence. However, it is also necessary
to carry a red warning triangle in case
of breakdown or accident and it would
be advisable, although not
compulsory, to take registration
documents and insurance certificates.

Lights
Automatic illumination of driving
lights is obligatory on all new
motorcars in Norway. Many older
vehicles also drive with lights on in the
daytime. Norwegians recommend the
use of lights even in daytime. Lights of
mopeds and motorcycles must always
be on even in sunshine. British drivers
must adjust their vehicle's headlamps
for driving on the right.

Tyres
If you are expecting snow or ice, bring

chains that fit the wheels. If the car has
summer tyres, you are forbidden to
drive on snow or ice-covered roads
without having chains. Use of tyres
with metal studs is forbidden from 1
May until 15 October.

Safety belts
The wearing of safety belts is
compulsory for both driver and front
seat passenger. In vehicles more recent
than 1 January 1984, it is also
compulsory to wear safety belts in the
back seats.

Vehicle widths
The maximum width for motor vehicles
is 2.5m and for foreign towed caravans,
2.30m. Wider vehicles need a special
permit which is available from
Vegdirektoralet (Central Road
Authority), P.O. Box 8109, N 0032
Oslo.

Limits for caravans and trailers
Some Norwegian roads are unsuitable
for caravans. A special map is
available from petrol stations. For a
motorcar with trailer without brakes
and an actual total weight of over
300kg, the speed limit is 60km/hr. For
a motorcar with trailer that has brakes
the speed limit is 80km/hr. For
vehicles having a total weight of over
3500kg, the speed limit is 80km/hr.
Buses have a speed limit of 80km/hr.
These speed limits apply to outside
built-up areas but only if there are no
signs showing a different speed limit.
(The speed limit in built-up areas is
50km/hr.)

Lane discipline
The right-hand side of the roadway
shall be used. The left-hand lane is for
overtaking or turning left. Overtaking
on the dotted warning line is
forbidden. Overtaking on an
unbroken line in the middle of the
road is forbidden.

Resting places
Are provided for resting. It is forbidden

to spend the night there. Tents and caravans should not be positioned less than 150m from a house or chalet. Caravans must not be parked in a layby. Fires must not be lit in fields or woodlands from 15 April to 16 September.

Alcohol, drugs and driving
Norway has very strict drink and drive regulations. To drive with more than 0.05 per cent alcohol in the blood is a punishable offence. Narcotics are also very dangerous to drivers. In Norway, medicines that represent a danger to drivers are marked with a red warning triangle.

Parking in Oslo
The City of Oslo has the usual traffic problems and in order to deal with these has introduced special parking regulations. They are sensible, but can be very confusing at first.

1. *Parking discs:* These are colour-coded according to the length of time one is allowed to park. Yellow means 1 hour, grey means 2 hours and brown means 3 hours. One can also buy special discs which allow parking for longer periods.

2. *Parking zones:* During working hours (Monday-Friday, 8am-5pm, Saturday, 8am-3pm) cars may only park at the kerb for up to half an hour in the city centre, or for up to 2 hours in the outer zones. Parking signs should be observed at all times.

3. *Parking at night:* There is an important regulation governing cars parked at the kerb overnight (midnight-7am). On odd days of the month, cars may only be parked on the side of the road next to the odd-numbered houses and correspondingly on even days. This is so that the streets can be cleaned overnight.

More exact information can be found in a leaflet entitled Parking in Oslo which is available from tourist information offices and petrol stations.

Road Signs
Envegskjøring — One-way street
Gjennomkjøring — No entry
  forbudt
Sakte — Slow
Se opp — Caution
Stopp — Stop
Toll — Customs
Veiarbeide — Road works

ACCOMMODATION

Hotels
All establishments offering overnight accommodation in Norway must be officially authorised. Hotels claiming *turisthotell* or *høyfjellshotell* must fulfill specific requirements. Vat and a service charge are included in the bill. Hotels often allow a 75 per cent reduction on *en pension* rate for children under 3 years old and a 50 per cent reduction for children aged 3 to 12 years old. This discount only applies however, when the child concerned occupies an extra bed in the parents' room.

Apartments/Cabins
Self-catering establishments usually have a high standard including a fully equipped kitchen with a fridge, shower, wc, electrical heating, parking space and sale of provisions nearby. All have duvets and pillows. Camp chalets/cabins have now been divided into four categories, from 0 - ★★★, according to facilities: 0 = a one-room furnished cabin; ★ = a cabin with electricity, heat, light and appliances, often with several rooms; ★★ = a cabin with electricity, water and separate bedroom; ★★★ = a cabin with electricity, hot and cold water, water drain, shower, toilet, cooking equipment and at least two rooms.

Camping

A new system of classification is being carried out: ★ = ordinary sites satisfying minimum requirements with regard to sanitary installations, drinking water, laundry facilities, entrance to the park is marked and there is access to telephone; ★★ = a well-equipped site offering one-star facilities as well as supervision from 7am-11pm, night lights on the sanitary installations, sanitary disposal, hot water in the laundry, outlet for electric razors, hotplate, postal service, kiosk and sale of provisions, telephone and electric points for caravans; ★★★ = a very well-appointed park which, in addition to the above facilities, has round the clock supervision, reception, tourist information, enclosed park area, playgrounds, recreation areas, sale of provisions as well as warm meals.

Youth Hostels

There are a total of 80 youth hostels in Norway, from Kristiansand in the south to Honningsvåg in the north. The hostels are noted for their high standard, whether it be a typical hostel or simpler accommodation at a farm. Norwegian youth hostels are classified according to facilities: ★ = a hostel which fulfills minimum requirements and provides simple facilities with regard to the size of the room, equipment available and sanitary facilities; ★★ = a hostel having four to six beds per room, laundry/shower in the corridor or on another floor, meal service or guest kitchen. Doors normally close at 11pm; ★★★ = a hostel with four beds to a room, hot and cold running water, comfortable sitting area, shower/toilet, meals provided and a guest kitchen. Closing hours are flexible.

Oslo

There is a wide selection of hotels and guest-houses covering a whole range of prices and categories of accommodation from the Grand Hotel down to the most modest Bed and Breakfast. Given the variety of block-booking arrangements, hotel vouchers and week end rates, it is important to get information from up-to-date brochures and lists from the Norwegian National Tourist Office or from the tourist information centre at Oslo Town Hall.

The Haraldsheim Youth Hostel is in the northern suburb of Grefsheim (Haraldsheimveien 4, Tel: (02) 218359.) It is on the tram route from the National Theatre to Sinsen and is open from May to September. Outside term times, it is also possible to stay in some of the various student hostels, such as Oslo Studentby og Summer-hotell (Tel: (02) 232880).

Oslo has a large number of camping sites but many are badly sited, crowded or noisy. Two that can be recommended are a long way out of town. The best site is Ekeberg Camping which is on a hill to the east of the city. The best route from the centre is along the Ekebergveien from Gamleby Cemetery - tents have to be pitched on a slope but there is a marvellous view of the city. The site is unfortunately closed from mid-August onwards, so later visitors must go to Bogstad Camping on the opposite side of the city. This well-appointed site is well-signposted.

Bergen

There are plenty of good hotels and guesthouses. A leaflet giving prices and categories is available from the tourist information centre.

The Montana Youth Hostel is beautifully situated at the foot of Ulriken and can be reached from the city centre on a No. 4 bus. The camping sites are Lone, Midttun, Grimen and Bergenshallen. Of these, Lone is the biggest and is situated by a lake along the E68 near Haukeland. The Midttun site near Nesttun is similarly well-appointed. The rather more primitive Grimen site is not far away from Halledal. Bergenshallen however, though nearer the city itself, is for caravans only.

Trondheim
There are two camping sites near Trondheim. Sandmoen Camping is near Heimdal on the E6 Oslo road. Vikhammer og Storsand Gård is on the E6 coast road near Malvik.

Full details of hotels and other accommodation can be obtained from the tourist information office in the Torget.

Stavanger
Brochures giving details of hotels and boarding houses are again available from the tourist information office in Muségate. The youth hostel and camping sites are both at Mosvangen and are open from May to September inclusive.

Kristiansand
There are several good hotels in the city centre. The youth hostel is at Bertesbukt, and there are several camping sites along the coast at Randesund, Søgne and Roligheden.

For a comprehensive guide to all forms of accommodation in Norway contact the Norwegian National Tourist Association.

Shopping in Norway

Tax-free Shopping
Norway has a unique system for foreign tourists. If you go to the right shops, everything you buy will be cheaper, so keep your eyes open for the Tax-free sign. In the whole of Norway, more than 2000 shops and department stores are affiliated to Norway Tax-free Shopping.

This is how you shop tax free:
1. You show your passport to prove you are not a resident of Scandinavia.
2. You may not use the article prior to leaving Norway.
3. The article must be taken out of the country no later than 4 weeks after it has been bought.
4. The shop assistant writes out a Tax-free Shopping Cheque when the article is bought (minimum purchase is 300nkr). You must fill in the reverse side. Upon leaving the country, you display the article and cheque. The amount on the cheque is repaid in cash.

The Oslo Card
The Oslo Card allows you to get to know the city cheaply. It entitles you to: free admission to museums etc.; unlimited free travel on buses, trains, ferries within Oslo; reduction on boat and coach sightseeing trips; special offers in restaurants; discounts on car hire; free admission to the Municipal baths; discounts on ski equipment, bicycle and windsurfing hire, renting squash courts, hairdressers, yacht rental, skin treatment and pedicure.

The Oslo Card costs:
*Price: 1 day
Adult 60nkr, Child 30nkr
*Price: 2 days
Adult 90nkr, Child 45nkr
*Price: 3 days
Adult 120nkr, Child 60nkr.

* Price subject to change.

The Oslo Card may be bought at hotels, tourist information offices, the Accommodation Bureau at Oslo Central Railway Station, campsites and some banks.

Souvenirs
Ideal souvenirs might include: gaily-coloured knitwear, wooden objects, pewter, enamel and brassware, tapestries and toys, reindeer skins and antlers.

International Dialling Codes
From UK to Norway: 01047
From US to Norway: 01147
From Norway to UK: 09544
From Norway to US: 0951

Emergency Calls in Oslo
NAF (Automobile Association) 24hr
Emergency Service: (02) 429400

Police: (02) 110011

Accident/Ambulance: (02) 114455

Fire: (001) 669050

For operator assistance: 093 (English speaking)
Telegrams: 013

The addresses and telephone numbers of tourist information offices in the major towns/cities mentioned in the guide are listed, followed by the telephone numbers for many other key areas. Opening times vary but most are open from at least 9am-4pm, daily, during summer. It is wise to telephone to check opening times before visiting.

Bergen
Torgalmenning
Bergen
Tel: (05) 321480

Hammerfest
P.O. Box 226
9601 Hammerfest
Tel: (084) 12185

Kristiansand
Henrik Wergelandsgt. 17
P.O. Box 592
N-4601 Kristiansand
Tel: (042) 26065

Lillehammer
P.O. Box 181
N-2601 Lillehammer
Tel: (062) 51098

Narvik
P.O. Box 318
8501 Narvik
Tel: (082) 43309

Oslo
City Hall
0037 Oslo 1
Tel: (02) 201517

Stavanger
The Tourist Pavilion
Muségate
Stavanger
Tel: (04) 528437

Trondheim
Torget
Trondheim
Tel: (07) 511466

Ålesund Tel: (071) 21202
Alta Tel: (084) 35041
Åndalsnes Tel: (072) 21622
Arendal Tel: (041) 22193
Aurland Tel: (056) 33313
Balestrand Tel: (056) 91255
Bodø Tel: (081) 21240
Brevik Tel: (035) 70200
Dombås Tel: (062) 41444
Drammen Tel: (03) 834094
Egersund Tel: (04) 490819
Eidfjord Tel: (054) 65177
Elverum Tel: (064) 10188
Fagernes Tel: (061) 30400
Fauske Tel: (081) 43303
Flekkefjord Tel: (043) 24254
Flesberg Tel: (03) 761028
Fredrikstad Tel: (032) 20330
Geilo Tel: (067) 85041
Geiranger Tel: (071) 63099
Gol Tel: (067) 74840
Grong Tel: (077) 31522
Halden Tel: (031) 82487
Hamar Tel: (065) 21217
Harstad Tel: (082) 63235

Haugesand   Tel: (047) 25255 ext. 276
Haukeligrand   Tel: (036) 73315
Hellesylt   Tel: (071) 65052
Hemsedal   Tel: (067) 78156
Hønefoss   Tel: (067) 23330
Horten   Tel: (033) 43390
Hovden   Tel: (043) 39630
Høydalsmo   Tel: (036) 76100 ext. 3109
Karasjok   Tel: (084) 66620
Kautokeino   Tel: (084) 56500
Kinsarvik   Tel: (054) 63450
Kirkenes   Tel: (085) 91751
Kongsberg   Tel: (03) 731526
Kragerø   Tel: (036) 82330
Kristiansund   Tel: (073) 77211
Lærdal   Tel: (056) 66508
Larvik   Tel: (034) 82623
Lakselv   Tel: (084) 61644
Levanger   Tel: (076) 86040
Lillesand   Tel: (041) 71449
Lom   Tel: (062) 11286
Mo i Rana   Tel: (087) 50421
Molde   Tel: (072) 52060
Mosjøen   Tel: (087) 71321
Moss   Tel: (032) 55451
Namsos   Tel: (077) 73470
Nesbyen   Tel: (067) 71249
Norheimsund   Tel: (05) 551767
Notodden   Tel: (036) 12633
Odda   Tel: (054) 41297
Oppdal   Tel: (074) 21760
Porsgrunn   Tel: (035) 51096
Ringebu   Tel: (062) 80960
Risør   Tel: (041) 51700
Røldal   Tel: (054) 47289
Sandefjord   Tel: (034) 65300
Sandnes   Tel: (04) 667773
Sarpsborg   Tel: (031) 54855
Sogndal   Tel: (056) 71161
Steinkjer   Tel: (077) 63495
Stjørdal   Tel: (07) 825500
Stryn   Tel: (057) 71526
Sunndalsøra   Tel: (073) 92552
Svinesund   Tel: (031) 95152
Svolvær   Tel: (088) 71053
Tønsberg   Tel: (033) 14819

Tromsø   Tel: (083) 84776
Ulvik   Tel: (05) 526360
Valle   Tel: (04) 337312
Vinstra   Tel: (06) 290166
Voss   Tel: (05) 511716
Ytre Vinje   Tel: (036) 71300

USEFUL ADDRESSES

British Embassy
Thomas Heftyesgate 8
N-Oslo 2
Tel: (02) 563890/97

Information Office for Guest Workers
Skippergt. 29
Oslo 1
Tel: (02) 204090

Guide Service
(Tourist Information)
City Hall
0037 Oslo
Tel: (02) 414863

The Hunting and Fishing Society
Prinsengate 21
Oslo

Norwegian Committee for International
  Information and Youth Work (NIU)
Grev Wedels Plass 5
N-0157
Oslo 1

Norwegian Guide and Scout Association
Storgt. 2
0155 Oslo 1
Tel: (02) 206379

Norwegian National Tourist Office
 (Britain)
20 Pall Mall
London SW1Y 5NE
Tel: (01) 839 6255

Norway Travel Association
H. Heyerdahlsgt.
Oslo 1
Tel: (02) 427044

The Norwegian Tourist Association
(Den Norske Turistforeningen)
Stortingsgt. 28
N-0161 Oslo 1
Tel: (02) 418020

Norwegian Tourist Board (Norway)
P.O. Box 499 Sentrum
N-0105 Oslo 1
Tel: (02) 427044

Norwegian Tourist Board (USA)
655 Third Avenue
s-New York, NY 10017
Tel: 1212 949 2333

Oslo Tourist Board (Head Office)
Rådmannsgården
Rådhusgt. 19
0158 Oslo 1
Tel: (02) 427170

Royal Norwegian Embassy (Britain)
25 Belgrave Square
London SW1X 8QD
Tel: (01) 235-7151

Royal Norwegian Embassy (USA)
2720 34th Street, NW,
Washington DC
20008 USA.
Tel: 3336000

NUH Travel Bureau (Youth Hostel
Assoc.)
Dronningensgt 26
N-0154 Oslo 1
Tel: (02) 421410

Skiforeningen
(Ski Society)
Kongeveien 5
Oslo 3
Tel: (02) 141690

Telephone, Telegraph and Telex
Kongensgt. 21
Oslo 1
(open 8am-10pm)

US Embassy
Drammensveien 18
N-Oslo
Tel: (02) 565880

YMCA and YWCA
Holbergspl. 1
0154 Oslo 1
Tel: (02) 204475

Motoring
Kongelig Norsk Automobilklub(KNA:
 Royal Norwegian Automobile Club)
Parkveien 68
N-Oslo 2
Tel: (02) 562690

Norges Automobil Forbund (NAF:
 Norwegian Automobile Association)
Storgate 2-6
N-Oslo 1
Tel: (02) 337080

Airlines
Braathens SAFE A/s
Ruseløkkveien 26
N-Oslo 2
Tel: (02) 411020

British Airways
Kronprinsesse Marthas Plass 1
N-Oslo 2
Tel: (02) 418750

SAS Scandinavian Airlines
52/53 Conduit Street
London W1 0AY
Tel: 01 734 4020

SAS Scandinavian Airlines
SAS Building
Ruseløkkveien 6
0251 Oslo 2
Tel: (02) 427760

Widerøes Flyselskap A/s
Mustadsveien 1
0283 Oslo 2
Tel: (02) 509130

By Sea
DFDS (UK) Ltd
Scandinavia House
Parkeston Quay
Essex C92 426
Tel: (0255) 554681

DFDS Norge A/s
Karl Johansgt. 1
N-0154 Oslo 1
Tel: (02) 429350

Fred Olsen Lines
11 Conduit Street
London W1R OLS
Tel: (01) 630 0033

Fred Olsen Lines
P.O. Box 82
4601 Kristiansand
Tel: (042) 26500

Norway Line
P.O. Box 4004
N-5015 Dreggen/Bergen
Tel: (05) 322780

Norway Line (UK)
Tyne Commission Quay
North Shields NE29 6EA
Tel: (0632) 585555

By rail
Norwegian State Railways (NSB)
21-24 Cockspur Street
London SW1
Tel: (01) 930 6666

Swiss Federal Railway
608 Fifth Avenue
New York NY 10020
Tel: (212) 7575944

Car Hire
Avis
Munkedamsveien 27
N-0250 Oslo 2
Tel: (02) 410060

Hertz
Wergelandsveien 1
NO-0167 Oslo 1
Tel: (02) 205212

Caravan Hire
Majorstuen Autoservice
Marcus Thranesgt. 2
N-0473 Oslo 4
Tel: (02) 381961

Dormobile Hire
Bislet Bilutleie
Pilestredet 70
N-0354 Oslo 3
Tel: (02) 600000

Interrent a.s.
Frysjaveien 31
N-0883 Oslo 8
Tel: (02) 236685

INDEX

Index to places

Norwegian dictionaries normally place
æ, ø and **å** (in that order) at the end of
the alphabet after **z**. But for the purposes
of this index they have been treated as
ae, oe and **aa** respectively.

239

Index to subjects